PARISIAN LIVES

Stonewall Inn Editions

Michael Denneny, General Editor

PARISIAN
LIVES

A NOVEL BY

Samuel M. Steward

ST. MARTIN'S PRESS   New York

Library of Congress Cataloging in Publication Data
Steward, Samuel M.
 Parisian lives.
 1. Stein, Gertrude, 1874–1946, in fiction, drama, poetry, etc. I. title.
PS3537.T479P3 1984 813'.54   83-15994
ISBN 0-312-59666-9
ISBN 0-312-03024-X (pbk.)

First Edition

10 9 8 7 6 5 4 3 2 1

PARISIAN LIVES

(1) July 18, 1935

It was once upon a time, all those years ago, that I first met Sir
Arthur Lyly at Gertrude Stein's house in Bilignin in eastern
France.

I was very young, then, and on my first trip to Europe—cal-
low, almost unplucked, and certainly unsophisticated, and more
overwhelmed than I had ever been in my life to be the house
guest of such a great woman.

It had come about quite naturally. At the university where I
had been enrolled, there had been a professor who was a great
devotee of Gertrude Stein's, and had talked much in his classes
about her and her writing. He had died quite suddenly of pneu-
monia, and I had taken it upon myself to write to tell her of his
death. She had responded graciously and sympathetically. I had
written again—and a correspondence had begun that came to a
climax with my visiting her at the old château where she and Alice
B. Toklas, her secretary and companion, used to spend every summer.

Gertrude was always marvelously kind to young people, and it
seemed she was especially so to me. I had had two books pub-
lished—one a volume of short stories in which she saw nothing at
all; the other—a novel—in which she said she saw a great deal of
promise. Her letters to me had warmed, had begun to bubble, and
eventually turned hot enough to invite me to come to see her.
Alas, her hopes for a literary life for me were never realized while
she lived.

All the world knew of Gertrude Stein then and still does, even
more today in the 1980s. She was perhaps the most famous of

expatriate American writers—not only for her obscure and difficult style, but for such things as her haircut and personality—all gaining for her a wider and more varied audience than Saint Paul. Her name was good copy for all the newspapers in America. Many persons joked about her and quoted her perplexing statements, such as "Rose is a rose is a rose is a rose" or "Pigeons in the grass alas." But she went serenely on her almost metaphysical way, obsessed with the many ideas her creative mind continually furnished her, and spending her time frequently knocking the daylight out of words. Across her threshold had passed the great, the near-great, and the not-nearly-great. Almost everyone worth knowing in the arts had sat in her salon at one time or another, listening to her wise and certain words, or else had been kicked out of it as Hemingway had been. To young artists and writers she was apologist, defender, and inspiration.

Sitting on the heavy horsehair sofa in Paris or in her rocking chair at Bilignin like a squat impassive Buddha with a Roman senator's haircut, she made her *ex cathedra* pronouncements about modern literature and art. And she came gradually to acquire some of that dusky magelike character that Coleridge had at Highgate—prophet and seer, speaking oracles that were sybilline and profound, and invariably correct. She and Alice lived in Paris from November until April. Then they would put their lecherous little Mexican chihuahua Pépé and the big white poodle Basket into the family Ford. They would take the manuscripts and kitchen utensils and chug merrily down to Bilignin in the lovely province of Ain. There they spent the summers among the poplars and the hills, talking, eating, walking, and receiving guests and disciples.

The house at Bilignin was an old ramshackle French château of the seventeenth century, somewhat modernized to the 1935 American ideal of comfort. Gertrude was very proud, for example, of the hot-water heater that had been installed. The first day I was there she led me into the bathroom, turned on a gush of steaming hot water, and exclaimed proudly: "There what do you think of that as hot as a hotel and quicker."

In the old house the original wallpaper still clung disconsolately but doggedly in some of the rooms; and on the walls of the living room were painted amber and purple columns and baskets of fruits, with hunting horns, in the *trompe l'oeil* manner. There also was Gertrude's rosewood desk, and opposite it a small, old-fashioned spinet that was rarely opened. A low round tea-table stood in the room centered between two reed rocking chairs. There Gertrude and Alice would sit after dinner in the long twilights, while the after-dinner infusions of verveine cooled in the paper-thin blue china cups, and the smoke of cigarettes drifted lazily out the door into the garden, over the low wall, and into the great wide pit of the valley below, from which the darkness rose slowly, gathering into little lakes that crept up to cover the trees.

It was in Gertrude's lovely rose garden, then, that I was lying on a sun-blanket in mid-July those many years ago, nearly naked, listening with closed eyes to the small sounds of the day. Down in the valley a cowbell tinkled remotely—a small silver interruption to the hum of a cicada in a eucalyptus tree nearby. From the old kitchen of the château came the rhythmic *clunt-clunt!* of the housekeeper Madame Roux beating something in a wooden bowl. On the road across the valley a peasant's cart was passing; I could barely hear the faint creaking of the wheels.

The sun sensually enfolded my body. It beat against my skin in pulsing waves and drew moisture from my pores the way it did from the ground. Lying there quietly, listening to the minute sounds, it was almost as if I became a part of the earth itself. I could feel the grass springing from the backs of my hands and arms. Within me, in the black soil of myself, life moved and burrowed. Beetles ran across my surface. The flagstones pressed heavily into me, and roots inched with imperceptible slowness through the red darkness behind my closed eyelids. Beads of moisture formed below me and rose with slow bubblings to the grainy rich loam from which the flowers sprang. . . .

Gertrude and Alice had gone off to the train to meet Sir Arthur Lyly at Culoz. He was arriving with an American friend to stay a few days.

"A friend indeed!" Alice had mildly snorted. "From Arthur's description he sounds like an American gangster."

"Arthur does more unpredictable things than most," said Gertrude. "Imagine bringing someone over here 'to get a job.' There are more jobs in America."

"This new one will probably be a handful for Arthur," said Alice, filing a fingernail. She flaked off a bit of crimson. "Zut! I've ruined one."

"I wonder what he looks like," Gertrude said.

Alice contemplated the rose bush. "He is probably about two meters tall with dark curly hair. He will look something like a boxer—not quite handsome but attractive enough. In that un-handled American way."

Gertrude and Alice had piled into the car and departed, leaving me behind because the luggage would have crowded the car too much. I was perfectly contented. They had told me some about Sir Arthur and I was curious to see him—and impressed too, because at that age I believed that anyone Gertrude said was good was really good.

They had been gone nearly three hours. It was twenty minutes of four when I heard them turn in at the gate on the other side of the château. There was a great slamming of car doors, loud and confused talk, shouted instructions, and over it all the wild and uninhibited barking of the two dogs. Arrivals and departures chez Gertrude were noisy things indeed.

I debated with myself whether to run upstairs and put on some more clothes. But I decided my body was all right—and I was already deeply tanned. I resolved to lie there quietly, perhaps even pretending to be asleep, although even an idiot would have realized that no one could sleep in such a racket as the one with which the four of them splintered the afternoon.

Listening, I followed their progress into the house. The windows were open and I could hear them clearly from the garden. Gertrude led Sir Arthur and his friend into the larger guest room, next to mine. She showed them the way to the bathroom, and I heard her exhibit the new water heater. Then all of a sudden there was a pause—Arthur had evidently looked out the window—for I heard a man's voice say:

"And who, my dear, is the charming young giant lying out in the garden?"

There was a quick muffling, something said that I could not understand—a sudden silence, a rustling whisper from Gertrude, and a kind of subdued grunt from a man. I resisted the reflex to open my eyes and kept them tightly closed.

After a moment Gertrude said in a natural tone: "I suppose you will want to wash, well do it, then come down, we will have something cool, the shade is coming around the house."

Oddly enough I began to feel flustered, although I was reasonably proud of my body. The near-nakedness perhaps had something to do with it. It was not that I minded Gertrude and Alice seeing me so; I had been similarly unclothed for almost every day for two weeks when there was sun. But the thought of being undressed in front of two men whom I had not met before was disturbing. I remembered a small blemish on my left shoulder, and was ill equipped at that age to understand why I was upset.

Deep within my subconscious secret powers laid hands on me, making me wish to seem attractive, compelling, desirable. The unvoiced question of which I was barely aware—and would have certainly rejected had it surfaced—was simply: "Are you well made enough to be considered by either of these men as a bedmate?"

Those who "double in brass" have an uneasy time. The ordinary man who follows the majority sexual practice is always a little concerned when he shows himself to women. He hates to grow old, to develop a paunch, to find his hair falling out—and therefore takes pains with his appearance, especially as he draws close to the hill of forty. But he can relax with other men since he is not trying to attract them.

The man's reaction, however, is nothing to the woman's. She must powder, paint, and perfume herself, broiling in reducing baths and under hair dryers, tortures designed to make her wanted by every man she sees. The man who has enjoyed both men and women, however, can never relax with anyone. He must keep himself attractive to all—before and after forty—for he considers every woman and every man as a conquest.

Thus all that was deeply buried in me urged me to leave the blanket, go to my room to dress, to meet the newcomers on at least an equal basis—in clothes. But I stayed flat on my back in the garden.

Presently I heard Gertrude at the door, shouting something to Alice on the second floor. Then I heard her footsteps as she crunched toward me on the gravel.

"Hullo," she said. "Are you still here and how has the sun been." She rarely pronounced her question marks. Everybody knows a question is a question so why use a question mark, she used to say—"It's all right for a brand on cattle but that is all it is all right for."

"It's been fine," I said, opening my eyes and looking into her strong square face under the close-cropped iron gray hair. Her figure was squat and solid as a block of granite, and her strong hands clutched Basket's leash across the front of her thighs against the rough brown skirt. She wore a pink quilted armless vest over a white blouse with a pleated front.

"Aren't you going to get dressed," she said. "We are going to have tea in a few moments now that we are all here. Arthur needs refreshment."

"I'm not all right just like this?"

"Of course you're all right any way you are, it is not a question of being all right, the sun will go down before long and then it will be chilly, so why not go upstairs and throw something on and then you can bathe after tea if you want to."

"All right," I said. It was difficult for me to talk with Gertrude because she awed me considerably. I was afraid that everything I said gave away the sad inadequacy of my brain. But I was a good listener, and consequently I was more silent—and adoring—with her and Alice than with any other two persons in the world. Neither of them ever saw what I really was, nor reached into what I fondly considered the sardonic and melancholy quality of my mind.

As I rose from the blanket and began to fold it I thought of something else. Upstairs my room was next to that of Sir Arthur and his friend. I had not met them. I would be certain to see them in the hallway or find them in the bathroom. I turned to Gertrude.

"I haven't met Sir Arthur and his friend yet," I said uncertainly.

Gertrude laughed. "Silly boy," she said. "If you see them just stick out your hand and tell them your name and don't worry, they won't bite you."

I must have been one of Gertrude's great head-shaking problems.

Of course I met them. A young man was just coming out of the bathroom with a towel wrapped around his middle. He was in his late twenties or early thirties—stocky and with a pleasant but not too intelligent face—rather ruddy, with a long mustache that looked untidy and scrubby. He caught me just as I was reaching for my own doorknob. Now I must do as Gertrude said . . .

I stuck out my hand. "Hello," I said. "I'm John McAndrews."

He shook my hand with a firm grip, peering intently at the

bridge of my nose—rather nearsightedly, it seemed to me.

"Hullo," he said. "I'm Arthur Lyly."

"You—" I was about to say it was a nice day to arrive but I was horror-struck at the banality. He saved me. "What do your friends call you?" he asked.

"Mac." I said.

He grinned. "I like that, Mac," he said. "Gertrude says that you are from Chicago."

"Yes," I said, strangling on the word.

"My friend is from Chicago too," he said, looking over his shoulder. Suddenly I felt cold and excluded. "My friend."

"Chicago is an exciting town," he went on. "I was there just last month. All that *meat*—"

"Did you go to the Stockyards?" I asked stupidly.

"Oh, yes," he said, seeming a little annoyed. "That, too."

The conversation was falling, dying. I had lost complete control of my wits. I could not think of a single thing to say.

At that harried moment, another young man appeared around the corner, drying his head and ears with a towel. He was tall and handsome—and completely naked. Around his upper right forearm was tattooed a green and red snake in coils, like an Egyptian ornament. It had a widespread mouth with white fangs opened at the lower edge of the shoulder pad. He was black haired and very good to look at, with a kind of sullen cruel set to his jaw and lips. His nose was not long, and had evidently been broken at one time. I could not keep my eyes from his crotch, hypnotized by what was there, and by the hair pattern that flowed down to it.

"Is this the guy Gertrude was talkin' about?" he said, advancing.

His grip was very strong. I felt my knuckles being cracked together.

"This is Wally Herrick—John McAndrews," said Sir Arthur.

"Hello," I said.

Naturally he did not recognize me. In the course of his work a masseur meets many people. They have no identities for him— they are merely bodies to be kneaded and pulled, thumped and whacked.

But I knew him at once. He was the masseur at the Lincoln Baths in Chicago—the tough "unmakeable" idol of hundreds of Chicago queens.

(2) July 19, 1935

The next morning was Friday, and sunny. My visit was drawing to a close. On that day I happened to rise a little earlier than anyone else—except Alice, of course.

"Good morning," I said to her at the doorway of her sacred terrain, the kitchen.

"Good morning, Johnny," she said. "You're up early. Do have a chair in the garden and I'll bring your breakfast to you in a while."

"Thank you very much," I said, turning to go.

"And Johnny," she said, with a wooden spoon suspended over the bubbling contents of a black iron pot, "today you may start calling her Gertrude, and drop the Miss Stein."

"Oh, thank you!" I said fervently. It was a sign I had passed my probation. I had arrived.

"But not too often," she warned. "Don't begin every sentence with it. That she finds annoying."

"*Bon*," I said. "*Entendu*."

The air was cool and fresh in the garden, the sun was warm on the lounge chair, and the clouds over the hills of Ain a tumbling and excited white. Alice brought the *petit déjeuner* on a large heavy silver tray—a steaming silver pot of coffee—strong and black enough to raise the hair on your neck, thick cream for the strawberries, some fried cornmeal mush (because of my allergies) with heavy golden syrup, and fresh hot croissants with a chunk of country butter.

When I had finished I carried the tray into the château.

"Gertrude will be down shortly," Alice said. "She wants to know if you will walk with her on the upper turn today."

"Delighted," I said, and returned to my chair.

Presently the great lady heaved into sight and hailed me from the doorway. "Are you ready Johnny, it's a nice day, let's take a walk, come along Pépé."

And we were off, Gertrude switching at the ragweeds with the dogleash as we passed, climbing up a hillside path behind the house, toward the low fence that surrounded the vineyards of her neighbors. Already the grapes were heavy on the vines—huge silvery-frosted clusters of purple, fragrance stirring and swirling around us as the vagrant breeze blew now in our direction and then away from us.

"What do you want to talk about," she threw back over her shoulder as we trudged along the narrow path. "Literature or art or what or just gossip."

"Tell me a little more about Sir Arthur Lyly, please," I said tentatively.

"Humph," she said. "That's gossip all right. He's a bad one he is, but you have to excuse him because of his talent, maybe he's got a lot of that and maybe not, I can't make up my mind yet but I buy his pictures even though I'm not sure.

"Good family background," she went on, "as British families go. Explorers and writers. Sir Jennifer Lyly sailed with Drake. John Lyly wrote *Euphues and His England*. Very elegant and artificial," she said.

Gertrude's narrative style was a little jumbled but I was able to rearrange it in a fair chronology. Arthur at eight had been sent to France with a competent French governess in Paris, who later turned out to be not quite the jewel her papers said she was—she ran off with a French sailor, or with lots of French sailors. Arthur was yanked back to England and when he grew old enough was sent to Eton, where he had (as he later told me with his wicked glint and the lascivious inflection) "lots of *fun*," a word he could pronounce more obscenely than any other. Then, said Gertrude, came Pembroke College at Cambridge, where he experimented with his roommate, a fellow named Ffinchffallowe.

"All kinds of experiments," Gertrude said briefly, slashing off the head of a marigold.

Then he decided to become a painter. He left Cambridge with considerably less than First Honors, and decided (heaven knows what obscure theory was at work!) that the greatest art comes from the worst experiences. He began to haunt the unsavory districts of London, always in ragged and filthy clothes. He met all sorts of people—sailors, cabbies, grooms, and painted several of them. He often dragged some filthy young man into the Lyly mansion until the portrait was finished—and the model ended by stealing a jewel or some silver plate. Once he got so drunk that he awoke the next morning to find he had enlisted in His Majesty's Navy.

His parents tried every way to get him released, but unsuccessfully. He was in for three years—Far East mainly, Singapore, India, Hong Kong. Once he missed his ship in New South Wales and had to make a dash overland to Queensland.

Understandably the Navy was glad to be rid of him when his enlistment ended.

"After that he went to Spain for a while," Gertrude said, "and they say he fathered a child on a Spanish girl."

". . . ?!" I made a noise of disbelief.

"Yes really. Then Paris. The toughs, *les durs*, he loved 'em. He wouldn't go to the usual cafés like the Deux Magots or Le Flore. Always up around Montmartre and the bad places."

"How old was he by now?" I asked.

"About twenty-six. Wasting his life. His father got him a diplomatic post in China for a coupla years. Then the old man died and his mother too, right together, and Arthur came back by way of America where I suppose he met this Wally Herrick person who's with him now. A broker. Hah. Bosh."

I decided that now was the time.

"Gertrude," I said and then stopped—and blushed. "Y-you d-don't mind if . . ."

"No of course not. I'm tired of Miss Stein."

"Well then," I said. I took a deep breath, and told her my story about seeing Wally at the baths in Chicago, and of the rumors that he was Dutch Shultz's mignon.

"Whew," said Gertrude when I had finished. "A masseur not a broker. Whew. Have you told Arthur."

"No," I said. "Should I?"

"By all means," she said. She frowned. "You tell him first and then after you leave I'll tell him too. And I'll have a talk with Mister Herrick, I know how to get things out of people, I'll find out for sure."

We went back to the château, not talking much, oddly silent—both of us, I am sure, sunk deep in the cellars of our imagination.

(3) August 2, 1935

There were only a few more days for me at Gertrude's before my departure for Algiers, where I planned to spend a week or so. They were busy times for our hostesses. It was inevitable that Gertrude should want to take us all driving as she did every newcomer. When I had arrived two weeks before, she and Alice and I had piled into the car with the two dogs to go flying about the countryside.

Gertrude's driving was a wild and wonderful thing. She would see that everyone was settled in place—Alice usually in front and the guests and dogs in the back. Then she would climb in, sit down very hard on the rubber cushion, wiggle a few times to adjust herself, clamp her big hands on the steering wheel in a clutch of death, tramp on the starter—and we would be off in a cloud of dust and squawking chickens, roaring at breakneck speed through the quiet country lanes, outraging and terrifying the peasants.

Both Sir Arthur and I had taken the introductory trip that Gertrude gave all first visitors—he many times and I once. But Wally was new and she had to show him the country. I doubted his enthusiasm for such a tour was very great. He remained a bit sullen and unlistening, staring out of the car window much of the time.

All in all, however, it was quite agreeable. We drove many kilometers that day through the lovely countryside of Ain. We passed vineyards heavy with their burdens of grapes and drove through valleys of poplar-lined roads, up mountains to look over vast blue-soaked panoramas dreaming under the hot sun. We saw castles here and there, and Roman ruins. We looked, absorbed, and listened, feeling the wind blow upon us, and quieted the dogs when they grew noisy. And we stopped at a roadside inn for a wonderful country meal—small scarlet crayfish, white wine, a curry of chicken and lamb, and delicate wild strawberries, with a thimble of benedictine after. We visited the Abbey of Hautecombe across Lamartine's lake from Aix-les-Bains, with Gertrude talking amiably to the *abbé* whom she had known for many years. And we wandered through the hush and gloom of the church and cloisters, peopled with gray marble effigies peaceful upon their tomb-tops under stained-glass windows like great stationary bursts of red and blue and gold and green fireworks.

It was late afternoon when we returned. Wally was tired and went upstairs to take a nap. Gertrude and Alice disappeared into their room. Sir Arthur seemed restless; I was keyed up. Undoubtedly Arthur knew who Wally was. He might have met him in the baths—and yet, and yet . . .

A vague uneasiness made me feel that I should find out definitely. It was a rather odd thing for a lord of Britain to be traveling with a masseur from a Turkish bath in America. I did not want Sir Arthur to feel that I was prying. Still, there can exist what might be called "friends at first sight"—not love exactly, but an awareness of certain mechanisms within two people meeting for the first time, small structures that reach out, touch, and quickly mesh in gear, drawing one close to the other, and making each feel that he has known the other for a long time. I sensed the existence of such mechanisms in myself, and had an almost psychic feeling that they were also to be found in Sir Arthur.

"Shall we go into the garden and sit down?" he asked.

"A very good idea," I said.

He pulled out the chased silver box he was always carrying and flipped open the lid on a black mess. "Some snuff?" he asked.

I hesitantly took a pinch of the moist and crumbly snuff and sniffed at it cautiously.

"Go ahead," said Sir Arthur, smiling a little beneath his scrubby mustache. "It is remarkably fine. Clears the head."

It was strongly, even brilliantly, perfumed, a kind of high-pitched erotic odor that suggested oriental brothels and hot nights in Moorish harems with flamboyant orange trees making the air sweetly intolerable. I put the stuff to my nostril and sniffed strongly upward as I had seen him do. At once my head was filled with the crash of cymbals, dancing girls took their positions around a smoking brazier—and the top of my head nearly came off.

Choking and spluttering, with tears in my eyes, I retreated from him and sneezed violently over Gertrude's sacred rose bush.

"Delightful, isn't it?" he smirked at me.

When I had recovered, we moved around the house. He had

the easily recognizable gait of a sailor who had been to sea. "I love this circle of blue hills," he said. "I shall always see their blue wherever I go. They and this garden are forever imprinted on my mind."

The hills stretched far away. From the retaining wall at the garden edge, with the little sort of cupola set in the wall's center, the valley fell sharply away from the house, down over fields and meadows to the narrow river far below. Then the land began to rise again, through patches of greenery and trees to the sharp-edged hills beyond. It was a clear day and you could see the far-away peak of Mont Blanc like a white veil dropped on the limit of the horizon.

The trees growing at one end of the wall had already shadowed a small section of it, and Sir Arthur waved languidly at it.

"Shall we sit here, Mac?" he said.

We sat down and looked at the hills for a moment. The silence was so heavy that it burred in the ears a little. And then I said— very softly, for Wally's window was open to the garden and I did not want him to hear: "Wally is very charming."

"Yes," said Arthur. "A fine fellow."

"Have you known him long?"

"No, not long. I met him in Chicago at a party given by Mrs. Brandon Harris. He was looking extremely bored with the whole affair, and I must confess I was too. Our eyes met, we walked toward each other, each with glass in hand, and looked at each other. 'It's a frightful bore,' I said to him. 'Yes, isn't it?' he said, and then we both had the same thought at once. 'Shall we leave?' we said together and then laughed. We put our glasses down on the table, got our coats, and slipped out the door without being noticed. We were not missed at all."

I knew the name of Mrs. Brandon Harris. She lived on Lake Shore Drive and was well placed in what there was of Chicago society. The whole affair grew more and more puzzling. What was a masseur at the Lincoln Baths doing on Lake Shore Drive at an elegant evening function?

"What did Wally do in Chicago?" I asked innocently.

"Oh, the poor chap was down on his luck in rather a beastly way. He was a kind of collector for a company that insured bars and nightclubs. He came of very good family—went to Yale as a matter of fact. Then a brokerage firm he was with went bankrupt and he turned to this other work. But I think he rather liked it," Sir Arthur said, crossing his legs and poking idly with a twig at a snail.

"Wally and I went to a number of bars that evening," he went on. "Every one of the owners seemed to know him and we had drinks, free ones, everywhere we went. Neither of us paid a shilling—a cent—all evening long. And we got roaring smashed, reely."

Curiouser and curiouser, I thought. Could it be that Arthur was as naive as he seemed? "A company that insured nightclubs," indeed! One did not have to be a Chicago native to recognize the protection racket and to realize its gangster connections.

Brokerage firm—and Yale! My eye!

Suddenly I had one of those flashes, when two elements lying side by side suddenly jump together violently to fuse into a conclusion. It was this: if Wally Herrick were a young Chicago gangster engaged in underhanded ways of making money, why should he not as a sideline (or even a main line) work in a notorious Turkish bath as a masseur? He could discover names with the aid of a conspiring attendant. They could look in wallets left at the desk. Then Wally could permit himself to be serviced by a wealthy customer, and after that—blackmail.

I saw the whole working of the scheme. A telephone call, or a knock at the door. A meeting, an explanation, a producing of a wallet in trembling fingers . . . , a sardonic smile, a finger flicked to the forehead, a murmured word about "I'll see you in two weeks." What a wonderful and profitable sideline to the nightclub collection!

"Arthur," I said, speaking rapidly and lowering my voice to a whisper. "We have become good friends quickly, but I am not sure that even that close bond can excuse the offense in what I've got to tell you. But there is something you ought to know about Wally."

An expression of great concern came over his face. His mouth opened a little. "Why—whatever do you mean?"

"I mean simply that you had better check on him. I think he never worked for an insurance company in Chicago. I do know where I've seen him—working as a masseur at the most notorious baths in Chicago. He's even given me a massage. I know it's the same guy. I couldn't forget that tattoo, and I never forget faces—

or bodies or dingdongs for that matter. How he got to Mrs. Harris's party I'll never know, but I imagine it was through some blackmail he'd been doing at the baths. And the 'insurance' business—well, it was probably collecting protection money for the syndicate."

Sir Arthur had paled a little when I began, but when I got to the collection matter a wide grin began to form on his generous mouth. When I finished he giggled a little and then reached with his fingertips to squeeze my kneecap.

"Mac," he said, "what a perfectly delightful romantic you are! What a wonderful thing it would be if he really were a gangster! I would even be more taken than I am at present. But you're quite wrong. He does come of very good family and he's never seen the inside of a Turkish bath except as a piece of trade . . . er . . . a customer, I mean. Your little head has simply created this charming and exciting tale, and I love you for it."

Like Cassandra prophesying the fall of Troy, I shook that little head bleakly. "I'm afraid you're wrong, Arthur. I see nothing but disaster ahead. You may be infatuated now, but it's nothing to what may happen later."

His merry laugh was loud. "I even find myself wishing you right," he said, "but alas, I'm afraid you're wrong. And now," he said, standing up and brushing his broad bottom with both hands, "shall we go clean up a bit?"

Two mornings after, I left for Marseilles to take the boat to Algiers. I did not see Arthur or Wally again that summer.

But from several sources—even before I sailed from France for the States a month later—I began to hear whisperings of a tale that rocked the international set in France, involved the Banque de Lyon, Gertrude and Alice, the British and American embassies—a tale that set ears flapping and mouths buzzing all over Europe.

It was the story of the great "taking" of Sir Arthur Lyly by a young American gangster from Chicago.

(4) April 14, 1937

Two years passed.

In that time the only word from Sir Arthur was his usual Christmas cards—by now, two of them, two line drawings that were very amusing. He always made two different designs, one to send to his decent friends, and one to his—shall we say?—indecent ones. I was flattered to be considered one of the second group. Once or twice I saw a word about him in an art magazine, and Gertrude once wrote in a letter: "And thank goodness that awful americain Wally has gone away forever we hope all of us."

Then it was my year again for Paris. By much wire pulling at the university I was able to shift schedules with another instructor in the classics department. I would teach in the summer if he would take my classes in the early term. For a long time I had wanted to see Paris in the spring, to learn if the songs about it were right.

Legends, reports, poetry, songs—all were correct, at least in that particular spring. Paris in April was wonderful. The air in the mornings was thin and clear like white wine with a little sparkling in it. In the afternoons the thinness turned into a golden haze, mellow and fine, and sometimes the sunsets were chill and lemon colored with the last of winter. The garnets of autumn were far ahead.

I arrived in the early days of the month when the trees were fair bursting to put out their leaves, and the avenues they lined seemed lost in a green mist. Tender blue and yellow flowers sprang from the rich soil around the bushes in the Luxembourg, and the broad lawns of the Tuileries were hazily soft and green.

Mysteriously there appeared from wintering quarters the old familiar army of those who kept the city beautiful—the shabby, huge-mustached caretakers, smoothing the gravel in every park with long-fibered brooms of brush and twigs. House painters dabbled industriously here and there, and others polished the memorial plaques found everywhere in the city. Chairs for the café terraces were scrubbed and brightened. Old men dozed along the Champs-Élysées in the warm sunlight under the awakening chestnut trees, and students walked hand in hand. A more youthful *beep!* sounded in the cab horns. New posters went up on all the kiosks, and the clouds above the Place de la Concorde were tumbling and excited white against the bluest of skies. Even the gendarmes directing traffic seemed to be affected: there was a kind of lackadaisical languor in their gestures as they tossed their short capes over their shoulders and lazily twirled their batons.

I gave way completely to the sweet gray spirit of the old city, and lived there almost without thinking or moving for a week, feeling the new blood of the spring enter under my skin. And in that one week—what changes! Paris was a misty green when I arrived; a week later it had deepened to a wild hunter's green. The Bois de Boulogne was a forest of freshness and sweet odor. Old women knitted in the enclosed gardens around the churches, slow as the fates in their movements; and old men talked of their youth on park benches in the sun. Young urchins dangled their rods over the Seine, hoping some fish would take their bait. Daily the piles of fresh vegetables in the market of Les Halles grew higher. Melons and oranges arrived from Algeria, the cabbages were heaped in huge green white pyramids; grapes appeared, and the onion soup grew sweeter. And the early twilights brought a soft gray golden blueness to the worn faces of the buildings, a blue in which small motes of silver seemed suspended.

On such an evening when the soul of Paris lay like a naked breast to the air and light, I walked down the Boulevard St. Germain from the restaurant where I had eaten. I passed the Café de Flore with a slight shudder. Somehow I could never enjoy coffee there for the ghosts of tourists haunted the place and the waiters' eyes were hard—so too with the Deux Magots. The little eye-games and the flirtations were too wearing. I wondered if I would be more peaceful at the Royale St. Germain across the street. Its waiters were no better than the others; clashes with my vulgar countrymen had made them tough and cynical. They brushed peanut shells over you and tried to cheat you. And yet at the Royale were one or two who were just a little polite—somewhat older they were, gentlemen with a savor of a vanished era of elegant ladies and top-hatted dandies.

I stood for a moment on the traffic island in the middle of the street, eyeing the Royale to find a favorite waiter, and located one with an empty table in his section. I made for the chair and sat down, beating another man to it by inches. I looked up with a half smile, ready to shrug a small excuse. The man who stood grinning at me was Sir Arthur.

"Arthur!" I exclaimed, and jumped to my feet.

"Mac!" he said rather loudly, and saluted me with a beery smack on both cheeks. Then he stood grinning, clutching my arms and shaking me hard twice.

"How wonderful to run into you," I said. "Do sit down."

"Why not?" he said. "I am always here now. I love to watch this crowd, this . . . fair. It always changes—new faces, new bodies, new loves. It's the most fascinating show in all the world."

We sat down. "Have you been here long?" he asked.

"I got here about a week ago," I said. "And what brings you to Paris, or have you been here all winter?"

"Some business," he said. "I've been designing wallpaper, believe it or not. Painting is very fine, but not many people trust my work. They hold my title against me. To be an artist I suppose I should starve in a garret and eat crusts and drink the cheapest *rouge*. You might think that money guarantees greatness—but not in Paris. And at present I do not have money. Have you seen Gertrude and Alice?"

"Not yet," I said, "and I must call. I've been having a whole week of rest, trying to get all this wonderful spring into my blood."

"They will want to see you," he said. "Both of them have talked a great deal about you. I think you mystify them a little, and that is a bother to Gertrude. She wants the lives of everyone to be laid out flat before her so that she can understand them at once. You have a puzzling region of shadow."

I laughed. "Don't you have one too?"

"Not I," he said. "I tell them all. They are my only confidantes."

I directed the talk away from such personal matters. "Sorry to hear you're having a hard time of it at the moment."

His perpetual grin suddenly vanished and his eyes changed. "I never wrote you about what happened two summers ago after you left," he said.

"I heard a little," I said discreetly, hoping my inflection would convey my sympathy.

He brushed back his downfalling lock of hair and looked for a moment like a teddy bear, rather worn and disheveled. "How right you were when you warned me about that American," he said at last.

Instead of turning the talk into harmless channels I had directed it into the worst terrain of all. Wild clutchings for a change of topic fluttered in my mind but the grasping closed on nothingness. The matter was at hand, and I wished I were elsewhere.

"I take it things didn't go so well," I said.

His laugh this time was a great upward lurch of a "Ha!" and then a bloated silence. At last he spoke. "No," he said, "not so well."

He looked down at his trousers and began to run a finger up and down the crease of his left leg. It would have been a small gesture in any other person, but in Arthur it was disturbing. His background had always made me think of him as one completely in control of any situation. His sophistication, the glitter and abundance of his experience, should have kept him always clear-eyed and amused. He always made you feel that he could *cope with*. Even in our brief first meeting two years before I had been struck by the fact that he always looked straight into one's eyes while he was speaking. Now he could not. Added to that was the almost shamed gesture of the crease. It dismayed me.

"Come now, cheer up," I said. "After all there are bad Americans just as there are bad Englishmen and Frenchmen. You had the misfortune to meet a bad American."

He suddenly put one hand to his eyes, keeping his face turned down. "Those are exactly the words that Gertrude used when she went to the British Embassy for me, to keep Wally out of England," he said, and for a moment I thought he was going to cry. Then he got control and looked at me directly.

"Won't I ever learn?" he murmured. "Won't I ever learn?"

A rhetorical question? I looked across the street and said nothing.

"We are all fools," he said after a moment. "We were created to be taken advantage of, to be used—yes, and blackmailed. Scapegoats for others' guilt. A joke . . . like village idiots."

"Fair game," I murmured. "At least everywhere in America."

"Here too, to a great extent," said Arthur, "despite the Napoleonic code and the freedom allowed in most of Europe."

"You'd have to live in the States to realize the frightening extent of the difference," I said, "but there are a few small signs of change."

The waiter came to hover. "Will you have another coffee?" Arthur said. "I'll have a *fine*."

"I guess so," I said, and he ordered.

"Are you doing anything this evening?" he asked.

"No, I'm free."

"Would you have a couple of hours?" he asked. "I'd like to tell you the whole story of Herrick, since you were there at the beginning."

"All right," I said.

"But not here," he said. "It's too long. And the place isn't right. Will you come back to the apartment with me? We can relax there."

"Certainly," I said.

The waiter came with our drinks, and I paid him. Then Arthur seemed to forget for a few moments about Wally Herrick, and was his old amusing self, commenting on the people passing. Not far away at another table was an elderly white-haired American man, with a high nasal voice and false teeth that clacked. All the qualities and airs of youth, which a good man gladly puts aside when the time comes, were obscenely preserved in him. His silver hair was carefully marcelled, and he was "my dear"-ing and "doll"-ing two middle-aged women at his table, name-dropping the persons he knew in the "theatuh" in New York. A large jade stone in a silver mounting flashed on his finger as he moved his hands—birdlike and limp wristed, fluttering with their points against his thin old chest when he said "You mean lil ole me?" and catching at the side of his hair to smooth it back with oh! such a ladylike gesture. And all the while his eyes were darting from side to side, the hunter's look, directed everywhere except at the two ladies, watching the young men pass fingering themselves, following them with beady little hungry eyes, like an elderly frosty spider looking for a plump and juicy fly.

Arthur looked at me and shook his head.

"America's leading export to Europe just now," I said.

Arthur smiled. "No wonder the French are convinced that all Americans are queer."

"Let's go," I said.

We took a cab from the standing place at the kiosk and headed through the dusk to the Île St. Louis, down the Boulevard St. Germain past the early evening strollers, by the Tour d'Argent across the bridge, and into the quiet downhill street where Arthur's apartment was. It was almost dark when we arrived. The Seine beyond the low wall was running smoothly like cold molten lead, steel gray in the last of the light, somber and gloomy under the dark violet sky.

Our heelplates rang on the stone flagging of the entryway. A bulb burned yellow in the lower hall. We went up the curving stairwell. Inside the apartment a single lamp under a rose shade was lighted.

It was a wonderful apartment, designed for intimate living. The ceilings were high and white, the walls a light gray, and the furniture very low and dark on a deep blue carpeting. On the walls were canvases by Arthur, two Picassos, a thing by Christian Bérard, a décor for a ballet by Cecil Beaton, and an erotic Tchelitchev. In one corner was a fluted section of a broken column from a Greek temple on which sat a head of classic statuary with great empty eyes.

A screen that Arthur had done, depicting fauns and centaurs engaged in some sort of horseplay, half-hid one side of the marble fireplace. Over the two wide ceiling-high windows of the main room hung thin yellowish blinds into the middle of which had been set two huge medieval vellums, now faintly illuminated by the streetlights outside. With his untiring collector's mania Arthur had filled the place with curiosities gathered from everywhere: a candelabrum that had lighted Marie Antoinette's boudoir, a *godémiche* said to have been Nell Gwyn's, the sextant that had reputedly belonged to Sir Francis Drake, a small sphinx with emerald eyes that Oscar Wilde had owned, and a profusion of others.

"How comfortable your apartment is," I said. "It's one that invites confidences and good talk and—"

"Lovemaking?" said Arthur with a kind of tense nervous giggle.

"Sure," I said.

"Sit anywhere," he said. "I'm going to change my clothes and put on something casual." He looked extremely hot in coat and striped trousers and black tie—and bowler hat. He told me that Gertrude once said to him, "Those clothes are the kind that beg to get you robbed." He agreed, but reminded her that an English baronet must keep up appearances.

"Of course," he said to me, "when I go out for an evening howl, the most disreputable *apache* is a credit to my appearance."

"What do you wear then?" I asked.

"Oh, some ragged blue trousers and a dirty striped French sailor's undershirt, with sometimes an old stained beret."

He disappeared into the bedroom, and I sank into a soft brown chair that rose around me and enfolded me as intimately as human arms would.

Perhaps there was already a vague feeling in my mind that one day I might write Arthur's story. I did not know then that I would fall heir to—through Alice's doing—all the background riches of his life. As I sat there, I began to prepare myself to hear an exciting tale. I tested the recorder stored at the back of my brain, my auditory memory being better than my visual. Sometimes that was unfortunate, for my mind was cluttered with worthless bits of information that an ordinary memory discards—old telephone numbers, street addresses, names without faces—all the useless things that make ragbags of our brains.

On that evening Arthur talked for nearly three hours. I left exhausted and exhilarated, filled with a wonderful story, and perishing to make notes while it was still fresh. That record, together with Arthur's diaries that Alice later gave me, a few letters from Wally (including the last one that still chills me with its perfidy), the notes from Gertrude's retelling of the same story, the stolen sketchbooks (which he *made* me steal), and the supplementary materials found in the two trunks that Alice kept for me, plus Alice's retelling of the same story much later—all these have been used to make what may be an awkward thing at best.

The bones might show through, but who has ever heard of a structure not built around a skeleton?

(5) August 3, 1935

In Arthur's journal under this date I read:

"It cannot be true, what the young American, John—or Mac what's-his-name, said. But it has somehow unconsciously *worried* me. I remember the business of the necklace on the ship—rather *nervy* thing that. But Wally made the whole story *sound* plausible. Still I wonder sometimes what Wally is *thinking* about when I come upon him as I did this afternoon. Seems to be living through some old violence in his past. He was cutting *viciously* at some stalks of weeds with Gertrude's old riding crop, which he had picked up in the house—swearing under his breath. His eyes mere *slits*. Rather *frightening*."

The business of the necklace had been a strange thing, certainly.

When Arthur had first suggested to Wally that the two of them go to France together, Wally had been delighted. They had arranged an understanding between themselves about men and women—that each was free to have whatever woman he wanted. But no men.

As a result the trip had been filled with pleasant and hilarious flirtations. A young green-eyed French countess, with an ancient husband who dozed away the days in his deck chair, had become enamored of Wally's arrow straightness, the hot daggers in his eyes, and the exciting lights in his curly black hair. They were always together—dancing, having cocktails, or walking the promenade deck under the silent windy stars. On the evening of the captain's dinner—when all the ship was drunk—Arthur returned from a little excursion of his own to the crew's quarters where he had left a string of happy souls behind. But he found the stateroom door locked, and had discreetly retired.

Afterward there was a lot of joshing, and just a twinge of jealousy in Arthur's heart. The countess that evening had been wearing a brilliant diamond pendant, which Arthur had noticed and praised.

He was much surprised, then, to see it fall from a pair of Wally's shorts as they were unpacking in Paris.

"Good fathers," said Arthur, wide eyed. "It's the comtesse's diamond pendant."

"Yeah, it was," said Wally. He retrieved it from the floor, and it hung silently swinging on its platinum chain like the pendulum of a fantastic clock.

"Where in the world—I mean, how does it happen that you—"

"She gave it to me," said Wally unconcernedly. He dropped it into the bag.

"For hevvin's sake, what for?"

Wally smirked. "Services rendered," he said.

"But it must be worth a thousand pounds," said Sir Arthur.

"Twelve hundred," Wally corrected. "I had it appraised at Cartier's while you went to the bank."

"She must have been out of her mind," said Arthur nervously.

"Oh, I dunno. Perhaps she was just feelin' generous that evening."

"You—you didn't s-steal it?" said Arthur after a long hideous moment.

"Of course not," said Wally evenly. "If I had, wouldn't there have been a fuss at the pier when we docked?"

"But the count—what will he say when he misses it? Or if she confesses she was in the cabin with you that night?"

"I think," Wally said with composure, "that part of the reason she gave it to me was so's he wouldn't find out anything. But of course I never said I'd tell, and she wouldn't let me think she was bribin' me not to. Hah. 'In memory of a sweet evening' she says, picking it up and wiping it off on her panties. Imagine that—a 'sweet' evening—with *me!*"

Sir Arthur sighed and returned to his journal:

"Wally is honest, of that I am sure. Not pure gold, of course. The poor boy's life was never very *pleasant*. Until he went to Yale. The necklace—well, would I have taken it had it been offered to *me*? Delicate morality—a *thousand* ways of looking at the matter. If it were a *souvenir—bien*. If he had demanded the necklace—*horror!* But he could not have done *that*. He went to Yale, and Yale men are *gentlemen*."

Sir Arthur wrote the last sentence without seeing any humor in it at all. The world was well arranged to him. The sun came up and went down with regularity, as it should. One season followed another. Christmas arrived when snow was on the ground. He had heard vaguely that below the equator—in Australia, say—Christmas weather came in July. That was odd and fantastic, but then no one ever went to Australia anyway.

If you were hungry you went to a restaurant for food. If you needed new clothes you bought them. Arthur's world had no squeaky doors in it, nor leaky rubbers, nor frayed collars, nor windows that stuck. Every family had a French or German maid, or at least a cook. Every robin was in its appointed tree, in this best of all possible worlds. Sir Arthur had *possessed* and *enjoyed* all his life long, and it had done things to him—made him soft where others were hard, and cynical where they were generous and open.

Against this backdrop of universal regularity, Sir Arthur had set his disordered life. The contrast pleased him. He would return from one of his romps sodden with drink, his eyeballs a thin network of red lacings, his clothes soiled with vomit or stiff with spillings, gait unsteady, body scratched or bitten. . . . But he knew that the quiet blue-and-white charm of his carpeted apartment waited for him beyond his door. Clean clothes, a tub for soaking, brandy to help him recover. Order—for everyone. His own money dulled him to its lack in others. He did not really believe that poor people existed except as a kind of philosophic balance—somewhere—to those like himself. They were creatures of dream and shadow. He thought that he was better than they, because the poor had to discover the rewards and havens of life for themselves.

Sir Arthur was not really an intelligent man. His money dulled his social responsibility, and kept his mind from developing deeply. He had a store of surface information, but knew nothing well. In winter, when alone, with the winds howling outside he sometimes sank far into himself, but never to the dark corners. If he ever asked himself what was the use of it all, he drew comfort from a remembered line from Whitman: "That you are here—that life exists and identity, that the powerful play goes on, and you may contribute a verse."

Of the many solutions to the universe and the problems of good and evil, Sir Arthur knew only one—and that not very well: the answer of the Catholic church. He had been born a Catholic and still made the motions. But the aura of holiness never lingered after his exit from the church on a Sunday morning; it evaporated as quickly as the holy water dried on his finger. He thought nothing of leaving the cathedral of Notre Dame into the crystal sunlight of the great square, there to see with darting eyes a young man leaning against a lamp post. He would move toward him across an invisible filament of the web always around him. A word, a proffer of money, a dull red on a yet unshaven cheek, and they would move away. His affection for his church was mostly pretense, but there was no question that he took a kind of sexual and masochistic delight in a Sunday submission to a higher power.

"Scourge me with Thy divine love, O Lord!" his thoughts might run, but the images of whips on naked flesh, of rampant genitals offered and accepted, of force and blood and agony on the fish-mouthed face—these took over, crowded out, and shattered the dreamy illuminations with which his meditations had begun.

Sir Arthur closed his journal and turned on the small table lamp. It was a wonderful evening outside. The sky lay in long violet and lavender strata of clouds, disappearing into the throbbing golden radiance that marked the vanishing point of the already sunken sun. The long shadow of the hills raced toward the little garden and the château, running so rapidly because of the hill-angle that it swallowed trees and meadows into its purple mouth as he watched it.

Below in the garden Wally lay alone, stretched out in the sunchair looking over the valley. One splendid forearm and hand hung over the side of the chair, holding a long-stemmed rose that he had plucked. He wore gray slacks and socks, and his ankles were lightly crossed like silver links. His white T-shirt set off the brown muscles of his strong arms. Arthur could not see his face—only the midnight tangle at the top of his head.

A wonderful young animal, and mine, all mine, Arthur thought happily as he leaned from the window and called down to him.

"It's a lovely evening, wot?" he said, trying to recall the exact wording of the love duet between Lorenzo and Jessica in *The Merchant of Venice*, but getting no farther than the repeated phrase: "In such a night . . ."

Wally turned his head and looked up. "Yeah. What're we gonna do?"

"We might walk over to the village," Arthur said. "It's Saturday and there'll be a dance in the square. Or we might play *boules* on the green."

"It doesn't sound very exciting," said Wally, and to him it was not. He missed Chicago or New York or Paris. To be caught down in the country with an eccentric British peer and two aging literary ladies was not his idea of a good time.

"It probably won't be," Arthur said. "But we can have a *fine* or two at a café and watch the country boys. And girls. Perhaps we can stir up a little excitement of our own."

"Come on down," Wally said. "We might as well go. There's nothin' else to do around here."

A few minutes later Gertrude heard the clang of the front gate and then Sir Arthur called her name. She put down her pen and went to the window. Arthur and Wally were outside the gate in the lane.

"We're walking over to Belley," he called out. "I don't know what time we'll be back."

"Stay out of trouble!" Gertrude yelled at them. "I'll leave the door open."

Sir Arthur waved to her and Wally said "So long!" and they walked down the narrow rutted road. Just before they turned the corner around a barn, Gertrude saw Sir Arthur's hand reach for Wally's and capture it.

She remained leaning on the windowsill for a long time, thinking, heavy as an Aztec idol of stone.

(6) August 4, 1935

The next morning Gertrude was scowling as she struggled into her blouse and buttoned the coarse burlap skirt around her waist. Alice, already dressed, was quietly tidying up the room.

"Did you hear them when they came in last night, Pussy, did you hear them," Gertrude asked, her voice rasping with irritation.

"Who could help?" Alice said. "It took them nearly fifteen minutes to get the front gate open, giggling and then swearing, until I'm sure all the community was awake."

"I am really very tired of drunks," said Gertrude, who rarely took a drop of anything herself. "And it seems that all our life long at least for the thirty years we've lived in France, we have been surrounded by drunks drunks and more drunks. It is stupid, it is a bore, it is a bother."

"Don't get excited, Lovey," said Alice calmly. "It's traditional for artists and writers to drink. It's the way they escape. They're all maladjusted and unhappy. If they weren't they wouldn't produce anything."

"Except me I ain't maladjusted," Gertrude grumbled. "Sometimes I wonder if what they produce is worth the trouble of having them around drunk until they produce it. They're none of them as sensible as Jo Davidson because he stopped."

"Only because," said Alice, "he broke his leg and was in a wheelchair and his wife wouldn't let him have any."

"Do you remember how his eyes were opened the time a coupla his drunken pals came to visit him in his wheelchair, Pussy, do you remember. He was disgusted with them entirely and when they left he said with a kind of sad bewilderment, 'Was I ever like that?' to his wife and she said 'Yes only worse,' and then he said 'Well then never again,' and he never did take a drink again and became worth knowing finally."

"Yes," said Alice, "but you can't expect Arthur and Wally Herrick to stop drinking yet. They're not old enough. And I suppose there's really no harm in their getting tight once in a while."

"That Wally Herrick," Gertrude said, and a frown darkened her forehead once again. "I'm going to have a talk with Mister Herrick because I think something is not quite what it seems it is on top with him. I think maybe Johnny McAndrews was right. Did he tell you what he told me."

"You mean about Wally's being a masseur in Chicago?" asked Alice.

"Yes and I wonder I really do wonder. Did Arthur meet him there or did he really meet him at Mrs. Harris's. You really can't depend on Arthur much more than you can on any stranger anymore."

"Or for that matter on Johnny McAndrew's stories," said Alice. "Maybe he was just jealous because Arthur had Wally tied up hand and foot."

"I think Johnny gets all he wants," said Gertrude, "but let's not be vulgar whatever we are. I am going to have a talk with Mister Herrick right after breakfast, so let us break our fast fast."

When Alice many years later repeated Gertrude's remark to me I did not know whether to be embarrassed, flattered, or irritated. For many years I had kept having sexual encounters with a kind of monotonous animal regularity, because they were good for one. Certainly not much escaped the careful eyes of those two ladies. . . .

Wally was sitting on the low stone garden wall looking out over the fresh green valley, idly picking snails off a rose bush and tossing them down into the brambles on the other side of the wall. There had been a little rain in the early dawn, and the landscape sparkled. It was a wonderful morning with lots of sunshine sliding about, and the sky at the mountaintops across the valley was filled with wild swirls and rumbles of thick white clouds, and bluer than blue above.

But Wally was irritated. Sir Arthur had been a very miser when Wally had asked that morning for a little pocket change. "Why don't you sell the necklace?" Arthur asked.

"That's a keepsake. I wouldn't part with it. And anyway, where would I sell it in this hick burg?"

"I'm sorry, I've got no extra change," Arthur said. "I have to go to the bank this afternoon myself. Then we can get some."

So Wally was mad. He squeezed a snail until it popped and left his fingers oozy. He did not see Gertrude nor hear her until she was nearly on top of him.

"It's a fine morning for a walk," she said and looked at him keenly, jamming her hands deep into her skirt pockets.

Her words and expression startled Wally, and for some vague reason he felt afraid. So must the victims of the Inquisition have felt when eyed by a monitor. But no one could say no to Gertrude. It was not a simple observation on the weather, but a command.

"Yes, it is," he said and got to his feet. "May I come along?"

"Do," she said. "Do you want to take the upper turn through the vineyards or the lower one through the valley."

"Either one. They're both new to me."

Gertrude turned to the house. "Come Pépé," she shouted and the little chihuahua stuck his nose around the corner of the door, and yelping joyfully ran toward her. She picked up a leather leash lying in the sunchair, "Quiet!" she shouted and then turned to Wally.

"We'll take the lower turn then," she said. "I don't think it'll be muddy."

They went out the gate. The small lane was scarcely wide enough for an oxcart to pass between the ancient crumbling walled-in houses on each side.

Bilignin was not even a village, but a hamlet close to Belley. There were only seven houses and some thirty-odd people—either quite aged or so young they could scarcely toddle. There were no adolescents. The women were withered, the men barely visible behind their long beards.

Gertrude walked swingingly and heavily, knocking at the bushes with the leather leash. She said nothing for quite a while. They followed the oxcart path that narrowed until it was barely wide enough for herself and Wally. It turned down the hill, entered the forest, and came out in a clearing.

Suddenly Gertrude asked abruptly, "What did you do in America."

"Why, uh, after I got out of Yale I worked in a brokerage office in Chicago—" he began automatically.

Gertrude cut him off. "I know lots of people at Yale," she said. "Do you know Donald Gallup or Thornton Wilder or Jessie McGonigle."

"No," said Wally after a thinking pause. "No, none of them."

"What did you major in while you were there," she continued.

"Banking and finance," said Wally. He began to feel a little hot.

"I never knew much about that department," Gertrude said. "What buildings were the classes held in."

"I—I don't remember the names offhand," said Wally, feeling that his face was getting red.

"Were the buildings around the Yard," Gertrude said, "and how long ago were you there."

"Three years," Wally said. "And yes, that's where they were, around the Yard."

Gertrude struck out viciously at a goldenrod and cut off its head. "That's very strange," she said, "because the Yard is at Harvard and Harvard is not Yale whatever it is."

Wally felt a drop of sweat roll down his armpit. He said nothing.

Gertrude looked at him. "Young man," she said sternly, "I don't know what your game is and perhaps it's better I don't know but if you are going to tell stories you ought to have practiced them better. As an author I know that. You are moving now in a world where lots of people know about Yale and it is different from the world you evidently did move in before. And just what world was that."

Wally was completely confused. In such moments he made use of a device of little-boy innocence that had generally proved effective. He hung his head and scuffed at the ground with his shoe. "Not a v-very n-nice one," he said. His voice was barely audible. "I reckon that's why I was glad for the chance to get away from it and come with Arthur."

"Were you a masseur at a Turkish bath in Chicago," Gertrude asked.

Wally nodded his head without saying anything but his brain was working fast. How had she—?

Gertrude was relentless. "Were you ever with gangsters in Chicago."

Wally nodded mutely.

"Doing what."

Suddenly he turned away, his jaw muscles working. It was simple but effective. He just bit down on his back teeth and the planes in his cheeks moved as if he were under a powerful emotional strain. "I—I was a collector for a while," he said. "Collecting protection money from nightclubs."

"Ah yes," said Gertrude and was silent for several seconds. "Now then," she said, "look at me, look here at me in the eye."

Wally looked at her. He had squeezed his eyes so hard while his head was lowered that luckily a little moisture had appeared in them.

"Now listen," she said. "I don't know whether I believe you, I never can tell when a man is lying to me especially nowadays. Maybe it's true that you are reformed and want to get away from it all. I don't know anything about that and as I said I don't know what your game is. But you listen to me—" and she shook a finger at him—"if your game involves Arthur I want you to forget about him right now and if you are planning any harm to him I want it stopped because I am fond of him and have been for a long time and I'm not going to have him hurt by you or by anybody else. Do you understand. And," she added, "stop biting down on your back teeth so hard, it will give you a toothache."

Wally was beginning to be really frightened by her. He protested. "I haven't got any game in mind for him or for anyone or anything. I was really tellin' the truth. I wanted to get away from America and this was a good chance. You can't understand how bad it really was—" He looked down again and let a muffled sob catch in his voice. "It was horrible."

"Well maybe I believe you and maybe I don't," Gertrude said. "I can't tell if you're acting or not. Hemingway knew how to lie better than anybody else and he was a ham actor too and he fooled me a lot."

Wally scuffed at the ground. "Are you gonna tell Arthur?"

Gertrude sniffed a little. "It wouldn't do any good at all, chances are he wouldn't believe me because he wouldn't want to or even if he did he would only want to help you that much more to get away from it so I won't tell him. But you listen to me, I'm going to keep an eye on you and you'd better walk a straight line from here on in." All her Pennsylvania Dutch was aroused. "And now come on and don't sniffle whatever you do, it doesn't impress me." She turned massively, farted, and stomped down the hill.

When Gertrude wanted to be cold, no one could be more frigid than she. Wally followed behind her in a small iced sphere of silence. They reached the bottom of the valley, where the path turned and started back up the hill. The only sounds were those of the gentle morning and Gertrude's heavy walking shoes breaking the twigs she stepped on, or making suction sounds as she crossed softer ground. Pépé danced around the silent pair, now and then barking at an ugly brown slug or something like it that he found on the path.

About halfway back up the hill Gertrude stopped suddenly. "Sh-h-h," she shushed. "Did you ever see a cuckoo," she whispered.

"Not until now," Wally said, looking straight at her.

"It's up there," she said. "Look."

A small yellow brown bird slid haltingly down a branch sidewise, placing one claw forward and pulling the other up to it. It sidled up questioningly to Gertrude, three feet above her, head cocked enigmatically, query and mystery in its tiny brown eyes. Gertrude and Wally did not move.

Apparently satisfied with what it saw as it looked into the deep anatomy of Gertrude's leathery face and the smooth plateaus of Wally's, it gave one little priming hop, looked into her eyes, and in a loud voice called: "Cuckoo, cuckoo, cuckoo!"

Immediately Gertrude grew very excited. She plunged one hand into the pocket of her old burlap skirt, and the startled bird flew away with a whir of wings. Gertrude pulled out some money. She counted it.

"Four thousand five hundred francs," she shouted, "and a check for two hundred dollars from my publisher. Oh how fine."

"But what's it all about?" asked Wally, mystified.

Gertrude grabbed him by the upper arm and shook him. "You silly boy," she shouted. "Don't you know the old superstition, if you have money in your pocket when you hear the first cuckoo of the year then you'll have money in your pocket for the next twelve months. And this one looked right at me and hollered three times."

"It sure did that," said Wally.

"—and I have a lot of money," said Gertrude jubilantly. Then she stopped. "Only. Only is a check money."

"It's as good as money," said Wally, "if it's good." Her speech habits were beginning to affect him.

"A lot of things are as good as money," Gertrude said impatiently. "And money is as good as a lot of things." Then she started to think out loud. "If a check eventually becomes money is it money after or as soon as it is written or does it have to be signed and cashed. It comes down to is 'money' money or isn't 'money' money. The answer is quite obvious, 'money' is always money. Anyone who can see anything at all can see that in a funny kind of way."

"Is the check endorsed?" Wally asked practically.

Gertrude turned it over. "Yes," she said exultantly.

"Then 'money' is really money."

Gertrude started rapidly up the path. "I must hurry and tell Pussy. This is fine. Superstitions are my new passion. Take spiders for instance, not in the morning but only in the evening when they are lucky, not at noon when they bring care and worry. I wrote a French poem about them but that doesn't keep me from giving cuckoos a whirl." She chuckled. "But I am a lot more interested in money than in spiders or cuckoos, and now we will have money all year round because the cuckoo said so."

"That'll be nice," said Wally. He was beginning to pant a little and so was Gertrude. She set a fast pace uphill. "I—I wish it had hollered at me but then I didn't have any money with me at the moment."

"Well it looked at me so it was meant for me and I did have money," Gertrude said. Her cheekbones were growing purple. They finally reached the main gate, and Gertrude began shouting even before. "Pussy. Oh Pussy. Alice."

Alice stuck her head out of the upstairs window. "Whatever is all the racket about, Lovey?" she yelled. "What do you want?"

Pépé barked and danced around Gertrude as she began to yell the wonderful story of the cuckoo up to Alice. Wally slammed the heavy iron gate with a shuddering clang. Below Alice's window, Madame Roux in the kitchen upset a dishpan full of pots and pans and began to swear loudly in her Brittany *patois*. A flock of geese passing on the road began to gabble and hiss, and Pépé barked even more shrilly. Sir Arthur yelled from inside the house somewhere, what was all the noise about, and above all the tumult came Gertrude's majestic voice narrating the sweet story of the cuckoo, while Alice kept screaming that she could not hear a word. Then Arthur stuck his head out of a lower window catty-cornered from Alice, and Gertrude began the story all over again. Pépé yapped so loudly that each yelp raised his tiny body from the ground.

Finally it was all finished. Congratulations descended, and Gertrude mopped her perspiring face with a blue bandana. Alice and Sir Arthur withdrew their heads from the windows, and Gertrude and Wally went inside. Wally went upstairs just as Arthur appeared in the lower hallway. He had a red silk handkerchief tied around the neck of his bright blue shirt, and a palette in his hand.

"Been painting," Gertrude asked, and he nodded.

"But more important," he said, "Madame Roux and I have finally got the mixing machine that I bought you all set up in the kitchen, and you and Alice must come to watch it work."

"Good," said Gertrude. "I want to see it. I love things that go round—eggbeaters, spiral staircases, whirling grouse in shooting galleries, merry-go-rounds, little poems written in circles, round robins, and—and the world. Come Pussy," she shouted up the stairs. "Arthur's going to work the mixer."

Alice descended with Pépé trailing after her, and Wally too

sauntered into the kitchen. The ancient oven took up half the west wall, and on the table in front of it stood the gleaming American mixing machine. Madame Roux with her bright red alcoholic cheeks and lanky black hair scowled a little, as if resenting this intrusion into her kingdom.

Sir Arthur waved toward the machine. "You see," he explained, "I had them put a special roundpin French plug on it. Because of the difference in voltages, it will run faster in Bilignin and slower in Paris."

"Such an arrangement of pace is against all nature," sighed Alice.

There was a vast moment of silence while Sir Arthur picked up the plug and with a certain aggressiveness sank it into the waiting socket. Then with a great whirring, all the gadgets on the machine started to spin at once. The fruit juicer turned, the eggbeater whirled madly, and the cake beater sang a note on F natural. There was a mixed chorus of "Oh's," "Ah's," "*Merveilleux*," and "*Épatant!*" Gertrude stared at it, fascinated.

"It makes me want to go around too," she shouted very excitedly, and turned around once completely. Then grinning broadly, eyes twinkling, she jammed her hands deep into her skirt pockets and stared at the machine.

Suddenly the smile faded. She fumbled in the pockets, drawing out a slip of white paper and the rumpled blue bandana. Surprise, astonishment, worry, and irritation slipped briefly and expressively across her face.

"Why, where—" she began. "Where's my francs."

No one said anything for a moment. Then Arthur reached over to shut off the chattering machine. "What francs?" he asked.

"Lost something again, Lovey?" said Alice calmly.

The scene must have been like a Rembrandt group or one by Goya—the dark colors of the old kitchen, the shining pots, the polished gleam from the scoured wooden table, with light pouring in the window in a kind of Vermeer illumination upon the five strangely contrasted figures—the stocky one of Gertrude and the slight birdlike Alice; the near-beefiness of Sir Arthur, the rolling lumps of Madame Roux, and the lean athletic grace of Wally as he lounged against the table corner.

Gertrude was always losing things and it was always annoying her, but somehow Alice always found them. It was Alice who picked up the dashboard cigarette lighter from the grassy ditch where I had thoughtlessly tossed it from the car window as we sped along the countryside one afternoon.

"Yes I've lost something," said Gertrude, nettled. "My four thousand five hundred francs that I had in my pocket when the cuckoo hollered at me. I counted 'em then." She turned to Wally. "You remember, don't you."

"Yup," he said. "The francs in the left pocket, the check in the right."

"Well what happened to them," said Gertrude, growing red in the face. "They're not there now, not anywhere. It is a bother."

"You put them back all right," said Wally, unperturbed.

"You probably missed your pocket or dropped them on the path," said Alice. She seemed to have lost interest in the affair. She was examining the adjustable speed switch on the machine, and peering into its innards.

"Well, we'll go look on the path for you," said Arthur. "Wally and I."

"And I'll come along," said Gertrude. She stalked out of the kitchen, seizing an old straw hat from a peg and jamming it on her head. "I know the exact spot. After all four thousand five hundred francs is four thousand five hundred francs."

"How much is that in American money?" asked Wally.

"About fourteen dollars," Arthur said.

"Oh, is that all?" said Wally. Sir Arthur looked narrowly at him.

The gullibility of the artistic personality is amazing. Being brought up in the dark alleys of Chicago's loop is bound to result in a kind of ingrained suspicion of everything seen and heard, and to result in a world view that everyone is guilty until proven innocent. That three such good minds as were grouped around that kitchen table should not have instantly perceived the suspicious nature of Wally's remark seems almost incredible. Sir Arthur did have a flash of uncertainty, but dismissed it as unworthy. For practical Alice, however, not to see the thing . . . baffling.

Gertrude heard the remark and turned sharply on him. "Young man," she said, "it's enough. If you had lived through the war of '14–'18 as Alice and I did, counting every *sou* and starving half the time and eating stale bread, you'd know what money is. Come on."

"You'll be late for lunch!" Alice called after them. Gertrude did not answer. She strode belligerently ahead, taking a narrow rake from the garden wall in passing.

They found nothing. Gertrude used the handle of the rake as a shepherd's staff as she hurried down the hill. She let the twigs of the bushes fly back in the faces of the two who followed. Sir Arthur looked extremely distressed as he dodged behind her. Now and then she muttered something.

They reached the tree where the cuckoo had hollered, and Gertrude planted the end of the rake in the dead leaf mold, her pose reminiscent of the Colossos of Rhodes, and addressed the black earth directly, demanding "Where is it," as if she thought the lips of the Sybil would open to answer her.

Wally looked up thoughtfully at the lately inhabited branch. Sir Arthur appeared confused and doubtful. In deep vexation, Gertrude began to paw the ground with her rake. She scattered the twigs this way and that, but uncovered nothing except a moss-grown Pernod bottle and two old used *caputes anglaises*.

"It's not here," she said finally. Sir Arthur was poking vaguely around an ancient cow disc. Wally tried to give the impression of concerned searching, but after all—fourteen dollars!

"Well, it's gone," said Gertrude. "Keep your eyes sharp as we go back. But I get it that it's gone." She started back toward the house, resigned, and the three of them puffed back up the hill.

(7) August 4, 1935 Afternoon

"There is a quality of *hardness* about Wally that is flintlike and a little *terrifying*," Sir Arthur wrote in his journal. "It creates one of two moods in me—not overlapping but distinctly *different*. I can never tell which one will win out. One of them is a kind of *sculptor's* mood; I want to seize a chisel and begin to *carve* something out of his solid *rock*. The other—a soft melting almost *feminine* one. I want to feel him press into my surface and leave his *imprint* there, like a signet ring in sealing wax."

A curious statement, indeed. It revealed Sir Arthur's personality, for in him the female vacillated against the male with a kind of musical beat of two against three. He hardly knew which would be uppermost at any given time, for the human personality is hair-delicate, web-fragile, and complicated beyond the most intricate electronic instrument.

But terms are relative, certainly. What Arthur referred to as the sculptor's mood or the wax mood might just as easily have been called male or female, or sadistic or masochistic.

Sir Arthur clearly saw the quality of hardness in Wally. Both before and after knowing him, he had known harder people—André Vignot, the Parisian tough, would have made Wally's "flint-like" quality seem like warm butter in comparison. But Wally was indeed hard in his own way; you could see it in many little things. He had a way of narrowing his eyes so that the top eyelid became almost a straight line; through the cruel slits you looked into a black fire burning. When he reached out to take something you handed him, there was a quick sharp decisiveness to the way he flicked his wrist. All of his body movements had this same quality. His muscles were hard, and moved him in clean gestures.

That hardness and half cruelty of Wally's temperment were quite evident to me the one time I had lain on the sheeted slab at the Lincoln Baths for a massage from him. He was excitingly and satisfyingly cruel and direct. As he worked me over I noted a certain sadistic tendency in his continued return to one sensitive spot on my body, low on the side of my groin above the peak of the pelvic bone in the soft and unprotected hollow of flesh. He massaged the spot with a penetrating power, a circular movement of strong fingers until—sweating—I had to ask him to lay off. He chuckled and said, "Can't take it, huh?" and with one final agonizing thrust returned to the place, holding my threshing body flat with one hand hard on my chest, until I actually whimpered with the pain.

I once saw his hardness illustrated in another way. Wally's massage cubicle at the baths had a curtain that pulled only partway shut. It was a great pastime to sit on a bench nearby so that one could watch him work. Ever the voyeur, I managed one evening to beat the others to the Peeping Tom post. Wally was massaging some little swish with bleached hair, a fragile flower with pipestem arms and legs who kept moving his hand up and down against the front of Wally's waist-towel. Suddenly Wally seized the kid by the shoulders and lifted him half up from the table, squeezing him so hard that the young queen—afraid to yell loudly—nonetheless opened his mouth in the beginning of a silent scream. With a quick gesture Wally bent his head and spat directly into the open mouth. At the same time he let go of the boy's right shoulder and cracked him flat on the cheek with his open hand. He said—low, tense, and violently—"Now cut out the foolin' around," and slammed the young man back against the slab.

After the losing of the francs the rest of the day passed quietly enough. After dinner there had been some literary talk over the verveine until about nine. Then Gertrude looked at the clock on the mantel, harrumphed loudly, and announced that it was bedtime.

Retiring chez Gertrude was almost as much of a ceremony as a coronation. Alice shooed Pépé and Basket out to take care of their gentlemanly duties, and after they came in she closed the door upon the fragrant night. Then the shutters had to be drawn and the bolts shot with great screechings, while Gertrude stood solidly at the door, her hand on the light switch. Everyone paraded through the dark dining room and up the stairs, and then Gertrude extinguished the light and followed.

"Heluvanhour to be sent to bed like kids," Wally muttered to Arthur.

"There's nothing else to do," Arthur said. "We'll go upstairs and I'll make some more sketches of you. I've been wanting to."

"Okay," Wally said, "but when we gonna leave? I'm gettin' bored."

"How about day after tomorrow? I'll get the tickets to Marseilles—"

"What we goin' there for?"

"Oh, just a trip," Arthur said vaguely. "Then we'll probably go on to Sanary-sur-mer for a while. Did you know I have a small villa there?"

"No," said Wally in astonishment. "How long you had it?"

"I bought it about four years ago."

"Where's Sanary—soor—whatever it is?" Wally asked.

"About twenty miles from Toulon," Arthur said. He opened

the door to their bedroom and switched on the light, a bulb hanging from the ceiling in a pink glass tulip shade that had a small yellow scarf hung over it, with tiny blown-glass ornaments twinkling at the four downhanging points.

Arthur crossed to the writing desk and turned on a lamp there. "Why don't you undress and lie down on the bed?" he asked. "I'll sit here under the light to make the sketches."

"Okay," Wally said.

Arthur reached into a portfolio beside the bed and drew out some paper. Then he sat in a small straightbacked chair directly under the ceiling light, which cast a grotesque shadow of his nose down his face.

Undressing was a kind of magic ritual with Wally. It was a ceremony in which like a consecrated priest he moved within an invisible circle inscribed on the floor, performing the holy rites as if awed by their meaning. He was alone within the limits of his circle, so intent on the magic that he seemed unaware of Arthur watching him. First the sweater was pulled slowly up over his head, his arms crossing in an X that grew smaller as they raised, disappearing at last into the reversed sweater and coming to a Gothic peak above his head. At the same time his torso gradually revealed itself as the sweater moved upward. You saw the muscles in their excited and tremulous interplay as the sweater came off his arms—the way they called to each other in a chain of action that flowed swiftly across his chest and caught echo patterns in his forearms.

With his head slightly lowered he grasped the end of his belt, pulling it momentarily tighter to release the hook. His fingers went to the trouser buttons, the left knee raising so that he could seize the bottom of his trouser leg—poised, steady, like a ballet dancer doing an elevation—and never moving from the sacred circle. Then with legs apart he fiddled with the trousers to straighten them, and hung them over the foot of the bed without moving from his stance. He sighed, pulled in his waist and expanded his great chest, slapped himself once on his flat hard belly, and put two fingers to the side of each hip under the top edge of the black French shorts he wore—a tiny *cache-sex*, no more—slipping the fingers down over his legs, repeating the knee-raising movements as he stepped out of his briefs. Then he stretched and yawned, arms up toward the ceiling, flinging the skimpy and shrunken triangle of black nylon into a chair.

Sir Arthur watched, almost breathless—the only worshiper at this mass. He never tired of the rite. Before the "Ite" there was the final movement of shoes and socks. Wally kneeled within the circle on one knee and untied one shoe; and then shifted, like a Russian dancer in a slow trepak, to the other knee to untie the lace. He stood again to remove the socks, knee angled, a finger at the heel pushing down, and threw the socks after the briefs.

Little blind and clutching fingers reached upward into the eyes of Sir Arthur; lyrics fled unformed and unvoiced through his mind. Chords sounded and harps rippled in his ears. His hand trembled on the paper.

"Well, how do you want me?" Wally said, arms easily at his sides. He had none of the self-consciousness that one man often has when he stands naked before one who is completely dressed.

"Any way," said Arthur. "Any way at all."

"Hell," Wally said, grinning. "I mean, how do you want me to pose?"

"Lie on the bed," Arthur said. "Relax on your right side, facing me." He was all business now; his tone was brisk. "Let your right leg hang down a little over the edge. Put your right hand cupped against your neck for support."

"Can I smoke?" Wally asked.

"Yes," said Arthur, "if you hold the cigarette in your left hand."

"I'll have to put the ashes on the floor."

"That's all right. We'll blow them under the bed."

It was Wally's turn to be amused. Sir Arthur settled himself, squinted at Wally, and began to draw rapidly with a soft pencil.

Sir Arthur's simplest sketches with their exquisite flowing broken line and their nuances of shadow and light were to my mind the greatest things he ever did. He was continually making them—on the backs of envelopes, on hard-surfaced paper napkins in the cafés, on the backs of menus, and then leaving them behind. I had salvaged a dozen of them at various times, wondering how many more were thrown away by careless and unseeing garçons de café, or again how many had been kept, framed, or sold. I could never decide whether I preferred the pencil drawings to those in India ink. He was unquestionably a master of pencil, but even in the hard boldness of ink his line kept its wonderful lightness and airy quality, strong at some points and almost invisible at others, a lyrical flowing thing of delicacy and sublety. Fire and grace in the cloudy-fair faces, naked figures with raised swords, flash and flicker, dark rays of defiance in the sensual proud line of thighs and curly touseled heads, lines of backs and buttocks like remembered dreams, giving a sense of fullness, an illusion of roundness as excellently as the drawings of Leonardo, as simply and dramatically as those of Cocteau. The *line* of Sir Arthur was like a living flame passing into the aesthetic consciousness, burning itself into the memory.

Arthur worked for an hour and made three sketches. Wally was growing restless. He had smoked innumerable cigarettes, filling the ashtray that he had finally put on the bed. The night air was growing cool, and once in a while he shivered slightly as a wayward gust puffed into the room, swinging a strand of ivy at the open window.

"You 'bout done?" he asked at last. "It's gettin' cold and this is hard."

"I'm all done now," Arthur said. "Three are enough for an evening."

Wally turned over on his back and stared at the gray ceiling. He did not look at Arthur. At last he said: "How's about gettin' out the ropes?"

Arthur came to quick attention. "You really want them?" he said excitedly.

"If I dint, would I say anything about 'em?" Wally growled.

Sir Arthur went to the bedroom door and turned the key. Then he flicked off the ceiling light. The glow through the pink blue shade of the table lamp turned Wally's body into that of a brown satyr, a sleepy deity of the forest. Arthur fumbled in a suitcase for a moment and drew out four five-foot lengths of ropes and approached the bed with them. Wally, lying on his back, stretched out his arms and legs toward the four corners of the mattress, spread-eagled like a victim on a medieval torture-cross. He did not resist, but let Sir Arthur skillfully knot the ropes around each ankle and wrist and tie them to the four corner posts of the bed. Only then, turning his head with closed eyes from side to side, did Wally commence to struggle and strain against the ropes that held him fast.

*   *   *

No one should wear the judge's robe to condemn anyone for practices that do not conform to what is foolishly called "normal." The term itself is meaningless, a snarl-word used by those who feel they have a monopoly on what is "right." Years ago André Gide taught me in two sentences to stop using the word. One was: "In the name of what god and what ideal do you prohibit me from living according to my desires?" and a little later: "My normal is your abnormal; your normal is my abnormal."

One's own actions are "normal" to oneself, and oneself alone. Nor could I ever refer to the actions of Wally and Sir Arthur as "unnatural"—a vulgarism, a semantic contradiction—for if it is in any single person's *nature* to perform an act, then how can the act be called "unnatural"?

But the business of the ropes is interesting. A search of the journals did not reveal anything especially illuminating. Once Arthur wrote: "Wally likes to be tied down on a bed, lying on his back. It pleases me to see the great animal helpless before me." There were other notations, phrases like "Roped Wally again tonight," "Tied him up," "*Cordes ce soir*," but no profound analyses.

But succeeding events helped explain. Not much was known of Wally's background except that he came from New England and one of the fundamentalist churches helped bring him up. Perhaps that fragment of information helped explain his unapproachable attitude in the baths. To become Arthur's "companion" he had to respond to something he did not enjoy. Was it a sin for him? If so, what easier way out of the dilemma than to say: "If I am tied to the bed and helpless, how am I to blame for what happens to me?"

Perhaps entirely wrong—perhaps right. I don't know.

Afterward, Wally sat up and yawned, swinging his handsome legs over the side of the bed and rubbing his wrists. He reached for a cigarette.

"God," he said, "I sure am tired. When did you say we're leaving?"

"Day after tomorrow," Arthur said. He wrapped a towel around himself and stood in the middle of the room. "I'm tired too. Shall we get some sleep? We can get the tickets on the train at Culoz." He started to hang up his clothes. "Will you take your trousers off the bed?"

"Sure," Wally said. He picked them up carelessly. Out of the inverted pocket some paper money fell to the floor, along with a clatter of metal francs. Wally stooped and swept them up quickly, before Arthur in the dim light could see more than that it was money.

There was a singing moment of silence in the room, so intense it hummed in their ears. Arthur stood motionless, a horrid suspicion rising. Then completely rattled he said: "Why—I—I thought you didn't have any money, only some loose change!"

Wally looked very composed. "Oh, after I asked you for some," he said, "I happened to look in the shorts in my bag and discovered some bills put there in Paris."

Arthur was uncertain whether he could ask the question he knew he must. "How much did you find?" It did not sound too suspicious.

Wally flicked through the money casually and stuck it back in his pocket. "A thousand franc note," he said, "and a five hundred one."

Arthur was relieved. He had to believe him, even if it were not true. "I'm going to wash," he said. "Are you coming?"

"After you're done."

Arthur went to the bathroom and Wally reached for the francs in his pocket. He took out the four thousand-franc notes with one five hundred, and separated three bills from the folded money, putting the fifteen hundred back into his trousers pocket. Then he looked around the room, walked swiftly to one wall, and thrust the three thousand francs behind an etching. The bottom of the picture frame held them against the wall, where Gertrude found them the following year during spring housecleaning.

She looked upon them as part of the great mystery of life.

(8) **August 19, 1935**

The train bore them rapidly toward the golden shores of southern, France, past the ancient city of Avignon for a glimpse of the gloomy Palace of the Popes brooding above the town. As they traveled farther into the south the landscape underwent subtle changes. The lively sky grew deeper blue, almost purple at the horizon. The great pilings of low and distant clouds took on a more dazzling whiteness, and the earth flattened itself into glowing apricot-colored plains and random far-spaced knolls with rugged outlines. Small castles and fragments of old ruins began to appear here and there. When there was green, there was much of it—the heavy lush dark green of laurels and olive trees, and the bright crystalline green of summer shrubs and grass. It was a wonderful countryside, intense with vivid colors. Here was a sunny kind of fairyland where even the beasts conversed with each other. In the fields the cows listened gravely and ruminatively to the chatter of the gossiping mares. The dogs and asses discussed the weather and spoke soberly of the prospects of the vintage, and fine red-wattled cocks clucked amorous court to shy and blushing pullets.

Arthur and Wally talked of many things—plans for Sanary-surmer, of Gertrude and Alice, of life in Chicago and London. Finally they fell silent, alone in their first-class compartment. Wally dozed in his corner, and when he wakened the afternoon shadows had grown very long, and poplars were stretching their somber shapes across the fields. They went into the dining car to eat a hasty and tasteless meal as the sun was setting, and the gold of its light brightened and reddened their faces, and glittered on the glasses and bottles and silverware.

Night had fallen in Marseilles when they arrived. A mantle of twinkling lights both near and far concealed the drabness of the seaport town, spreading a glamorous magic and brilliance over the streets and parks, and made mere tall shadows of the monstrous cranes and girders along the quais.

From the station on the hill they took a taxi that bumped them down a street of switchbacks until they careened around a final corner to burst upon the wild and exciting melee of the Rue de la Cannebière that led to the swarming vibrant center of the city, with the sea basin gleaming like a mobile square black pearl beneath the moon.

Sir Arthur inhaled the noise and clatter, the insolent impatience of the taxi horns, the strumming of café orchestras on the sidewalk terraces, the cries of the orange and flower sellers and the calls of newsboys.

"Marseilles is wonderful!" he exclaimed. "There's no place in France quite like it."

"So?" Wally was a little indifferent. He liked the place without knowing why. "How's dat?"

"Well—oh, I don't know. For one thing, the people. People from all over the world. Meeting, flowing apart. Blackamoors from the Sudan. Tall black Senegalese soldiers with thick lips and scarlet *chéchias* on their heads. Arabs in burnooses—and sailors! From every Navy in the world—big sailors, little sailors! Turkish rug sellers, dope fiends, sailors, *trucqueurs*, sailors, stevedores, and sailors!" He pointed excitedly. "Look—look at that tall black with the red cummerbund and the blondined eyebrows! And that sailor—oh, wonderful!"

Wally looked at everything. "The way you describe it," he said, "it sounds a little like Chicago."

"It is, it is!" said Sir Arthur, "except that there are more sailors." His eye was then on a handsome young gendarme swinging his white baton. "It is the French Chicago and even a little more dangerous."

"I never found Chicago so dangerous," Wally said.

"Well, that's your opinion as a native," said Arthur. "There are even more gangsters here in proportion, but they dress with . . . er . . . more chic than the Chicago ones. You know—tight-fitting neckless sweaters with short sleeves, and tight wide flaring trousers . . ."

Wally stiffened at the mention of gangsters and then relaxed. "What's their line?" he asked.

"The French call it *chantage*. That's mostly it. Blackmail."

Wally stiffened again, but he said, "Lotsa big shots, huh?"

"Oh, big shots all right," Arthur said, "but not the way you mean it. No rackets, as you call them. Each does his own work. Very individualistic."

"Huh!" said Wally in disgust. "They'd oughta organize. I bet if they all got together they could run this town. Protection, see? Everybody needs protection. Say, I wish I could talk French."

Arthur looked at him coldly. "I'm very glad you can't," he said. "I am afraid you knew too many people like that in America. And when we spoke of a job in France I didn't mean getting you work as a racket organizer. And as for forming a syndicate of—*chanteurs* —well, I'm not sure how far you'd get."

Wally did not pay much attention to him. "Chee," he said, his eyes shining. "I think I'm gonna like Marsay. I feel right at home. Oughta be able to make some good contacts here."

"The only contacts you make will be engineered by me," Arthur said frigidly. Then his mood melted and a faraway look came into his eyes. "But," he added, "I know one or two that might be arranged. If little Albert happens to be still here . . . and then there's M. Le Bonniquéjadis . . ."

"Who's he?"

"A nice old man, the consul-général of Belgium. A reely sweet person. Nearly eighty but still quite active. He loves to show young people around the old part of Marseilles."

"No comment," said Wally.

The taxi jolted to a stop in front of the Hôtel Beauveau. A small bellboy in a red jacket with gold buttons was at the door of their car. He had curly yellow hair and sparkling eyes.

"Les messieurs, they have some reservations?"

Sir Arthur patted his head paternally. "But yes," he said in French, "my little friend who has the air so young it would appear that he could not make ascend the baggages all alone."

The boy grinned. "It makes nothing, monsieur. The hotel has a good ascender." But he staggered as he vanished inside the door with the suitcases.

It was a small hotel with a quiet and dignified lobby and many mirrors around, giving one glimpses of oneself at unexpected moments and places. Arthur filled out their blanks for the prefect of police, and the bellboy showed them to their room—a large airy one with a double bed. The window looked out on the diplomatic offices of one or two extinct republics. Arthur glanced around. There was a connecting door between their room and the next. He went to it at once, tried the handle (locked), and examined the paneling carefully.

"These French," he said. "They never want to miss anything."

"What now?" said Wally.

"See the tiny hole bored in the wood? It focuses on the bed."

"That's what I like about the French," Wally grinned.

Arthur yawned. "Yes," he said. "Shall we go down for something to eat, or phone and have the hotel send up a boy?"

Wally looked startled. "—with a menu, silly," Sir Arthur added.

"Oh, let's go down," said Wally. "It's more fun. We can see Marsay."

They dined that evening at the Café Metropole, the food on the train having been all too unsatisfactory. Their table was in front of a wide curved plate-glass window that looked upon the twinkling lights of the basin and the twin-towered bridge of the *transbordeur*—high in the night air like a structure of cobweb and dream. Through the glass filtered the noise of the city as they watched the crowds outside and caught fragments of small street dramas.

In France there is always something happening on the streets. Perhaps the wine at breakfast, lunch, and dinner has something to do with it. A fight will break out between a café patron and a waiter; a man buying a newspaper will throw the money into the seller's face. A drunk will try to embrace two nuns. Nothing is too small for a Frenchman to stop to watch the dramas unfold, or to become involved in the scene himself.

Wally and Arthur had come to the end of their fantastic bouillabaisse, which had been prepared almost before their eyes with four kinds of fish, a lobster, saffron and garlic and other herbs. Sir Arthur, looking idly out the window, saw a drunken sailor collapse on the sidewalk. Arthur half-rose and then sank back in the chair.

"Perhaps not," he murmured to himself. "One must not be greedy."

A crowd began to gather but everyone seemed reluctant to touch the fallen sailor—held off from him by the curious isolating power that surrounds a person in distress. Then suddenly a small urchin—a flower seller with a tray of small red roses tied in miniature corsages—came through the crowd. He could not have been more than twelve years old. He put down the tray of flowers, kneeled, and got the sailor's arm around his neck, picked up the tray. The sailor, lurching against the slight frame of his good Samaritan, walked unsteadily off into the night.

"Charming," murmured Arthur. "A beautifully engineered pickup."

"Two to one the kid rolls him before breakfast," said Wally.

Sir Arthur looked at him, fighting against the slowly rising uncertainty that Wally was perhaps not the best choice he could have made of Americans.

Wally picked up a card on the table as the waiter brought Arthur's change. "What does this say?" he asked.

Arthur looked at it. "Oh, the restaurant has a person who analyzes handwriting," he said. "'Madame Suzanne, the Past Unfolded, the Future Revealed.' Shall we let her have a go at ours?"

"She couldn't make nuttin' out of mine," Wally said. "Mine's hen tracks."

"I guess I've never seen your handwriting," Arthur said. He pulled a pad from his pocket and pushed it across the table. "Here—write your name."

Wally scribbled it down—"Walter Richard Herrick."

Arthur looked at it. "It's pretty bad," he said.

"Yeah," Wally said. He tore off the leaf and crumpled it with one of his sharp clean movements, tendons dancing in wrist and hands. "Now let's see yours. Guess I never seen it either."

Arthur wrote in his large and most schizoid flourish, "Sir Arthur Lyly, Bart.," and handed it back to Wally.

"When you sign your name do you always put the 'Sir' and 'Bart.' on it? 'Bart.'—what's that mean?"

"Baronet," Arthur said. "Yes, that's what I use on all legal papers. Naturally I wouldn't sign a friendly letter like that." He pushed back his chair and rose. "Shall we wander over into the Old Port? You might like the excitement."

As they got up, Wally's hand closed over the slip of paper on which Arthur had written his name. He stuck it, unfolded, into the pocket of his jacket. Then he followed Arthur out of the dining room, his eyes dark and enigmatic, narrowed, catlike.

The anchor line of the web trembled, and held fast.

(9) August 20, 1935

It was the next day at the hour of apéritifs, and Wally and Sir Arthur were sitting in the crystal and gold Victorian jumble of the high-ceilinged music room of the consul-général of Belgium, Monsieur Le Bonniquéjadis.

Arthur chuckled as the consul finished his story. "And do you mean that Max the sailor and the Apache actually stood in Noël Acharde's living room and put on that scene? with a real pistol?"

The consul smiled, smoothed an elegant hand with a large amethyst ring (a gift of the then prince of Abyssinia) over his white-fringed pink bald pate, tugged gently at his silver mustache, and crossed his ankles delicately.

"But certainly," he said with his too-white teeth showing.

Wally listened with interest, watching the reflection of the old man in one of the ornate gilt mirrors hung upon the wall.

Monsieur Le Bonniquéjadis went on. "Noël had never known that Max had been interested in the other side of the coin—though sailors traditionally are—nor that Max had on the string the Apache and a fiancée as well."

"Fantastic," Arthur murmured, "and delicious." He fingered a small statue of a satyr sentimentalizing over a wood nymph's breasts, and took a sip of cool sauterne. "I suppose dear fragile Noël was frightened to death."

The consul inserted a cigarette into his long gold and ivory holder. "He was indeed. He called the servants after he had talked the hot-blooded Max out of killing his Apache friend, and everything went well . . . and after, Noël became very fond of the sailor lad." He considered the glowing tip of his cigarette. "Do you remember the fearful poetry Noël used to write about Madame Récamier?"

"Oh too well!" Arthur cried in horror.

"I have just recalled," said the consul, rising with a few creaks and going to his ornate rosewood desk, on which sat a fine picture of the youthful and beloved king of his country, "that I have a copy in Noël's own handwriting of a poem he wrote about Max and his fiancée, signed with his own hand."

"Oh, spare us!" cried Arthur.

"All except the last two lines," Le Bonniquéjadis said, returning to his chair with a paper. "Like this: '*Et parfois—*'" he began, and then looked apologetically at Wally. "I really will have to read it in French," he said.

"Do," said Arthur. "I'll explain it to Monsieur Herrick."

"'*Et parfois, Max mon cher marin, je te ferai enceint,/Et vous, ma chère, je vous rejetterai dans la mer!*'" The consul chuckled. "Is it not charming?"

"Very amusing," Arthur said, turning to Wally. "Noël explains that he will make Max pregnant, and throw the fiancée back into the sea—where the sailor should go. A delightful twist, isn't it?"

"Yeah," said Wally, spreading his long legs and fondling himself; a little drool appeared on the consul's lips. "This Noël Acharde—ain't he the guy we met in Paris the night you got so damned drunk? The little banker?"

"No less. The president of the Banque de Lyon."

"Not a bad chap," said the consul, wiping his lips fastidiously.

Arthur shuddered. "Such a frightful bore. I can't endure him. I think the blackheads in the part of his hair finished me."

The consul took a sip of wine and nibbled with his large white teeth at a sweet biscuit. "He is not very clean, it is true."

Arthur rose. "Will you excuse me a moment?" he said. "And while I am gone perhaps you will show Wally around your treasures."

"I shall be delighted," the consul smiled. He got up slowly as Arthur disappeared through a door, and approached Wally. "I have not much," he said. "They are mementoes of my past." He laid a trembling fine old white hand on Wally's forearm, squeezing it gently to read the muscles through Wally's jacket. He led Wally to two glass cases at one side of the room. They were filled with diplomatic medals and decorations—sunbursts of gold and silver here, dully gleaming profile medals there. The scarlet and blue ribbons had faded to ancient tones of rose and lavender. In his gentle, faintly Oxonian accents the consul told little stories about them—forgotten missions, deeds of valor, sentimental anecdotes. And as he spoke his thin pale blue-veined hand crept upward on Wally's arm until it reached the hard flesh of his biceps, and Wally could feel the fingers express their astonishment. He looked down at the consul's kindly face with the beginning of a scowl, and then the sun passed over his features and he smiled at him. The consul's heart fluttered with a forlorn happiness, and he sighed.

"Such a pity," he said, "that you are Arthur's."

"Oh, I dunno that I am," said Wally. "Dyuh see his brand on me?" He put a large arm around the consul's shoulders and squeezed, looking directly into the old man's face, smiling more widely.

The consul clutched at his wildly fluttering heart in the sudden ecstasy of the moment. Then he put one hand into his pocket and drew out a small piece of gummed paper. On it was printed: "Alex. Tel: 34–897."

"Here is my number," he said in a low voice. "If you are free, call me."

Wally turned the paper over, feeling the glassy gum on the reverse side. He had seen many such stickers unobtrusively glued to the tiles of the métro in Paris, or high against the glass at the top of the pissoirs around the Opéra. . . .

"I'll arrange it," he said, grinning infectiously, pocketing the sticker.

"It would bring me much happiness," the consul said with a conspiratorial wink. "And now to continue—"

They moved around the room, hung with its many photographs of the royal family, and the young friends of the consul in their Army and Navy uniforms, and some in dresses. There was scarcely a vacant spot on the walls. The top of the darkly gleaming grand piano was filled with pictures, a forest of young gods in gilt and silver, mahogany and glass, the terrain of the consul's memories, to be taken up and sighed over, while the mind tasted again the young lips (now withered, shrunken), and the phantom hands stirred restlessly through the curly hair—blond, red, chestnut (now bald and shining).

There was a tragedy in growing old for men like the consul, who never again (save rarely) would feel young thighs threshing beside or above or beneath them. Rarely—perhaps when someone like Wally came along. Happily there were still some "vicious" ones in the world, so that the poorly put-together ones, the *mal foutus* and the old ones, could still know love.

Old Le Bonniquéjadis with his gray Homburg hat, his stick,

and his velvet-collared coat was a fine and familiar figure in Marseilles. The people looked indulgently on his little sins, for not everyone in life had such a fearsome tragedy as he. He had been a career diplomat with a charming wife who had wanted many children, but none ever came, and his young wife grew old. With age came a kind of desperation that—some said—drove her insane. The consul, returning home late one night from a secret mission to the young and handsome secretary to a foreign power, had descended from the train expecting to be greeted by his wife's kiss. Instead, he stepped from the train directly upon her head, lying in a puddle of rainwater.

The shock hospitalized the consul for many months. For a while he disappeared from public life, to turn up much later in Marseilles, far from Paris, with vacant eyes and a haunted look. The people of Marseilles understood. Even the gendarmes looked the other way when they saw the old man with a bag of bonbons looking for urchins with a sweet tooth, or as his tastes changed, sailors with a thirst. He was only trying to make people happy, said those of Marseilles. . . .

Sir Arthur returned. "Is it not a wonderful collection?" he said. He bent down to examine a shelf. "I love those snuffboxes," he said.

The consul was in a generous mood. "Please have one as a souvenir," he said, "in memory of all the good times we have had."

"Oh, thank you!" Arthur's face broke into a hundred pieces of joy. He picked a small one inlaid with white and black mother-of-pearl.

"And perhaps Monsieur Herrick would like a small souvenir too."

Wally's hand moved involuntarily toward his jacket pocket and he smiled secretly at the consul. "No, thanks just the same."

"Ah, but I insist!" He opened the case door and took out a small silver object on a thin chain. "I got it many years ago in Pompeii," he said, "but I never had the courage to wear it. It is a guarantee that you will never be . . . er . . ."

It was a small winged phallus exquisitely carved in silver. "You are young enough to get away with it and big enough to protect yourself against laughter." He pressed it into Wally's hand, feeling the flesh a little overlong.

The butler appeared at the door. *"Monsieur est servi,"* he announced. The three of them linked arms and walked toward the dining room, gleaming white and silver and crystal through the mahogany doors

They went back to the Hôtel Beauveau about midnight. While Sir Arthur was splashing in the tub, Wally sat on the bed and fished the evening's haul out of his pocket. It was not bad. A small slip of gummed paper with the consul's telephone number. A silver ornament hanging from a chain. And a larger piece of good stiff bond paper, engraved with the words *Banque de Lyon* and signed with the signature of Noël Acharde. He folded it into his wallet.

"Damn it," he said. "I wish I knew French a little better."

(10) September 3, 1935

Blackmail is an ugly word to most people. It flourishes in America. If your instincts and practices violate the puritan folkways of the community you are an easy mark. In Chicago the fearful paradox was that policemen—who should protect the citizens—were themselves the great practitioners of blackmail. Of course, there are masochists who find the idea delightful, particularly if sex and not money is involved; they can think of nothing more pleasant than being visited by a tall curly-haired tough cop demanding his weekly "payment" in a special service.

Wally with unerring underworld intuition chose the best subjects for his prey. The blackmail of Sir Arthur might have been difficult since Arthur seemed not to care who knew of his obliquities. But through Sir Arthur—what others! Noël, a bank president, and a wealthy old Belgian consul—not bad for a beginning.

The preliminary shadows of his play, although perhaps moving like fog-shapes in Wally's deeper mind, were not evident on his handsome face as the train took him and Arthur toward Sanary-sur-mer a few days later. They were certainly invisible to Arthur, enmeshed as he was in the comfortable and muscular tangle of Wally's long legs across the compartment from him. Arthur was happy—he was going "home," he was going to paint. Ideas were formed, broken, discarded, saved in his kaleidoscopic mind, and he hummed a little as he looked out the window. The ocher landscape was now filled with olive and mulberry trees, and occasionally the incredible mauve of the Middlesea gleamed at them beyond the jagged yellow promontories. The bright sun shone in great plenty, and the lacy tendrils of vines and shrubs along the rail bed quivered as they passed.

The last two days in Marseilles had been good ones for Wally. He had managed to slip away from Sir Arthur one afternoon to do two things. The more difficult one was accomplished only after many gestures in explanation to a news seller who spoke a little English. But the man had at last understood. For a fee he gave Wally the name of a lawyer who spoke a lot of English and would do anything for a price. Wally went to the attorney, and after much haggling the man drew up a document giving Wally the power of attorney for Sir Arthur Lyly, witnessed it, affixed a seal, and gave it to Wally—who copied the signature of Sir Arthur Lyly, Bart., on it with no trouble at all.

The second thing was easier. Wally visited M. Le Bonniqué-jadis, and in a darkened room at the top of the house, naked upon a lace coverlet, with one arm beneath his head in boredom—but simulating the highest pleasure with his moans and twisting—he let the hot cavern of the consul's mouth enfold him, while he idly clacked the consul's dentures as they lay on the nightstand beside the bed.

All in all, it was working out well. But the psychological moment had not yet arrived. Wally trusted in his star, waiting patiently for its light to shine on him. When the moment came, he would know it and act.

The train reached Sanary-sur-mer, with its blue green bay lying in the hollow of a bent arm of land. Even Wally could not repress a whistle of pleasure. "Sheez," he said, "sure is swell."

"It is nice," Sir Arthur admitted, "and it is small and quiet, not gaudy and lurid like Cannes or Nice."

They stood on the station sidewalk. The train departed and the golden silence rose around them—the quiet of the countryside in which they could hear the drone of summer insects, the clucking of hens, the far-off tinkle of a cowbell in the humming emptiness.

"Where's your house?" Wally said.

Sir Arthur waved to the left, toward a woody knoll set about a kilometer from the bay. "You can just see one of the chimney pots from here."

They climbed into the lone taxi waiting at the station, and drove up an attractive small street with high walls on each side, over which the tops of still more olive trees cast the light imponderable shade of their lance-shaped leaves. The taxi stopped in front of a high wrought-iron gate. At Arthur's direction the driver jumped out and pulled the bell.

Soon a bent and grizzled Frenchman in the eternal blue blouse and trousers and old blue cap shuffled down the driveway and unlocked the gate. Sir Arthur climbed from the taxi with a shout of "Franz!" He seized the gnarled old man and kissed him loudly on each cheek. Wally climbed out too, and there were greetings and laughter and introductions, though Wally could barely understand a word. The taxi pulled into the wide deep yard, heavily overhung with trees that cast a thick green gloom. Borders of shrubs and yellow flowers bloomed along the sunny edges of the place, and the high tawny walls of the villa were just beyond, brilliant in the Midi sun. The graying shutters stood open to the good light.

"It's nothing extraordinary," said Sir Arthur modestly. "Only eleven rooms and two baths. But the kitchen is rather large." He paid the taxi driver and the sputtering car backed out and disappeared. The quiet returned. A bird sang and another answered it. The leaves rustled in the warm wind from the sea. Under their feet the gravel crunched as they followed old Franz to the door.

"Peaceful, isn't it?" Sir Arthur said. He stretched his arms contentedly.

"Sure is."

"Would you like to have a look about inside?"

"Yeah."

It was a mid-seventeenth-century house with a graceful winding staircase to the gabled roof. In many of the rooms the original paint and gilt still clung dimly to the walls. There were gold and blue damask chairs about, and *trompe l'oeil* decorations of columns and hunting horns and lilies in the main room and salon. The rose and yellow brocades draped above the tall windows downstairs were somewhat dull and faded with the light, and the stone floors worn a little at the thresholds. Everywhere were the ashes of magnificence and an air of elegant decay. The dusky furniture of the dining room and the delicate spindliness of the ancient harpsichord had a fragile time-eaten quality about them. The windows were all open, and from the small garden behind the house there blew in the rich yet mild perfume of verbena and early roses, and the sharper acid smell of fresh-spread dung.

Sir Arthur collapsed on a divan in the living room after the tour, and Wally stood by the mantelpiece arranging his *armement*, one leg crossed against the other, an arm resting on the marble shelf.

"Say, boy, this is all right!" he said. "Must've set you back plenty."

"I'm glad you like it," said Arthur. "Actually, I paid about—" he computed a moment, changing francs into pounds and pounds to dollars—"about fourteen thousand dollars for it. With all the modernizations it should bring more on the market today."

"You're not thinkin' of sellin' it?" said Wally with faint alarm.

"No, not now," Arthur said. "And speaking of modernizations—would you like to take a shower? Then we can go down on the beach and have a Pernod at a café. Put on your trunks and perhaps we'll have a dip."

"Suits me fine," Wally said.

An hour later they were sitting in front of a café under a gaudy striped umbrella pulled against the sun, watching the ladylike wavelets of the calm purple Mediterranean roll politely on the golden sand not far away. In front of them some tawny young men were playing a kind of Latin leapfrog, while nearby some young ladies looked decorously and thoughtfully at them. Two boys close together on assback rode by.

"This wonderful sun!" Arthur exclaimed, sticking his head from under the umbrella and turning his face full into it. "You can actually feel it enter your lungs."

"What the hell are we sittin' here with our pants on for?" Wally grumbled.

"It's an achievement to end a sentence with two prepositions," said Arthur. "Undress and get into them if you want."

"Into them? Right here on the beach?" said Wally. "Ain't that indecent?"

"Pooh," Arthur said. "You're in France now. Anyway, I meant the waves, not the boys."

One of the leapfrogging boys shrieked something in French. Arthur laughed.

"What'd he say?"

"He said they needed to be organized," Arthur said. "A pun on the word."

"Why don't we speak French more? Maybe that way I'd learn it."

Arthur looked doubtful. "Yes, perhaps," he said, "but you really ought to get the grammar first. But what need do you have of it now? I'm your translator."

"I'd just like to know some," Wally said. "But I reckon I'll get along. That day in Marsay while you was asleep I got some stamps, had lunch, bought some shorts and a lottery ticket, had a drink, and went to a pay toilet. I don't need much more than that."

"The sign language can do wonders," Arthur said. He finished the last sip of his greenish yellow poison and stood up. "Shall we go back or stay? Franz will put a chair out for you to read. Or you can go swimming or sunbathing."

"I'll stay and look the place over," Wally said. For the last few minutes he had been eyeing a small yellow-haired girl sitting at a nearby table, and with their glances they had exchanged silent greetings.

Wally was not so adept at the sign language as a Frenchman, nor as the young woman with the golden coronet braids in polished tiara across her head, but his comprehension was magnificently intuitive. When your friend leaves, she said, why not come to sit with me? For look you, am I not all alone, and are not you? And her eyes lowered demurely.

Sir Arthur walked away with a kind of seesaw movement of his rear. Wally watched him amble down the sidewalk under the palms, turn a corner, and disappear. Then Wally stood up and stretched. Conscious of the girl's dark eyes upon him (imagine—a black-eyed blonde!), he pulled his sweater over his head, unfastened his belt, undid the buttons of his fly, and then—looking straight at her he stepped slowly out of his white trousers. His muscular brown legs were given a kind of grave softness by the glint of the sun on the hair of them, making him seem to stand in a dusky luminous haze that rose from his ankles to his crotch. He laid the trousers over the chair, picked up the unfinished Pernod, and with eyes upon her boring deep, a half smile on his lips and his teeth shining, he walked across to her table. His dark eyes were full of confidence and the bold look that women love, and some men. She watched him with a pleasant moment of panic flutter. He pulled back the vacant chair and sat down, still smiling.

"Hello," he said. *"Parlez-vous anglais?"*

(*11*) September 3—12, 1935

Sympathiser in French means more than merely to love. It is like the final dissolving of the ache that the Greek idealists described when they said that man is created double, then split so that each half ran wildly through life looking for the other half. It is the end for which man was made.

Wally and the small blonde girl, Margarita Ngûyen-Khoa, "sympathised" at once with each other. She was the wife of a small, sleek-haired, slant-eyed young Indo-Chinese, an Anamite whose father was minister of agricultural economy. He had wanted to study art in Paris and there he had gone, where he met this charming yellow-haired goddess with her high Slavic cheekbones, and the snow and ivory quality of her native Scandinavia.

It was a strange alliance. She lived alone at present, waiting for her husband to come down from Paris to spend his vacation with her in their villa. She had a strong social consciousness. She ate in a workingmen's café, and talked long and passionately about conditions, freedom, parties, liberation, and revolution, and now and then permitted two or three of her comrades to come home with her when it grew late, after the last train from Paris had arrived.

This was the charming and amoral Cressida whom Wally met and loved for a little while, grinding his weaponry deep into her soft body. His life became a lazy sensual routine, with evenings given to Heliogabalan revelry between himself and Arthur; and the afternoons—while Arthur painted or napped—almost invariably spent with Madame Margarita Ngûyen-Khoa, who had become quite attached to Wally's penetrating charms, and to the faintly cruel way his large and ruthless hands caressed her. The two lay in the sun in her garden that ran rockily down to a corner of the sea, or they quietly sweated belly to belly in the lavender and pink shadows of her frilly boudoir. Their love had more than a touch of danger for the little husband liked to surprise his wife, who never knew when he was coming.

"He has the hot blood of the Indochine," she warned Wally one day, "and he is quick with a knife. It would be fatal for you to be discovered here." She looked nervously toward the bedroom door that she had locked from inside.

"Naked and unprotected," Wally laughed, toying with one of her undone braids, curling it around his finger, and then elsewhere in a moment of whimsy. "I can take care of myself."

"No, no—it is really dangerous," she said. He liked her accent, husky and faintly faltering, teetering uncertainly now and then on the peak of a word to await his confirming nod or impatient correction. But he could not break her of trying to talk with her mouth full.

"Can't you fix it with Suzette to keep her eye peeled while I'm here?"

"I—I would be afraid to trust her," said Margarita, trembling.

"Oh hell," said Wally. "She's French. She knows what it's all about. You think she don't know? And anyway, I'm not the only—" He stopped in time to keep from a remark that would be insulting to any woman.

"Perhaps, perhaps," she said. She looked tenderly at Wally, at his touseled hair and the dear cleft in his chin, at the tattooing on his arm, at the resting father of all evil, and said something in her furry soft language.

"I don't understand," he said.

"Never mind." She touched the edge of his sideburn where it crept down a trifle too far toward the hollow of his smooth cheek. Then she said, "Why can't you come in the evening sometime?"

"I—I don't see how I could," Wally said. "I—well, my friend and me are generally f— er . . . together in the evening. We spend . . . that is, we—well . . ."

"But why not bring him along?" she said brightly. "It is often amusing for three to be together, not so? We would not lack for things to do, and the evenings are very lonely and dull . . . unless I go to the café."

"Er . . . I—I don't really think he'd like it," Wally said. "He's generally got something planned. His work's all laid out for him and he likes to get at it while it's ready and waiting."

"And you? Is your work laid out for you too?"

"Well, I'm usually tied up," said Wally lamely. "But I might try."

And try he did, and did succeed. It was not the first time that alcohol had been used as a narcotic, but it was a successful one. Wally left Arthur at seven o'clock one evening after they had been drinking all afternoon. Sir Arthur was flat on his back on the bedroom floor, his nose pointed at the ceiling and his mouth open, snoring to shake the shutters. By Wally's estimate he was good for at least five or six hours.

But the husband, the little Indochine with the hot blood, came down from Paris unexpectedly. True to the best Hollywood tradition, Wally escaped through the window that came down sharply on his ankle, and as he fled through the garden stepping on the flowers, he heard the beginnings of a frightful scene in the bedroom that smelled of American cigarettes and the musky odors of sweat and sex.

He went limping down the quiet streets of Sanary-sur-mer about eleven o'clock at night, looking over his shoulder and swearing. He let himself in noiselessly at the gate. A light burned in Arthur's room.

"God damn it," Wally said. "That's all I need right now." His ankle pained him sharply. He went softly across the yard in the dark, wondering just what kind of story he might tell. There was always the one of going for a walk, but that would not account for his ankle.

When he opened the bedroom door, all thought of alibis left his mind. Sir Arthur was sitting on the edge of the bed and his eyes were wild. His hair was in great disarray, and with both hands he pointed a small pearl-handled revolver directly at Wally.

"Hey-yey-yey!" Wally yelled in alarm. "Put that down!" He raised one hand in front of him as if to ward off a bullet.

"Where have you been?" Arthur asked in a cold voice.

Suddenly Wally decided to tell the truth. He gulped. "With a young lady," he said, strangling. "Margarita."

"You are limping," said Sir Arthur. "Did she bite you?"

"No," Wally said. "Say—t-turn that thing away, will you?"

"How did you hurt yourself?" Arthur asked, ignoring the request.

"The damned window came down on my ankle."

"Oh!" With the sudden shift of a still-drunk man, Arthur was all tenderness. His mood changed at once. "Oh, that's too bad. You poor boy." He put the pistol down and got up from the bed, staggering a little. "Are you in pain?"

"Yes, I am," Wally admitted.

"Come into the bathroom and we'll fix it up."

Wally took off his trousers and limped down the hallway, his arm around Arthur's neck. In the bathroom he took off his shoes and socks. His ankle looked quite badly battered. Arthur drew some water in a pan and put it on the floor. Then he kneeled before Wally and washed his foot and ankle carefully. Afterward he applied ointment and wrapped it with a bandage. He seemed entirely sober, and had not again referred to Margarita.

They returned to the bedroom. "Does it feel better?" Arthur asked.

"Lots," said Wally. "I feel as if I could go to sleep now."

Arthur turned to the nightstand. He poured a half glass of cognac from the nearly empty bottle and swallowed it horsily. "Not yet," he said in a steely tone and picked up the gun again. Wally's eyes went wide, then narrowed. He got up and took a step toward Sir Arthur.

"Listen, Lyly," he said in a hard flat voice. "Stop this god-damned—"

At that moment Sir Arthur fired.

A small scarlet centipede appeared on the back of Wally's hand. In the silence following the shot they both looked at it, fascinated, watching it elongate into an earthworm, an eel, and drip, drip, slowly on the floor.

"You bastard," said Wally in a low tight voice.

"My aim never was good," Sir Arthur said. He threw the pistol on the bed, walked over to Wally, and picked up the injured hand. Wally did not resist him. Arthur raised the hand toward his mouth as if to kiss it, but instead he sank his teeth into the fleshy part of Wally's palm, and at the same moment kicked him viciously on his naked shin.

"Ye-ow!" yowled Wally. He swung his uninjured fist at Sir

Arthur and cracked him mightily under the chin. Arthur staggered backward and fell on the bed, where he lay groaning.

Wally hopped in pain, and swore at the top of his voice.

There were steps outside. There was a knock at the door. "What is it that the messieurs have therein?" came old Franz's quavering voice.

A sudden silence bloomed in the room. Arthur half-raised himself on the bed, holding his hand tenderly along his jaw and over his mouth. Wally hesitated, then stepped to the bed and picked up the gun.

"*Entrez*," he said. "Nothing is wrong. I was cleaning the gun and it went off in my hand."

To his surprise Wally found himself speaking French with almost no trouble at all.

(12) September 13–22, 1935

A lamentable chill descended over the Château du Lys after the deplorable shooting, and well it might. Perhaps both of the boys were equally to be blamed. Wally should have been able to control his emotions better, to accomplish his wicked purpose; and Sir Arthur, on the other hand, had been the one to suggest originally that women were quite all right for both of them, but no men.

When two men attempt to live together in "wedded bliss," there is often difficulty. The basis of such affairs is quicksilver, the foundations of sand, the house itself of milkweed down. Talk of constancy is as ridiculous as it would be among rabbits in a warren. They are the animals of pleasure, not the apes of wedlock.

Wally was quite furious about the entire episode. He had a wounded hand and a bruised ankle. While they were healing, he could not forget. Shaving was difficult, bathing an irritation. To crown his annoyance, Margarita was his no longer because the little husband was at home; he could not even have walked to her house. He spent much time looking at comic books in the garden, his foot propped on a low hassock, planning Iagoan revenge while nursing his body and feelings.

Sir Arthur was naturally sobered by the incident for a while. When he finally realized what he had done, he was overcome. He edged into the garden where Wally was reading. Wally did not look up. Arthur plucked at a fern and cleared his throat several times. Wally continued to read, and the scowl on his face deepened with anger.

"I—I'm reely sorry," said Sir Arthur finally.

"Let's not talk about it," said Wally curtly.

For the next ten days or so, scarcely a dozen sentences passed between the two. Each hour raised the formidable wall higher. Sometimes they would sit next to each other in sun chairs, sourly silent, reading or staring moodily into the distance. Finally Arthur forsook the garden for his painting, and locked himself in the studio room for hours at a time.

One of the strange things about Sir Arthur was that the more embroiled and tangled his life became the greater his work grew. Some of his best canvases came from the days when he was actively hunting evil in the bistros of Montmartre or courting the truck drivers at the Porte de Vincennes; at such times the dead hands of the great were upon his shoulders and the paintings fairly leaped upon the canvas from the surrounding air.

"All art is fantasy, and all fantasy is escape." It is easy to understand why Arthur could paint best when troubled; the quarrel with Wally kept biting his mind, and in painting perhaps he experienced a forgetting, or perhaps he squeezed from the tubes of color an ointment for the rash on his emotions.

The ten days of the "cold period" produced three excellent paintings: *The Dream, The Man with a Tattoo*, and *The Two Friends*. The last was revelatory.

In front of a Roman boxer knelt a young man, who was applying a salve to an open wound on the boxer's hand. The boxer's right leg, foreshortened, extended past the young man into the foreground of the picture. The boxer's unhurt hand rested on the knee of his long sweeping and muscled leg, and from that hand dangled the leather spike-armed knuckleband that Roman boxers wore. And on the fighter's face, turned slightly down toward the head before him, was an expression of friendliness or love—a kind of enigmatic half smile that has since drawn almost as much critical speculation as that of the Mona Lisa, an expression in which there was also mixed a cruel sensuality. In tones of warm ivory, brown, and deep red, the whole thing glowed.

On the tenth day, Sir Arthur was exhausted. He had not bathed or shaved for three, and there were daubs of paint on his shoulders and in his mustache. He finished *The Two Friends* about three o'clock one afternoon, took a long pull at a bottle of marc, and spilled turpentine on his hands to take off the worst of the paint. He had long ago examined for himself the old myth that artists do their best work while drinking, and found it false. For if you cannot see the canvas, how can you paint? The paints and brushes disappeared in little puffs of fog, the thinner cups upset themselves, and the shirtsleeve wiped large streaks of damp paint across the already finished picture.

His three paintings were done. Arthur sank to a footstool, bottle still in hand, and so he sat for nearly an hour. From time to time he upended the bottle and took another gulp. He saw some last touches that should have been made, but resisted the temptation to putter with alterations. A great part of the glory of his paintings—and of his drawings too—came from his knowing the precise moment to stop working on them.

At the hour's end he arose. He staggered a bit as he went from the studio to the bathroom, still clutching the bottle of marc. He managed to shave—nicking himself only once. Then he soaped his heavy body under the shower and dressed in a clean light sweater and a pair of clean slacks. He peeked from the window and saw Wally reading in the garden below—saw him, it is true, through a wavering opalescent haze that put a small purple edge around him like a mysterious aura. Suddenly Wally seemed the most desirable of all men on earth.

With a final swig at the marc, Arthur lurched from the bathroom. Clutching the banister for support, he went unsteadily down the stairs singing softly to himself, and into the open sunlight of the garden. With the bravado of a liter of green brandy in him, he made one quick swoop from the steps across the gravel, a kind of skittering ballet movement with his feet working, but seeming merely to graze the surface of the garden stones. He waved his arms wildly to keep his balance, as might a hoisted ballerina wire-drawn across the stage. He grabbed for the back of Wally's chair in passing, and stopped.

Wally looked up at him coldly. At that moment Arthur bent and put his lips in a resounding wet smack on Wally's forehead. At the same time he said thickly, but in what he took to be a bright and charming voice: "I love you!" And he smiled toothily.

Wally looked steadily at him with no warmth, friendliness, or amusement. The furrows between his eyes were so tightly drawn that they were pale, the tan pushed out of them. "You're drunk," he said.

Arthur grinned foolishly. "I yam indeed," he said. He laid a thick-fingered hand high on Wally's inner thigh. Wally slapped it away.

"Cut it out," he growled. "Knock it off." He pushed hard against Arthur's stomach. And Arthur, with a balance currently none too steady, stumbled back toward the edge of the path. His foot caught on one of the border stones, and yelping a little he went over backward into the pansy bed, his legs flung high above his head before they came down with a thud. Then he lay still.

Despite his anger Wally got to his feet. "The damfool must've hit his head," he muttered and moved toward the flower bed. He bent over Sir Arthur. "Hey!" he said and shook him by the shoulder. "What gives?"

Sir Arthur opened one eye, and the foolish grin reappeared on his face. "You do love me then," he said.

Wally's lips grew tight with anger. "You're drunk," he said again, controlling an impulse to kick Arthur in his soft belly. "Get up outa there and go to bed and sleep it off."

"Won't," said Sir Arthur petulantly.

Wally grabbed him by the hand and attempted to pull him up. Sir Arthur made himself very heavy to lift and refused to budge.

"You're comin' outa there!" Suddenly Wally stooped, reached down, and heaved Sir Arthur out in a fireman's lift. He flung him over his shoulder like an old bag of oats. Sir Arthur struggled.

"You big bull!" he bellowed. "Who do you think I am—Europa?" Then he giggled and relaxed. It was funny. "Moo-o-o!" he mooed.

Wally carried him up the stairs and into the bedroom, where he flung him down on the bed. "Now undress—or will I have to undress you?"

Arthur lifted his face, closed his eyes, and slowly inhaled and exhaled. A kind of ecstatic bovine smile appeared. "Jove . . . you'll have to," he breathed.

With many tuggings and liftings Wally relieved him of sweater and trousers. Sir Arthur's unlovely shapeless body, hairy and muscled like that of a tough old satyr of the woods, lay on the coverlet. He blinked upward at the elaborate arched and coffin-frilled canopy over him. Suddenly he turned and seized Wally by the hand and drew him down to the edge of the bed.

"Wally," he said, and his voice almost broke. "Wally, please . . . it's all over, isn't it? Please tell me it is. The quarrel, I mean."

Wally sat silent for a long minute, eyes fixed on a far corner of the room. Finally he looked at Arthur, into his red-laced eyes. A faint smile flickered at the corner of his mouth.

"Yeah," he said, "it's all over, boy. It's all over."

Had Sir Arthur been not quite so drunk, he would have heard the odd note in the inflection, and seen the warning light—for Wally was not referring to the quarrel at all.

The sun was sinking with quite a Turner look of glory when Wally slipped out of the house somewhat later, and went down to the post and telegraph office in Sanary-sur-mer. There he called a number in Marseilles.

When the lawyer answered, Wally said: "Will you fix it to have the wire sent from London now?" And then he hung up.

The spider sat fat and satisfied in the middle of its completed web, and bounced a little to test the springiness of its marvelous trap.

(13) September 23, 1935

For a while the next day Sir Arthur was infinitely happy. The world was right. His lover had forgiven him. The sunlight warmed him; birds sang, and his heart answered. The colors of the house inside were rich and unfaded—deep dusky scarlets, piercing blues, glowing threads of antique gold in the draperies. The sky was so dazzlingly blue that it was intolerable to the eye, the few white clouds a blinding, almost indecent white. And Sir Arthur, with a true romantic's soul, judged it right that nature should reflect his mood, not he the mood of nature.

Arthur later remembered that single day, his last of happiness for quite a while. Late in the afternoon he sat in the garden with Wally—the *new* Wally, all friendliness and large smiles and high-spirited whimsy that made him a more delightful animal than he had ever seemed before, the gloom and tension gone. His face was free of frowning; his laugh seemed honest and sincere. Indeed, the euphoria was almost as if it were induced by a sniff of cocaine, or caused by four martinis on an empty stomach. Arthur was glad that his friend was happy, the wall between them destroyed, the minds and bodies fitted together again.

Old Franz shuffled toward them down the graveled walk, carrying an envelope. *"Un télégramme pour monsieur, qui est arrivé à l'instant,"* he said.

"Merci bien, Franz," Sir Arthur said. He tore it open and read. Then he suddenly sat upright in his sun chair. "Good hevvings!" he exclaimed.

Wally turned his head to look at him. "What is it?" he said.

Sir Arthur beamed with delight. "You'd never imagine," he said. "It's from Martin Baylor in London!"

"Who's Martin Baylor?"

"Oh, I've told you many times," Arthur said a little crossly. "The owner of the Baylor Galleries, the most important in London. And what do you think? He wants me to come to London by Thursday, to discuss a one-man show for me."

"Sounds good," said Wally indifferently. "This's Monday. You can make it by train."

"Good?" Arthur said. "It's the most wonderful thing that ever happened to me!" He leaped from his chair in excitement, and did a little sidelong hop from an old Chinese temple dance. "At last—some recognition! I wonder whatever got him in the mind to do it. Yes, I'll go by train. I hate flying unless it's absolutely necessary. Have to save me wings, y'know," he burbled. Then he stopped prancing. "Will you come along with me?" he asked.

Wally shook his head. "I'd only be in the way," he said. "I'll wait here. How long will you be?"

"Oh, I should be back within ten days," Arthur said. It *would* be a nuisance to take Wally along, in a way. He would have to leave him alone in London. . . . Besides, there was a young man in Paris, and he could manage a night there. . . . "Do you really want to stay here?"

Wally looked at him enigmatically. "Yeah," he said. "I'm real comfortable here, pal. Real comfortable."

"You'll find something to do? You won't be bored?"

"Nope."

"Then I'll go pack," Arthur said. "If I hurry I can get the night train to Paris—and I'll spend a while there before going to London. A day and a half. There're a couple of things to be done."

Wally nodded, his eyes closed. Sir Arthur went toward the house. Then he opened his eyes, yawned, and stood up. He moved the sun chair into the full hot glare of the sun. He stretched and pulled his sweater over his head. His clean-limbed torso was a hot Gauguin brown, and the tattooed snake moved and curled and flashed in the sunlight as if it were made of emeralds and garnets. Then he settled himself in the chair and closed his eyes.

The sun of the Midi is stronger than other suns. It beats upon the earth and your body with visible pulsations and waves. It enters every pore and chokes it, until—blind and heated—the protesting moisture starts to rise. People do lie wholly naked in the sun, though it would seem to be too much. Strange hot dreams beat about the brain, and vapors and imaginings rise from the body to the head, and the brain seems to shrink like a baked nut in a shell; in the wing room left inside, there is space for wild and improbable fancies and lusts to fly. Even Wally's brain, cold and iced and steel-like as it was, must have felt the power, and reacted in its own way as the sun shone down upon him to temper his hard plan.

A light sweat began to cover his naked chest, and he felt a first cool drop run down the back of his neck, gathering speed until it touched the fabric of the chair and disappeared. Idly he took his left nipple between brown thumb and forefinger, rolling it until small chills of pleasure spread over him, and his trunks grew tighter above the stretching expanding mound. Arthur would get to Paris on Tuesday morning, and would probably stay there until Wednesday noon. He would go to the imaginary interview with Martin Baylor at one o'clock Thursday afternoon. Mr. Baylor would be astonished at first, then incredulous. They would try to discover what had happened. Arthur would be dazed and unbelieving, and would return. Or call or wire. Or get drunk. At any rate, Wally would not be there.

Wally's plan was worked out in its broad lines, not in detail. In the past he had always trusted to his luck, his "star"—and found out that everything worked out for the best. Years of training in Chicago—in lying, cheating, turning the chance coincidence to profit—had convinced him it was better not to plan too carefully. There had been created a kind of serene fatalism in him, and he always shifted the unexpected to his own advantage—a kind of modern Iago at the solemn and joyous work of destroying his enemy. But in a sense he was superior to Iago. For Wally understood, as Othello's tormentor did not, the spring that uncurled inside him to furnish the motive power. It was not that he hated Arthur, or wanted to increase his own feeling of importance by bringing Sir Arthur down; he merely wanted his money.

There would be two full days, Tuesday and Wednesday. And then . . .

He had fallen asleep when Sir Arthur descended an hour later. Dressed in his traveling outfit, complete to ascot tie and bowler hat, Arthur stood on the steps leading to the garden and called to Franz, who appeared behind him carrying a heavy suitcase.

"You have commanded the taxi?" he asked.

"*Mais oui, monsieur.*"

Wally awakened at the noise, drenched in his own juices, wet and uncomfortably hot. He shook his head like a dog and climbed out of the chair.

Sir Arthur looked at him fondly as he stretched. "Will my Adonis miss me?" he asked somewhat coyly.

Wally blinked at him. "Will I, though?" he said.

"Let me know if anything goes wrong."

"I figger nuthin' will."

The taxi appeared at the gate, and for a moment there was a flurry until Arthur was installed. As he climbed in, he suddenly turned and gave a secret kiss to Wally, aimed at his mouth but hitting him in the eye. Then he leaned out the window, waving. "I'll see you next week!" he called.

Wally stood for a moment, fists on hips, looking after the cab. "I may not look like a goose," he muttered, "but I sure as hell have laid a golden egg."

He turned and walked rapidly into the château.

* * *

An hour later he was entirely done with his packing. He buckled the suitcase straps and looked around. Then he began a check of the room, his slow sensual movements now quick and lithe. His animal grace took him from closet to chest of drawers. In his absorption, his heavy cruel lips parted and his mouth stayed a little opened.

Nothing left—not a scrap. He turned to the small pile of papers on the bed, and leafed through them. The power of attorney, with Arthur's forged signature. The Paris address and private telephone number of Noël Acharde, stolen from Arthur's address book the day before. The copy of Noël's poem, in his own handwriting. The street address and telephone number of Monsieur Le Bonniquéjadis in Marseilles. The deed to the Château du Lys, abstracted from Sir Arthur's strongbox, and three bank books taken from the same place. A small package of negotiable bonds on Burberry's, Ltd. The countess's necklace—safe in his suitcase in an old sock—together with the Cartier appraisal. The key to Sir Arthur's house in Brampton Row in London—who could tell? it might come in handy. The key to the front door of the Château du Lys—for you could not sell a house without delivering the key to the new owner.

He smiled briefly, satisfied. Then he distributed the papers and objects in his pockets. When it was done he picked up his bag and went downstairs. There he called loudly: "Franz!" and when the old man appeared, Wally pointed to the telephone and said, "*Un taxi, s'il vous plaît?*" with a rising inflection.

The old man could not understand at first. Milord had said monsieur would remain . . . But the monsieur had changed his mind. *Bien alors* . . . Franz dialed a number. Would the monsieur be back? Yes, very soon. . . .

When the taxi came, Wally climbed in. He waved goodbye to Franz, standing still puzzled, clutching the five thousand franc note Wally had given him—baffled but beaming.

"*Au 'voir!*" he called. The taxi left and Franz turned back into the house. It would be nice to have a few days' rest. Les messieurs were very nice, oh very amiable, but it was good to be alone now and then.

(14) April 14, 1937

I remember quite clearly that April evening when Arthur took me eager captive to tell the story of Wally Herrick. Just after he finished about Wally's departure from the Château du Lys, he stopped suddenly and did not go on. He had paused several times before—to take snuff, to find a picture to show me, to mix a little *pastis* and water for us—so I thought it an ordinary pause to arrange and collect his thoughts.

But the minutes went on to four or five, and still he said nothing. He sat with head lowered, elbows on knees, hands clasped together. His dull lank hair fell fanwise, concealing his face. The ancient clock ticked, and the old rafters of the house settled for the night. The window, open on the convent garden, let in only a thick silence; the sounds of Paris had been removed completely, and the shadows in the corners of the high-ceilinged room seemed to spread as I watched.

At last I leaned forward and said, "Are you too tired to go on?"

He raised his head, an intense bitterness in his eyes. "No," he said, "I—I guess I was living it over too completely." He sat back in his chair. "The truth is it took me nearly a year to find out exactly what happened, and even now I'm not certain of all the details of his trickery. It was monstrous and amoral."

"Who has ever expected morality from gangsters?" I murmured. "Except, of course, the odd kind of 'honor' by which they live among themselves."

Arthur nodded, an impish smile on his face for a moment. "That's why I always found them fascinating, reely."

I laughed with him. "What strain draws us to such people?"

He shook his head. The moment was restored, and his blackness dissolved. He leaned back and went on with his story. Pieced together and shortened, the tale amounted to this:

Sir Arthur had gone his leisurely way to London, arriving late Wednesday night. On Thursday he went to see Martin Baylor. But Baylor had been in the West End and had not returned until four o'clock, and by that time Arthur was nervous and irritated. It had not taken long to discover that Baylor had sent no wire. Distraught and bewildered, Arthur left. He still had no inkling of disaster, and certainly no suspicion that Wally had anything to do with it. He went immediately back to Paris. At his apartment the concierge gave him a note from Noël Acharde, begging him to call.

Noël, it seemed, had been visited by an utter stranger the day before, an American named Herrick who had asked to see him as a friend of Sir Arthur Lyly. Everything had seemed quite all right. The young man had called Noël on the private phone number given only to Noël's intimate friends. And Noël, delighted at the prospect of a new "contact," had cordially invited him to the house. He had been fascinated with the tall brute's good looks and sensual mouth, his teasing *déshabillement*, the strong tanned legs moving, the hips arching. . . . Judge then the little banker's surprise and horror when Wally dressed and quietly asked Noël for a million francs as a purchase price for a rare holograph poem having to do with a sailor named Max and his Apache friend. Sweating profusely, Noël bought the single-sheet manuscript, paying the American in hundred thousand notes taken from his wall safe.

Aghast to hear this, Arthur continued his journey to the south. In Marseilles he learned from Monsieur Le Bonniquéjadis that the "American gangster" on threat of exposure to the government of Belgium had extracted a similar sum from the gentle old diplomat. Arthur spoke to his ancient friend in the hospital, where the police had taken him on finding him with his two fine old wrists meticulously sliced with a razor blade. The consul's face was drained of blood and very white indeed, and his lips were pale blue—so that with his white hair and closed eyelids he blended with the white sheets. Arthur had the ghostly sensation that he was talking to an empty bed, on the crushed pillow of which two disembodied lips lay moving slightly in the twilight, and ghostly fragments of words sighed almost soundlessly past his ear.

More than ever alarmed, Arthur turned to the two friends who had always helped him through his crises. From Marseilles he called Gertrude at Bilignin. The connection was bad, but not all the crackling came from the wires. Gertrude exploded, demanding to know where he had been and what was up—for with her uncanny way of learning what was happening in any part of the world almost as soon as it occurred, she had heard of the Noël episode, although not the one involving the consul. She further told him that the gangster was planning to go to London and could he get into Arthur's house, now could he, and ought he not to be stopped. Frantic, Arthur begged her to call the British Embassy in Paris to see if she could keep Wally from entering England. She assured him that she could, through a man she knew, and advised him to get on to Sanary-sur-mer to see what had happened at his villa.

It was a gray soggy day, raining all the way from Marseilles, when Arthur drove up to the Château du Lys. Packing cases stood in the graveled courtyard, truckmen were about, and two new owners—an American millionaire and his wife—were installing themselves in his house. And Franz? He had gone to Toulon; there was his address. The millionaire had purchased the house from a real-estate dealer in Marseilles; there was the bill of sale—thirty thousand good hard American dollars. Everything was quite legal. The house had been sold by a Sir Arthur Lyly through arrangement with his attorney, a Walter Herrick, nice chap, working with a lawyer in Marseilles. The millionaire was surprised to learn that the bedraggled figure before him was Sir Arthur Lyly—and even more astonished to hear what had happened. The whole transaction, however, was perfectly legal, and he would fight any efforts of Mr. Lyly, Sir or not, to expel him; and no, by God, he was not going to get out that very minute. It had not been a pleasant scene, and Arthur found himself seized by one of the truckmen at the collar and the seat of the trousers, and forcibly put into the roadway beyond the gate, which was slammed and locked behind him.

How Arthur ever found his way back to Marseilles and from there to Gertrude's, he was never quite sure. He moved through a mist of Wally's making. His consciousness was askew, and he groped through billowing clouds of confusion and unreality. There was a moment of awareness when Gertrude stood before him, her arms wide outspread; and he remembered that he collapsed within them, drawn to her great bosom and weeping like a child, completely broken under the strain. And Gertrude put him to bed between fresh lavender sheets, and Alice brewed special broths and bouillons in the vast gray kitchen. Doctors came and stuck him with dream-filled needles, and nightmare fever-steeds pranced and neighed through his empty head.

Then one morning he awakened and saw the sun filling the room, heard the quiet of the countryside, and knew that he was well. He staggered from the bed and dressed, and holding to the banister he went downstairs and into the rose garden to look at the fresh new world. Gertrude and Alice and the doctors were delighted, for a recovery from "brain fever"—the only name they had for it—in two weeks' time was rare indeed.

By then all France was buzzing with the story. Gertrude had turned a dozen reporters from the door, and finally refused to answer the telephone at all. She had been successful in getting the British Embassy in Paris to refuse an entry visa to Mr. Herrick; and various actions had been started against him, but all too late. Sensing the moment, Wally Herrick had slipped away and was back in the United States heavy laden with his booty; Arthur and Gertrude estimated it at approximately two hundred and twenty thousand dollars, if one included the countess's necklace. Refused confirmation of the story, the French newspapers had to be content with letting their gossip columnists peck away at the details, and add wild small inventions of greasy minds to the tale.

Arthur told the last part of the story haltingly. I had no comment to make when he finished. The part of me that liked Arthur as a friend was in tatters of sympathy and outrage for him. The other part—not pleasant to confess—so much admired the well-executed completeness of the plot that I felt an itch to see Wally again, if only to congratulate him.

Sir Arthur rose and went to his small desk to rummage among the papers. He found a letter and took it carefully from its envelope. "I shall never lose this," he said, "for I intend to reread it often, to remind me that I am a fool. . . . It is from—from him." He handed it to me.

A copy of it is before me now. It was written in pencil originally; had it been ink, it would not have survived its long watery immersion. It was sent from "Lk Plasid, N.Y." and is reproduced with all its poor spellings and punctuation.

Dear Arthur, Well here we are at Lk Plasid Dick and me and we sure are having a swell time. The wether is good the winter season just begun the other day. Artie, I cant understand why you seemed to turn aginst me so much before I left France and why you wouldnt see me agin. Or why you fixd it so I couldnt get to England and had to leave France in a hurry. Dont our freindship mean nothin to you, Did you get tired of me that quick. We usedta have real good times in bed, hot stuff???!? (ha-ha). I spose you have found somebody new by now and left me all alone by the telephone except for Dick, he's one of the boys I usedta know in good ole Chi, he knows lotsa tricks specialy with ropes (ha-ha). We expect to be hear for two-three months, and then mebbe head for the Sunny Southland, Dixie for me, to give em some Yankee Doodlin down there with my ole nine incher. I dont know what your freinds say about me but it is all lies, and I cant understand why you wouldnt say goodbye to me when I calld up Missus Stine's house, I knew you was there but she wouldnt even listen to who I was, just hung up and said something in french. But gee whiz we hadda lotta fun while we was together, aint we ever goin to see each othr again. I would like very soon to come back to France because it was very profitible to me while I was there, meeting all those new people and learnin about Life with a capitol L, I sure learned a lot off of you, your one of the smartest nice people I ever knew and I cant understand why you seemd like you was real anxious to get rid of me. Why dont you come to Lk Plasid, it's fine hear right now, lotsa beautiful babes and some swell lookin college boys from Harvard and Dartmuth and even some from Yale, we talk about the ole school a lot (ha-ha). Youd like some of those college athaletes for sure, most of em real well-hung, whoppers if you know what I mean (HA-HA!) Well so long Pal and drop me a line at Lk Plasid before Dec first, we are plannin to go south with the birds by then to see what if anything we can stir up around Miame, hear theres lotsa big bucks around Miame just waitin for a big hunka man with a big whang like I got. Love, Wally.

P.S. Say hello to Missus Stine and Alice for me. Dont forget to write.

(15) **April 16, 1937**

After that April evening with Arthur, when I heard the story of Wally and read the illiterate letter, I managed to rouse myself from the passive orgy of sensuous pleasure into which I had been sunk for a week after my arrival. There were many things to be done. I paid a call to Gertrude and Alice and was greeted enthusiastically; there was an excellent meal of chicken steamed over white wine—and talk, talk, talk. I gave them the package of kitchen gadgets I had brought from America; their pleasure was immense.

And there were other things waiting too—walks to be taken in the Luxembourg gardens, and dreaming to be done before the white statue of a sullen stone god looking off toward his remembered Olympus with great blank eyes. There was a late-night half hour to be spent at the gently peaked center of the Carousel bridge near the Louvre, staring down into the hypnotic black waters of the Seine until the flickering eels of light seemed to rise to envelop you, and the shattered daggers of the streetlamps' reflections seemed to draw close. There were wanderings to be made in the Tuileries gardens in the late afternoons when the shadows of tree trunks and the sunlight between them made a dizzying checkerboard of black and brilliance.

And there were old friends to be seen once more. There was Jacques Guerre—suave, vocal, eloquent—long legged and crop headed and glintingly devilish. And handsome Marco Soudain, with his chatter and his vivid mind that turned everything into concretely hilarious images, a delightful acrobat of the mind, always dressed like a young elegant of the Toulouse-Lautrec period. And of course Fitzie—old companion of many frisks in Paris, a young thin wicked American art student who had forsaken the States, and whose blue denim outfit made everyone turn to look, with whitened dungarees clinging like a second skin to his leanly sexual legs. An early visit to Fitzie was a necessity, to learn who was who in the quarter, and who was popping into bed with what new lover—all the current gossip of the shadow world on which so many ordinary individuals looked with disgust or curiosity. Fitz knew it all, and at brief notice could furnish you with the name and phone number of someone who exactly fitted your moment's mood—whip wielders, foot fetishists, lovers of the rose petals, butch numbers, willowy ones—the whole strange populace of the twilit lands. So far Fitzie had resisted the disease of Paris—the slow rot of morals and ambition that the café life could spread through the unguarded system. . . .

And Herbert Baudy . . . whimsical and wholesome, an intern at the Sorbonne who dreamed of the day when he might travel as a doctor all over the world—seemingly the most "normal" young man ever, hairy chested, ready fisted, laughing, unafraid—yet falling head-over-heels for young tawny-skinned boys from Italy, only Italians, no other race. And Georges Raveau, lately released aviator from Algiers, with his dark-red hair burnished, metallically lustrous, struggling to adjust to civil life, with his glamorous tales of the Casbah and the desert, and his blue eyes darkened by sun on sand.

Like an unending mobile frieze, the young men of Paris moved slowly on their way through time—a frieze from which a figure dropped and was replaced even before you saw the gap. "For I may comfort me to think/The lads come on and on." The frieze changed continually. In two years it could alter so that it could not be recognized. But everyone cut some segments from it to cherish, segments filled with sturdy thighs and sculptured chests, with towers of firm young necks and the rising hillocks of the beautiful terrain of torsos as perfect as that of the faun of Praxiteles. . . . I saw the frieze again, now in the spring in Paris, and laughed and chatted and panted and sighed with the young ones on it. . . .

One evening I returned to the Hôtel Sainte Marie-Gallia to find a *pneumatique* from Sir Arthur waiting. Inside the tiny sheet he had mussily scrawled: "I hope you are free tonight—let us have a romp. The Royale St. Germain at nine? If not, ring me."

I was not exactly in the mood for a romp, having passed a rather exhausting afternoon in the bedroom of a young acquaintance. But a shower and apéritif and dinner would restore me, and an evening with Arthur was usually fun. As I undressed in a cubicle of the "Grand Baths of the Rue du Four," I hoped that Arthur would not mention Wally Herrick again, for I had had enough of that recital, but when he had something on his mind he talked of it forever.

Early, at eight-thirty, I captured a table at the Royale, having eaten at the Vagenende. Dining there had made me mellow. It was a forest of mirrors in dark rich beveled woodwork, so that the place seemed four times larger than it really was, peopled by thousands of reflections of pieces of persons. The waiters had been there for twenty years, and the mosaic floor worn by thousands of feet. The linens were very white and starched and the silver good. I always sat facing the red velvet drapery at the door, for I expected Lillian Russell or the Divine Sarah herself to come sweeping in at any moment, ostrich plumes and rustling silks and all.

The mood of the restaurant lingered in the more businesslike Royale. I ordered a coffee and opened my newspaper, but did not read it, for the lovely twilight and clean air and new spring clothes on the people passing were more attractive than the news. I had not been sitting long when I had the odd feeling that someone was looking at me, just a bit out of range of the rods and cones of my side vision.

At the sidewalk café tables in Paris you can stare if you want to, as long and hard as the desire commands. Sometimes it is disconcerting, when someone two tables in front turns to stare directly at you. A novice will drop his eyes and feel the color mount. But you soon learn to return the stare with either a frown or a smile-flicker, depending on your mood. I shifted my chair a little, raised my paper, and looked directly at the person.

It was a young sailor in the uniform of the British Navy!

He must have read my expression of astonishment for one of recognition, for he smiled at me. He could hardly have known that my surprise was due to my wondering how he had slipped in without my seeing him (a sailor, especially!) or how I had missed him when I sat down.

At any rate, I recovered quickly and smiled back. "Are you alone?" I asked.

"Yes, I am," he said.

"Why not join me?"

"I will," he said. He picked up his cup of chocolate and carried it to my table. I put out my hand but did not rise—you never rise at the sidewalk tables of St. Germain, even for ladies. "My name's McAndrews," I said. "John."

"I'm Peter Quint," he said, and seized my hand in a grip that nearly raised me from my chair. Lord, it hurt! He seemed much too thin—lean is the word—to have a grip like that. I rubbed my knuckles wryly.

"Good heavens, man," I said. "You nearly broke my hand."

He grinned, seeming pleased. "Pretty strong, wot? Exercises, y'know."

I liked his grin, and looking further decided that I liked Peter Quint. He was tall, about six feet—and well balanced, with good long legs dramatized by the tight-fitting sweeping bell-cut of his sailor trousers. His black-banded white-topped hat sat well back on his head, and there was a pleasant tangle of short yellow curls in front of it. The eyebrows had a good arch, the lips a strong full male cut. He rested one hand in a sailor's gesture on the inside of his thigh, palm down and fingers spread. The flare of his jumper opened wider than that on an American navy uniform, and the dark blue edging of the revealed undershirt cut a sharp line across the base of his throat. He was extremely good to look at, and I looked. A giggle rose inside of me, as I pictured Arthur's surprise when he saw what I had trapped.

The problem of the uniform puzzled me for many years—why it was so appealing, so attractive. For a long time the sailor's uniform topped the list of favorites. Its cut was beguiling; it fit so closely that it added a strange and sexual darkness, a kind of magic to the body underneath. It decorated and adorned the wearer, from the sharp contrast of the white piping on collar and sleeves to the tight clutch of dark wool upon the buttocks. Genet once wrote that the function of the French Navy was to ornament the coast, not defend it.

But there was more to the uniform's appeal than its sensual cut and fitting. The sailor's uniform had a kind of psychic pull not to be found on that of a mailman or bus driver. It was glamorous, I decided, because it represented a way of life that most of us could never know. We think: the sailor knows far suns and seas, the bamboo huts of savages, the stone lacework of far-off castles, crystal pools and sands, white columns against dark blue Greek skies, the golden suns and fountains of red-walled Rome. His life is romantic, dark, and strange. And when he takes us in strong young arms, we feel that beneath the rough black wool there beats a heart more brave and gallant than we have ever known, that his thighs have known the caresses of mermaids beneath the sea, and that his lips have tasted the sweet brown flavor of Arabian throats.

It is all hogwash, of course. The sailor's body is formed like any other. He is frightened and delighted by the same things that terrify and please the stay-at-homes. But the uniform surrounds him with the shimmering glitter of an illusion; it was the psychic link, the gazing glass through which we looked into another world.

I was not thinking of all those things when I met Peter Quint. Here beside me was a uniform, inhabited by a lean and sinewy body, and it had to be kept there until Arthur arrived. I mentally flipped through a half-dozen topics and discarded them all for the one he had mentioned.

"Exercising?" I said with a friendly interest. "What kind?"

"Oh, all kinds," said Peter Quint. "I've just taken up barbells recently. Great fun. Smashing good for the shoulders."

"You look fairly strong as it is," I said, looking him over. "But isn't it rather difficult for you to do such exercise while you're a sailor? I mean—well, here you are in Paris, You certainly don't carry a barbell with you in your duffle bag."

He laughed with invigorating freshness. "Oh, I say now, that's very good," he said. "No, of course I don't. I've been in Paris for quite a bit of time, stationed at the ministry, y'know. They've got a good gym there and I work out every day. I've been lifting for about three months and there's a shattering improvement already. Look, feel this—" he said, and drew his right arm to a bent position. Before my fingers touched and squeezed it, my eyes saw how it filled his sleeve. It was rock hard. I made an appropriate sound of admiration.

"Quite a muscle," I said.

"And this—" He flexed his upper thigh by drawing back his foot, and the flesh jumped upward into a tight and mighty mound. I reached to dig my fingers into it, smothering a crazy urge to giggle over the picture of myself sitting at a Paris café, reaching over to feel a sailor's arm and leg! But I kept a straight face and a grave air of sober approval. "Working with weights must really pay off," I said.

"It does that," he said. "When I began I could barely lift five stone—that's about seventy pounds, American," he explained a bit apologetically. "Now I can do ten—jerk and snatch, that is—not press." I noticed that the weight lifters' terminology was the same all over the world.

"You say you've been in Paris about three months?" I asked.

"At the ministry. About four months in all," he said. "I live right down there on the Rue de Grenelle—" He waved toward the left.

"I suppose you've been having a lot of fun here," I said. "I mean—when you're not weight lifting."

"That's an odd thing," he said quite seriously. "I really don't go out much at all. Not good for you, y'know, if you're a weight lifter. Runs you down. No late hours. Have to be in the sack early to get my rest. No wine, either. Strange, ain't it? Here where there's such fine wine."

I sighed inwardly as a number of embryonic plans vanished abruptly from my mind. The new ascetics—the weight lifters! The ones I had known in Chicago were all the same. "Well," I said, "of the three traditional delights that leaves only two—women and song."

He grinned at me. Oh, lord—his white, white teeth, and the yellow of his hair! "I have a jolly good baritone," he said, "but women don't bother me much. Besides, they're really—"

"Not good for you, y'know, if you're a weight lifter." We said it in unison, and then laughed together. "No sex at all?" I pursued, cocking an eyebrow at him quizzically.

That was a very dangerous question—a loaded question . . . for Paris.

"Oh, a little," he said and looked down at his crotch, running his hands nervously up and down both thighs at the same time. "A bloke's got to have a bit of sport now and then, wot?"

"Right you are," I said, feeling foolish with my British inflection. One of the plans that had vanished from my mind suddenly returned with a small tinkling. Perhaps there was some hope, after all.

"Yes, a fellow's got to have some fun occasionally," I went on. I was on my own shoreline, a well-mapped territory—sex. "I keep having sex with a kind of monotonous animal regularity," I said, "because they say it's good for you. But somehow it lacks the careless rapture if it goes on too long. I'm a burned-out husk of a Don Juan."

He looked a little blank. The communication level may have been too high.

"I don't understand—'it's good for you,'" he said. "All the journals say you ought to conserve your—your self," he finished. "You don't look burned out to me," he said simply. His glance passed over me. I drew one foot back slightly under my chair.

"Well, I guess I'm really not," I said.

At that moment I saw Sir Arthur round the corner of the Rue de Rennes. I caught his eye with a wave of the hand. He saw me and grinned, his eyes opening wide when he saw Peter Quint as well. He came quickly to our table.

"And who is this?" he said a little thickly. He had been drinking.

"A countryman of yours," I said. "Peter Quint, Arthur Pickett." We had devised names between us for use with strangers— he was Arthur Pickett, and I was "Mr. Belvedere."

It was like a meeting of two fraternity brothers twenty years after graduation. There is a tie that binds sailors together, and when they meet it is in a room away from the rest of the world. What a hubbub of talk they struck up at once! Ships they knew and sailed on, persons, commanders and officers, pubs in London, people and places in Paris. I felt left out, and after a few moments paid them little attention. Someone else had taken a table to my right, and my interest shifted to the newcomer. He was pretending to read his newspaper, but he watched us over the top edge. He wore a pair of bright flame-red wool socks, and a brown velour sweatshirt of the shiny material the French thought chic that season. I was staring at him when I felt Arthur touch my arm.

"Peter and I are going to my apartment so that he can see some of my sketchbooks and photographs from the Navy days," he said. "Will you come?"

He was smiling, but at the same time squeezing my arm nervously. I was expected to say no. I smiled at him.

"*Non, merci,*" I said in French. "I wouldn't come along for all the world, not even a little voyeurism. Besides, I am quite occupied, and happily, here." I nodded toward the tall red-socked Frenchman. Arthur glanced at him and smiled with relief and comprehension.

"Then you won't be angry if we postpone our hunt for a while?"

"Not at all. Haven't you the fox already? Enjoy yourself."

"*Merci*—that, I will try to do." He stood up and Peter with him, towering over. Peter reached to shake hands and I folded my knuckles roundly together, prepared for the squeeze.

"Jolly seeing you," he said—so correctly British. "We'll meet again?"

"Indubitably," I said, clipping it off crisply.

They were gone, a curiously assorted pair, through the evening parade of the passersby on St. Germain. A small green mist of envy befogged me for a moment, but not for long. I looked at the lean young Frenchman and shrugged and smiled. He saw it, and hitched his chair closer to mine.

"They will amuse themselves well?" he asked in French.

"Without doubt," I said.

He leaned forward, put his hand on my knee under the table, and picked up a small mound of flesh with two fingers, pinching it—*hard!*

"*Je suis un peu vicieux*," he said. "*Et vous?*"

My mouth formed a scream that was not uttered. I nodded mutely, sudden tears in my eyes from the pain, and moved my knee away.

"Then," he said, standing up, "let us go to my apartment. I live not far away." There was a glint in his eyes that I had seen before among such "*specialistes*," but—well, why not go? "It's good for you . . ." and his suggestion contained an inflection of command I could not resist. I would probably be black and blue tomorrow. . . .

It is so easy to meet the damned in Paris.

(16) April 17–27, 1937

During the next ten days I saw Arthur and his sailor three times. Each meeting revealed more of the curious tangle that was the weight-lifter mind, recalling for me details of the type that I had forgotten. Peter Quint talked long and enthusiastically of the benefits of blackstrap molasses, yogurt, brewers' yeast, the vitamin complexes, and the comparative value of green and white leaves of cabbage. He held interested monologues with himself and the empty air on the horrors of sleeping pills, alcohol, and coffee, while Sir Arthur and I sipped our benedictine or brandy or eternal *café noir*, and looked at each other.

I was fascinated with Peter—what he said and the way he looked at life. He was like a young male vestal virgin tending the shrine lamp before his body's perfection, typical of the vast group of those in America who spent hours a day in exercises to increase the size of thigh and shoulder. Like the priests of a new cult of self-denial, they do not smoke or drink. Marriage will waste their juices; some sleep with a towel knotted in the middle of their back, so that their energy will not spill from them at midnight. Oh, their chastity! When will they not realize that of all the "aberrations," chastity is the most abnormal!

On one of those meetings, perhaps the third, Arthur arrived before his sailor did.

"Well, how's it going?" I asked, aware that the flood of his reply might drown me before Peter came.

Arthur passed the back of his hand across his forehead in a Victorian gesture. "I really think, Johnny," he said, "that this is the great affair of my life—the one thing I've been looking for all these years."

I was annoyed. "Nonsense, Arthur," I said impatiently. "I've heard that from you before in the two years we've known each other. You can't expect me to take you seriously. It's a summer interlude, and it'll fade like all the rest."

"No, it will not," he said. "I insist it will not. It's really love this time. All the others have been leading up to this. The boy has everything I've always wanted in myself—good mind, good body, wonderful personality. He's solid and sound, and—" He stopped and looked thoughtful.

I said ironically, "Not one single weakness at all?"

"Not a weakness exactly," Arthur said. "Something a bit strange, perhaps. He's the moodiest creature I've ever known—some days completely depressed, and at other times so high spirited you'd think him drunk—if he drank. When he's happy he almost dances around the room. Picks me up and hugs me. Tender, charming, sprightly. Thoughtful and considerate. But when he's depressed—good hevvings! I sometimes wonder for his sanity. But those periods don't last long. He comes out of them quickly. But lord, the demands he makes on me!"

Sir Arthur grinned one of his gargoyle grins on which rode

meanings of paralyzing obscenity. "Y'know," he said, leaning closer, "I often wonder if he doesn't believe—obscurely, of course—as do the African savages whom Frazer mentions in *The Golden Bough*—that . . . well, d'you remember? He says they eat the parts of animals that they think contain the animal's virtues. A lion's heart will make them as brave as a lion. Sometimes I believe Peter thinks the same way, and the easiest method for growing strong and manly . . . is to swallow—you see what I mean." He smiled crookedly. "He's drained me dry."

"Good lord!" I said. "So? That's primitive."

"The French believe that eating rabbit makes you able to run fast and have lots of children," Arthur said, amused.

"Let's talk about something else," I said. "How's your painting coming along?"

"Splendidly! When I'm in love I do my best work. I've begun another this week. It's a garden scene—" he took a piece of paper and a pencil from his pocket—"I'll show you the composition."

He began to sketch rapidly. While he was in the midst of it Peter came to the table. "Sit down, Peter," Arthur said, pausing to shake his hand. Peter shook it briefly and then took mine. I folded my knuckles just in time.

"What're you doing?" he said. He raised a long leg and straddled the chair to sit down, rather than collapsing in it.

"Just showing Mac the composition of my new painting," he said, and handed me the paper. "Here—the background in blues, greens, and reds—and the two men sitting on the edge of the fountain. Rather, one's on the ground with his head in the other's lap. The girl with the parasol here, as if she'd come on them by mistake. I don't know what to call it yet—perhaps *The Blind*. Or *L'Affaire à Trois*."

"Who's blind?" I asked.

"I haven't the foggiest," he shrugged. "People can interpret how they want."

The sketch lay on the table. I kept my eye on it because I was planning to stuff it in my pocket before we left.

"How've you been, Peter?" I asked.

"A bit of all right," he said, smiling. "Arthur and I get along very well. 'E's old china, 'e is—lovely drippin's, that's wot."

"Good hevvings!" Arthur exclaimed. "Don't use that vile cockney slang!"

Peter's pale blue eyes glinted with amusement.

"I don't know what he means," I said.

"'Old china' means I'm an 'old dear,' and the other means—I guess you'd say 'swell stuff,'" Arthur said.

I smiled and nodded, but my eye was on Peter. He had picked up Arthur's sketch and turned it over, and his fingers were idly toying with the pencil. I could not stop him, of course—and then it occurred to me that it would be interesting to see what he doodled. He took the pencil and wrote, tentatively, the word "One." Then he frowned a little and wrote "Two" beneath it. Then "Three." He drew the paper toward himself and scowled. Then he began again: "One, two, three"—and at last set absorbedly to work, writing the three words over and over in a column down the sheet. I watched, fascinated. When he came to the bottom of the paper he began another column beside the first one—another line of "one, two, three."

I awakened to hear the end of Arthur's question: "—and what of that?"

"Sorry," I said. "Thinking of something. What did you say?"

"I said I was thinking of asking Peter to live with me. Reely, he stays in a dreadful hole. Do you think people would talk? He could be my cousin . . ."

I shrugged. It was hard to believe that Arthur's sophisticated friends in Paris did not know of the long line of "cousins," "sons of old friends," and "houseboys" that moved through his apartment from year to year.

"And what if they do talk?" I said. "In Paris no one cares what you do."

"Well, I have a reputation . . . a certain front to keep up," he said.

"You're keeping it up, all right," I said wryly. The concierge might believe that a handsome blond sailor was Arthur's cousin—and again she might not.

"How would you like to help Peter move in tomorrow?" Arthur asked. "I have to spend all day with the wallpaper people."

I chuckled. Arthur hated physical work and avoided it whenever he could. I indicated Peter with my head. "You mean you'd trust me alone with him?"

Peter did not hear us at all. His face was close to the paper and he was writing furiously.

"Of course I don't trust you," Arthur said, grinning. "But it's a small price to pay to get him moved . . ." A toothy grin, evil and conspiratorial—a full permission.

"I'd be delighted to help," I said quickly, with a new interest.

"What time shall he come over, Peter?" Arthur asked, speaking to him directly. "Peter! What on earth are you writing? *Peter!*"

Peter did not look up. Arthur put a hand on his arm and shook him a little. "Peter!"

The young man finally looked up. His eyes were blank and there was a light sheen of sweat on his forehead. He seemed completely detached and lost. "W-what?" he asked in bewilderment.

"I asked if you wanted Johnny to help you move. But what are you writing?"

Arthur picked up the paper and looked at it. Peter buried his face in his arm on the table. "Why, it's nothing except 'one, two, three' over and over," Arthur said, baffled. He showed me the paper, with six or seven columns filling the page, one column not completed.

I lifted one shoulder a little, to show I too was puzzled. Sir Arthur turned to the young man and shook his shoulder.

"Peter, what does this mean?"

Peter raised his head. In a peculiar way, *he* had returned to his eyes.

"Nothing," he said. "Nothing at all." He took the paper and held it at arm's length. "But it's pretty, isn't it?"

(17) **April 28, 1937**

The next morning was bright and sunny, and the air again had the thin purity that one finds in white wines of great delicacy. It dazzled the eye and filled the lungs freshly, and laid itself gently against my face as I walked toward the Rue de Grenelle.

I was still thinking about the odd occurrence of the evening before, the "one, two, three" affair. Somewhere in my mind there lurked a reference—a previous mention of "compulsive repetition"—ailment or symptom? The identification was tantalizingly close, yet I could not get at it. In Chicago I could have found it in my reference books. My grandfather had been an old-fashioned country doctor, and when he died I had appropriated several medical volumes—among them a psychiatric dictionary in which I thought I remembered seeing an explanation of Peter's unusual action, or a description of it.

I located the number on the Rue de Grenelle without difficulty. The concierge was a half-wit, like so many in Paris, but she brightened when one of her neurons connected with "a young British sailor." Then she pointed out the *ascenseur* so that I would not have to climb to the fourth floor. I got into the rickety contraption with my usual prayer, but this one bore me upward on a column of steel that rose mysteriously from the depths below the cage, and exhaled a vast hydraulic sigh when I got out and pushed the return button.

I pulled the doorbell. In a moment there were footsteps. Peter had said that he "had a room in an apartment"—a usual enough arrangement in Paris among families feeling the pinch, who often rented out single rooms.

Peter opened the door. "Come in!" he said, grabbing my hand. "Jolly nice of you to come. It's this way." I followed him into the gloom. "Watch your way around these corners," he said. I trailed after the white shadow of his undershirt into a maze of dark right-angling turns.

"Dark in here," I said. There was an ancient dinginess to everything I could see—a damp odor, too, that you find in many old houses in Paris. We turned into a corridor with a window at the end. The white shadow of Peter now became a black silhouette against the morning sun, and the light was trapped in the outline-edge of his hair. He stopped in front of a door, motioning me in with a naked arm outstretched and a wide grin on his face. "'Ere's me diggin's," he said. "And Artie was fair right about its bein' a 'ole. A cubicle, I calls it."

I walked into the depressing little room—clean enough but bare. A naked light bulb dangled like a casual suicide from the ceiling. A table was topped with a disordered chaos of magazines, books, and letters, and was pulled close to the window to catch what gray light there was from a narrow sunless airshaft. Cardboard cartons sat on the floor beside the table. The faded wallpaper was patched here and there, the ceiling cracked. A gray muslin screen, tilted at a nervous angle, stood partly concealing a washbowl. Beneath the bowl crouched the eternal bidet, a washcloth draped on its edge. A single bed under an empty bookshelf had a dirty gray green cover pulled over it. On the walls were several photographs of Peter's current weight-lifting idols; I was amused to see one of a husky hustler from Chicago, with whom I had had several encounters. There was a strange aromatic smell, a little spicy, that I noticed as I walked toward the bed—my nose caught it along with the undertone of urine from the washbowl; I had a whiff of the same curious odor from Peter the first evening I met him. It was not unpleasant. It suggested an Arabian spice—ginger, perhaps—or some odd rich cologne; but beneath it there was a vaguely disturbing sexual smell, male and sweaty—quite stimulating. Peter's very own smell . . .

"Well, wot d'you think? Not much, is it?"

I shook my head. "You'll be much happier at Arthur's place," I said.

"Righto!" he said. "You sit there half a mo'—I'm almost done with this." He shoved one of the cartons closer to the table and began grabbing the papers with his big capable hands. "I'll straighten things when I get over there," he said.

"What can I do to help you?" I asked.

"Not a thing, really," he said. "You can help carry things down when they're boxed, and tell the taxi where to go. I don't know a word of French."

It did not take him long. I lay on one elbow and watched his quick movements. They gave me the same shoulder-chill that poetry does, or some music. He created a visual lyric for me with the sweep of his long legs, his bendings that showed his back muscles through the thin cotton undershirt, and the tight small buttocks with deep hollows in their sides. As I watched the beauty of the rapid shifting line that his body motions made I felt a terrible weakness inside, a melting into a symphonic chorus of sweeping violins.

Michelangelo said that the highest object for art was man. For those who know art and do not use it as a springboard into erotic fantasy, the body of a man is superior to that of a woman. I thought of a discussion I once had with a young married couple—the wife insisting on this same point, that the male body was more beautiful (she had been trained in art); the husband held out for the female. "But how about your own body?" the wife asked him at one point, for the husband was indeed well formed, and had been a lifeguard. "Oh," he said, "but I'm a special case. . . ."

Those who have beauty have a definite obligation to the rest of us. They should share it with all the world, not with just one woman or one man. They are the temporary trustees of a treasure that should be divided with the less fortunate. Their bodies should be caressed and adored for the brief years that beauty stays, but alas! how little they realize their obligations during the golden time.

I doubted that Peter would appreciate the reasoning of such an argument if I presented it; his brain was capable, but hardly subtle. A nice kid, however.

He threw the last papers into the box and looked around the room.

"All finished?" I asked.

"Right you are," he said. He opened the door of the armoire and saw its emptiness, then slammed it. The mirror in the door rattled and then the door slowly swung open again. "Now I have to put on my dress blues. Won't take long."

There was a kind of muted joy in him as he realized that here was another chance to unveil his body before a possible worshiper. I could sense his excitement and pleasure in the trembling of his fingers as they worked at the buttons of his trouser-bridge. And within myself I could feel the exact moment when the adrenalin poured through the floodgate into my blood. My heart began to pound heavily, my breathing grew quicker and shorter. My mouth became dry. And at the hollow of my throat a great artery chugged.

He stepped out of his trousers. The room seemed more illuminated than it had been. His body was indeed good to see. The tanned skin was covered with a golden down, heavy upon the legs and chest, and lighter—a mere breath, a mist of gold upon his arms; and deeper toned in the triangle rising upon his belly above the sharp low line of the narrow black nylon French briefs he wore.

I could say nothing, not even compliment him. The moment was silent. Perhaps he could sense the tribute of my eyes' glitter and understand the dryness of my mouth.

He stepped backward so that he could see himself in the full-length mirror of the armoire. With his legs spread and his feet well planted, he stretched his arms toward the ceiling and let his head fall back. I saw the white gleam of his armpit like the belly of a trout, the tight-drawn line of the arch of his ribs. . . .

And suddenly I was on my knees in front of him, clasping him around the thighs, my cheek pressed against the black pouch. The odor of ginger and musk was overpowering. I looked up at his face, towering in a strange perspective atop the ridges of his abdomen; I looked through the golden hair of his chest into his nostrils above the cutting of his full lips. He looked down at me, his fingers threading through my hair, and then he raised his eyes to watch us in the mirror. He rolled his shoulders forward like a boxer and spread his feet farther apart, bending his knees slightly. He gripped my head with his hands pressed hard over my ears, and like an echo down a long and empty corridor I heard his words come from far away:

"Take it, Mac . . . take it . . . please . . . please . . ."

With fingers at his hips I pulled at the black pouch that covered him, and freed from its tight confinement, his cock sprang forth. It rose as if by magic, with tiny jerks as if some small machine within were pumping the empty girders into a threatening rigidity. Engorged, the helmet head began to glisten with the growing tautness of the skin; it shone with a red and purple brilliance, and glittered with a morning star at its tip. I opened my mouth and slowly closed my lips around the hot flesh, feeling the smooth column push over my lips and tongue, filling my mouth and gliding through the magic ring, and coming to rest at the back wall of my throat.

It did not take him long.

Late that afternoon, little Monsieur Charles rapped on my hotel door to call me to the telephone. "*C'est un monsieur qui vous appelle,*" he grinned.

"*Mais bien sûr,*" I said, knotting my robe to go to the phone. "Who else would be calling me?" I winked largely at him.

"Monsieur is a droll of a person," he giggled.

It was Arthur. He sounded distraught and terrified. "Are you there?" he asked. "My God, whatever did you do to Peter this morning? He's been weeping all day and now seems to be having some sort of a fit. He's absolutely unconscious on the bed—his breathing is shallow and he's in a cold sweat, but his forehead's hot. Whatever happened?"

I was startled. "Why, n-nothing particularly," I stuttered. "You as much as told me you wouldn't object if I had him once—"

"No, of course not, once," he said. "But was that all? Were there no scenes of any kind? No arguments? Nothing unusual?"

"No—and moreover, he asked me, not I him," I said shortly, irritated. If the young man had fits, it was hardly my doing.

"We had a dreadful scene. He kept bawling that he'd been unfaithful. And the more I told him it didn't matter, the worse it got. Said I didn't love him . . ."

"Worse in what way?" I asked.

"Well, at one point he grew rigid and I was afraid he was going to suffocate. He really began to turn blue in the face."

"Fits," I said. "Is there epilepsy in his family?"

"Not that I know of," Arthur said. "I've just called a friend . . . a doctor. Good hevvings . . . what a worry!"

"Evidently the boy is very sick," I said. "There is really something wrong. Do you think it's some kind of mental disorder?"

"I don't know. I'm almost distracted." He was silent for a moment. I could picture him trying to bite the end of his mustache with his lower lip, a habit he had when upset. Then he said, "I must go put some more cold presses on his forehead. The doctor told me to do that. And keep him well covered."

"Do you want me to come over?"

"Yes, why don't you? Or—wait a minute. If he's having some sort of remorse or conscience fit, the sight of you might set him off again. Why not wait until we hear what the doctor says?"

"Are you going to tell the doctor everything?"

"Oh, of course. He's a club member. Jean Lalongue. Awfly nice. And awfly long too." He giggled a bit hysterically.

"Tell him about the one-two-three business," I said, "and let me know as soon as you learn anything."

"Very well," he said, and hung up.

I went back to my room and lay on the bed for a long time, thinking.

(18) **April, 1937**

Excerpts from Sir Arthur's journal:

Peter spends long hours in front of the mirror, posing, turning this way and that, *admiring* himself. He is truly justified—something to admire, really—a *delight* to the eye. Like Narcissus, must have a pool to reflect his *beauty*. Told me he came of extremely *Low Church* parents, moralistic, narrow, bigoted. Beauty *sinful* to them, therefore sinful to touch oneself in adoration of one's beauty. Last night Peter described the *agonies* he went through as an adolescent while trying to stop "those" early habits. Weight lifting has been an activity to stand between himself and his "sin," just as becoming a sailor was successfully accomplished. Very *obvious*. The more activity, the less playing with oneself. (Masturbation = hand rape, *manus + turbare*, according to Johnny.) Peter now full of sense of right-doing, offsets early wrongdoing. His beauty and his "solitary" habits still tangled with guilt and sin. All caused by parents' *philistinism*. Think I can help him, though not a psychiatrist. Guidance may remove worries, even some of his *narcissism*, make him a *child of nature*, like me. Flush the stables *clean*. Yet—am I Narcissus also? Aren't all artists? Does not painting represent psychic projection of own personality? Is not artist a creator who *recreates himself* on canvas? Must talk about this with Gertrude and Alice. They *know*.

From the very first, have noticed strange—almost *exotic*—odour clinging to Peter and his clothes. Smelled it in his room, very strong. He says he uses no *scent or cologne* of any kind. Very *strange*. But not unpleasant. It calls up *visions*. I see him *naked* in a pool where lilies float, and a blue-footed Nubian slave pours a scented liquid from a red jar with a curved lip into the black water. Perhaps that would make a nice painting. His odour calls up *Gauguin's* colours—rich amber, purple, brown red. Hard to think of Peter's being blond with that odour—rather, suggests his skin should be *dark olive*, and his hair black and oiled. Curly.

When Peter is in a good mood I am in a good mood too. His humour is reflected in me the way his body is in the mirror. Three weeks now since we have met—*exhausting, wonderful* nights. I am humming in studio all day, thinking of seeing him after his work. I have made three small tempera paintings, using Peter's *"essence"* as a binder. That means I must *spit* it into a mixing dish without his seeing me. The temperas smell dreadful whilst *"curing."* These little experiments are all the dearer to me because—in a very *real* way—they *are* Peter *himself* and *myself*, added later because there is never enough to make even a small painting. We are mingled forever together in a work of art for all to see. If the world *knew* . . .

My sailor lad continues to offer me surprises. Last night he confessed that he had a passion for *leather*. I had noticed that every time he took his wallet from his pocket, he *smelled* it. His liking for it goes back to childhood. He became enamoured of an uncle who wore a pair of high leather *boots* laced to the knee. Remembered several years ago purchasing a pair of American motorcycle boots, with metal buckle and strap at the arch. Dug them out of bottom of armoire. Peter *delighted* with them. Sat in chair *fondling* them, putting them to his face, *smelling* them. When he thought I was not looking, he actually *licked* one of them. Then he kicked off his shoes and tried them on. Good size for him. Pranced around room, standing with legs spread apart, *swaggering* like a pirate or *dur*. He ran into bedroom, stood before mirror, I following. Unbuttoned his trousers, took them off. Had some trouble getting them off over boots, but managed. I drew him into bed with his boots on. Sex very *exciting*. He still had his jumper on. Sheets got *terribly* dirty. His personality completely *altered* while he had boots on. More dominant and *commanding*. Straddled me forcefully whilst he held my head up at very uncomfortable angle, nearly *choking* me to death. Both of us sweaty and exhausted. Such little games are *fun*.

Dinner with Johnny McAndrews tonight. He full of talk about projected visit to Rome, never having been there except as child. Told him great deal about it, best places for cruising, dangers, baths near Trevi fountain, Pincio, Borghese gardens, etc. Rome is wonderful. Sex comes out of the *walls* there. Would be nice if Peter and I could go there on his free fortnight. Peter did a strange thing this evening. Wrote the words *one, two, three* in columns on a piece of paper, over & over. Seemed weak & ill afterward, though made quick recovery. What can this be? He is a strange person, with *very unhappy* life. Father *rejected* him early. Mother boxed ears, was a *whore* despite religious narrowness. But this one-two-three suggests grave disorder. Afterward, he was *moody*. Fell asleep in chair, almost. Hope it is not *serious*. He *looks* so very healthy. But who can tell about brain's dark interior? Would break my heart if I *lost* him.

Horrible and exhausting day. Peter now sleeping. Jean Lalongue just left, gave Peter an injection to make him sleep. He & Johnny McA. moved Peter's things over to my apt. this morning. I came home from Cirman's about three o'clock, called for Peter when I came in. No *answer*, but great *splashings* from bathroom. Went in. Peter naked at washbowl, washing cock over & over with soap and water. Floor covered with water. He looked at me, eyes red & swollen. "Artie, oh Artie!" he sobbed & threw himself against me, wet & covered with lather. Tried to comfort him. "I've sinned against you, I've sinned!" Sobbed out whole story. I tried to wipe off lather from my gray suit. Ruined. It had just been *cleaned*, too. Now will have to send it out again. Nuisance, with such slow service in Paris . . . Well, seems he & Mac (Johnny) had little fling this morning. I had told J. it was all right. Told Peter same thing, that it didn't matter. Then P. grew *angry* with me, said I cared *nothing* for him, handed him around to all my friends, that I was *evil* & that God would *punish* me. That frightened me. Then his mind seemed to *shift* & he said *he* would punish me because I was a wicked sinner &c., and *he* was God and would strike me *down*. Threw a vase at me but missed. By now really alarmed. Got to phone and called Jean Lalongue & then went back to see what I could do. Peter *lunged* at me. I hit him on jaw—hard, knocked him out. In a feverish distraction until Jean came. He gave Peter an injection & then asked a lot of questions. Told him about the one-two-three as Johnny suggested. Jean asked if any insanity in Peter's family. Told him no, nothing I knew about. Jean gave me some sedative pills for Peter, also prescription to be filled at chemist's. Told me to take one pill myself. Peter sleeping peacefully now (eight o'clock) but his face still white & tortured. In God's name, what is the matter with him? How can I ever *paint* if I have this worry on my mind?

Peter much better this morning. Even went back to work. Seemed to remember very little of yesterday. Did not talk much except to apologize for his "spell." I asked if he had them often. "Once in a while." I persisted—what had doctors said about them? Nothing, he said, except that he was very *high strung* and *nervous*. Had been warned against intense *emotional* excitement—might "trigger" him at any moment. If I can recover from this shock I may even learn to *enjoy* his illness—gives a sense of living with *danger*. Keeps me continually alert and *stimulated*. Only must not go too far, i.e., provoke him *deliberately* if things get too dull. But I always do my best work when excited.

For the next two weeks until mid-May the entries are uninteresting. Then:

Peter and I were looking through some old photographs I had in a box. We found some that I had taken in Madrid many years ago, many of Juanita Ramirez. Peter asked who she was & I reluctantly told him she was the daughter of a *very* famous Spanish gypsy dancer. He was not satisfied & pressed me further, inquiring why there were so many pictures of her, more than fifty perhaps, even several of the two of us. Finally had to confess I had an affair with her. "An affair with a *woman*?" Of course, I said, somewhat irritated that he should think I could not. Then still *nettled*, I told him of the child and how I had offered to settle £5000 on Juanita when I learned she was pregnant, and how the mother made Juanita refuse it. Gypsy pride. "And the child was really born?" he asked. I said I supposed it was but that it was not a matter of consequence one way or another, that I had done the *honourable* thing and then when my gesture was refused I simply put the whole affair out of mind. Peter much disturbed over this, & esp. over the affair with a *woman*. I said why not, many men liked them. Not content with his misery I continued to peck at him, telling him of Juanita's charms—my God, why do I do such things? He had *never been with* a woman, thought they were vile & unclean. I told him women furnished a *superior sensation*. Naturally they do not but I liked to see him squirm. He turned very pale & got up from chair. Think I could see what was going on in his mind. I was taking away from him a feeling of his *value* to me, hence of his *raison d'être*. I followed him, taunting his inexperience. Suddenly he began weeping again—great shaking sobs. Put my arm around his shoulders and comforted him. Made me feel *very* good to have this wonderful young *animal* at my mercy & be able to console him. But not certain I *did* console him. When we went to bed he turned on his side & would not even let me kiss him goodnight. Things have been rather *dull* for the past two weeks. Perhaps it is time to stir up some excitement. My painting is losing *fire & colour*. It does need a new *stimulus* of some kind.

To Antoine's today. Ordered a pair of briefs for Peter, to be made from a *very thin* black leather, very *glossy* & very *high cut*, or is it called *low cut*. Antoine suggested kid, which seemed a good idea. Perhaps now he won't pout. At least I will *enjoy* seeing him in them. It will be *stimulating*.

Peter had to work late at the ministry this evening. Rang up Johnny McAndrews, had dinner with him at a place called the Vagenende—rather horrible *bourgeois* establishment on the Boulevard St. Germain, filled with middle-class Frenchmen and their wives & fly-speckled mirrors. Johnny persists in worrying about the one-two-three business. Said it is called stereotypy, which is a symptom of cat—catta—I can't spell it—catatonic dementia præcox. Told him Jean Lalongue *had* asked if there were insanity in Peter's family. This *worried* me. Would not relish having an insane person around, or be bothered with taking care of him, getting to an asylum, &c. But Johnny is a Cassandra, always prophesies the *worst*. Troy will fall at any minute. Bombs will explode any moment. The cow, the old cow, she is dead. *Das Untergang des Abendlandes*. He says *he* is never disappointed since he *always expects* the worst, the bad things, to happen. He added that he thought he had identified Peter's odour—says it is phenylpyruvic acid (simply *know* that is not spelled right!), which is to be found in urine of certain "low-grade mental defectives." Imagine that! Never heard of any kind of insanity producing an odour! Quite *impossible!* There is nothing wrong with Peter my love for him won't cure. Created an imaginary engagement and left Johnny after we had dined—somewhat *irritated* with him.

Peter seems to have an *obsession* about Juanita. His talk filled with references to her. "Did you & Juanita ever—?" "Am I better looking than she was?" "I'll wager Juanita couldn't do *this!*" "How old would Juanita be now?" Finally told him not to mention her again, that she was dead as far as I was concerned. Peter promised. He has developed an *annoying* habit, pulling at lobe of his left ear. Evidently pulls it (i.e., his ear) even at work, because it is swollen in the evening when he gets home. He pulls at it & then *makes a fist*, which he holds at the point of his jawline. Then tugs again. About once every eight seconds. If he is not in a position so that he can rest his elbow on a chair-arm or table after making a fist, he *moves* to a chair where he can. Have also noticed a tic in his left eyelid that recurs *frequently*. Is something really wrong or did the fit he had (and all that talk from Johnny and Lalongue) make me look for things? He loved the *leather* shorts, which arrived today. Tried them on at once. A perfect fit, tight as his own skin and *very revealing*, bunching him all together there in a bulge as big as an orange (and just as tasty!). A little hair and skin pop out between the fly buttons *most amusingly*. He can wear them even under his sailor trousers. They leave no line.

Telephone call today from a young American sent to me by George Platt Lynes—with the improbable name of *Tony Midnight!* Know what *that* means since George sends me only the best. Arranged to have him call at the apt. tomorrow when Peter is safely at work—he is so *extraordinarily jealous!* And of course without any reason at all . . .

(19) May 10–24, 1937

Remembering what Alice had once said to me about Italy, one day in May I suddenly packed and left for Rome. My departure was as unexpected to the hotel as to myself. I retained my room. But Alice had complained that since I had been all over Europe in the past, and twice to Algiers, if I didn't go to Italy this time it would almost amount to a criticism of the place. Moreover, I had become acquainted with a charming young expatriate American artist (his specialty was to paint collections of family jewels for their wealthy owners), and he had talked as enchantingly of the city as had Sir Arthur.

There had been two mental blocks working against the trip—an utter ignorance of the language, and the dread of a twenty-four-hour train trip as the engine snaked up and down the Alps. I overcame the first block by remembering the hordes of tourists who went everywhere in Europe and got along with "Oh yeah?" and "So what?" in their multiple inflectional forms. And I overcame the second one by flying to Rome, which took four hours.

The city was all that had been promised. The ancient town lay in languor beneath a golden sun in such an intense blue sky that the eye could not look at it long—a sun and sky that had baked the city to a red brown ocher tone. The color of Paris was gray, but Rome was red, and its air smelled of dusky-ripe melons and grapes. There was the noise of water everywhere—fountains with a deafening enfolding roar held you in the circle of rush and fury at almost every corner you turned. I took a conveniently isolated room at the Pensione California—which had even a private elevator, so that I could get to my bed without passing the concierge. The windows looked over the dark green treetops of the Borghese gardens and the Pincio. I was only a block from the fleshpots of the Via Veneto, and not much farther from the lolling gamins of Rome on the Spanish steps.

And the people! Tall, deep-olive-skinned, black-haired and black-eyed, the most beautiful people in the world! The men walked with a proud animal grace and arrogance, straight limbed and tight thighed, heads back, nostrils aquiver like panthers prowling, infinitely aware of themselves as citizens of Rome, proud to call themselves "*un vero Romano di Roma*"—a true Roman of Rome. The women were wonderful to look at—elegantly coiffed, gowned in heavy silks and stiff dark brocades, with a great deal more chic than the women of Paris.

I dutifully took tours through museums, churches, and catacombs—and in the caves stole a fragment of vertebras from the skeleton of an early Christian martyr; then with a free conscience I devoted afternoons and nights to the subtler delights for which Rome had its reputation. The language gave me no difficulty; if the citizens did not know English, they knew French. And on one memorable afternoon in the Baths of Rome, the Terme di Roma, I even found myself speaking Latin with an American accent, and being perfectly understood.

I met many new people—a middleweight boxer who had toured America, and a young man who had the proud bearing of a gladiator. I met the handsomest sailor of my life—Luciano, with his midnight hair and high brown copper coloring and his smooth dusky limbs, who walked hand in hand with me in the Italian fashion through the Borghese gardens while I—poor creature conditioned by the Bible Belt—felt fussed and uneasy when anyone saw his warm brown hand clasping mine. Or did they look, or was it only that I thought they noticed? In Paris the life of the oblique ones is at best sneaky and furtive; the tradition there is that of a man and his mistress, even though the town is filled with *pédés*. But in Rome all was golden and sunlit—open and happy and animal.

There was even a moment of magic in the Colosseum. One night I dressed in my oldest clothes, a night when the moon was full and silver, and went to the old ruins, remembering that a friend had once said that no one had ever really lived until he had seen the full moon in the Colosseum shining through the hairy legs of a young sergeant. I went under one of the great entry arches into the pool of black and light, for the moon was pouring over the edge of the great cup of high crumbled walls. It illuminated half of the circular bowl, leaving the rest in shadow blacker than black. The noise of the city traffic was reduced to a distant humming and the stars stood out above. I was transported to an ancient time, steeped in romance, degraded, wonderful. Then I became aware that the great bowl was filled with a faint *rustling* made of many whisperings. I saw the moving shadows, while here and there a match flickered to light a cigarette, and there were young men sitting wide legged and motionless on the low walls, looking . . . and waiting, silently, their hands cupping their crotches or fallen between their thighs, caressing. . . And there I met the little soldier Pasquale who knew no English or French, and yet who understood and smiled in the darkness. And afterward a rendezvous for the following night—when I knew I would be back in Paris, and that as I came down at Orly he might still be waiting . . . but not for long alone.

When I did get back to Paris, exactly two weeks after leaving, I was shocked at what I saw. The city was still at its leafy loveliness, the avenues broad and beautiful—but what in God's name had happened to the people? Were these runty ones the same that I had left only fourteen days before? They had shrunken, somehow—or so it seemed, because for two weeks my sight had been filled with the image of man as he *ought* to look.

Among the notes and letters waiting was one from Sir Arthur, saying that if I returned by the twenty-fifth, to call so that we might have dinner together. It was then the twenty-fourth, so I gave him a ring. He listened politely to my enthusiasm about Rome, and finally I remembered to ask after his health and Peter's.

"I'm very well," he said. "And Peter is improved. Doctor Jean is giving him massive injections of vitamins and doses of tonics, and he's quite calm. He works only a half day at the ministry now because Jean wrote a note for him, saying that he should not get overtired. He looks a bit thinner—that's all."

"Happy to hear that," I murmured. "How do you think he feels about me?"

"Forgotten, dear boy, completely forgotten. And that reminds me. I hope you can come over to dinner tomorrow evening—just a simple thing. We're eating at home these days. You must tell me *all* about Rome."

"You're quite sure it will be all right? I wouldn't want—"

"Quite sure," Arthur said. "I even asked him. He talks about you quite freely, and says he finds you attractive." He giggled. "Shall I get jealous? No, of course not. So have no worries about disturbing him. We can expect you at seven-thirty, then?"

"I'll be there," I said, and hung up.

Peter did look very well indeed, aside from cheeks slightly hollowed, but the hollows threw his cheekbones into high relief and trapped fragments of pale blue shadow as he turned his fine head. I saw planes and angles not there before.

"You're looking quite well, Peter," I said.

"Thank you," he said. His handclasp did not make me wince this time. "I'm feeling quite fit now."

Outwardly the evening seemed very calm. The dinner was satisfying, though simple: a mushroom soup, lamb chops, a salad of romaine and *fines herbes*, and a good red wine. Arthur seemed his old genial self, a polished host, guiding the small talk into unimportant but charming rivulets. He had been painting wildly and had got a great deal done, but the wallpaper people were taking much of his time, always wanting new designs. "I resent every hour spent with them on their work," he confessed as we got up from the table and went to the salon for brandy, "because I feel that it's an hour taken away from—from the *Permanent*, shall we say?"

He picked up a rose petal that had fallen on the floor. "There's a new youngster in Paris," he said, "who's been sending me a lot of his artwork for my opinion. I've told him repeatedly that I'm no critic, that I have no authority, and that I'm just beginning myself. But nothing stops him. He writes almost every week, or sends sketches. I've got so now that I just tell the messenger to turn around and take them back."

"Arthur!" I said reprovingly. "Of all people, you should know that's no way to treat a youngster just beginning."

"Really, Mac," he said petulantly, "one could spend all one's time with such persons and get nothing at all done."

"But don't you have an obligation to them since you're an artist?" I persisted. "Granted, there are more without talent than with it. But mixed in, at last comes *the one*. You don't meet him often—maybe he looks like all the others. Behaves like them. But—he sees the things others don't, hears sounds we never hear. Sometimes he'll stop talking, and his eyes sparkle with something only he hears. The god is speaking—maybe soft and unclear now, but some day loud—and he'll step over the line into immortality. And you've already rejected him? Suppose Gertrude had rejected the early things you sent to her?"

It was a long speech for me. Arthur was quiet. Peter lay back in the deep chair that almost swallowed him from view with its side wings; one of his hands rested on an arm of it, the four fingers moving in a slow tattoo of four beats, from the little finger to the index, pausing, then beginning again. It made a soft little ghost-sound on the chair-arm fabric.

"That's well put," Arthur said. "Perhaps I've been too harsh. I'll have a look at the next things he sends around. But—" he pushed at his forelock—"the poor fellow's so *ugly*."

I did not know if he would. Despite all that had passed between him and me, I felt that as usual his mind was locked to me. I felt there were secret rooms, bolted to outsiders, behind which lay things one could not even suspect. At times I felt a barrier between us, composed of some invisible potent force or substance, like a wall of glass. We could see each other moving on our separate sides, but could not hear each other.

And Peter—drumming on the chair-arm—what lay in his secret room? What fogs or pains? Despite Arthur's assurances and Peter's appearance, I could see that all was not well. Outwardly, as I said, the evening seemed calm indeed, but inwardly there was a sense of tension, apprehension.

I could understand why Arthur liked a way of life stretched taut and quivering. A furious kind of internal excitement seemed to be necessary to him for creation. It would have worn me thin in very little time and carried me to the edge of a breakdown. But not Arthur. He lived on drama—as Alice would have said: "He ate it with a spoon." A calm life bored him. For the twilit ones a calm life was difficult at best; they found it full of messes and odors, lying and evasions, pretenses and hypocrisies—a hard business even when it seemed to roll smoothly. Why Arthur wanted to complicate it with tension was beyond my grasp. He had chosen to fall in love with a man marked with a mania of some sort, who trembled continuously on the thin edge between sanity and some awful doom. Why could he not have found a "normally abnormal" good companion? Had I been Arthur I would have found my sleep uneasy, wondering if the sailor's supporting thread might snap, and that Peter, crouched like a darker shadow in a darkened room, panting hard and wet with sweat, clutching a blade that caught a gleam from the streetlight, might not with questing fingers delicately raise the sleeper's chin, to sever the defenseless throat with one swift sweep of steel.

I came away from my little fantasy perspiring, to hear Arthur say: "It's a wonderful evening. Shall we stroll along the Seine? Peter?"

His inflection reminded me of a nurse speaking to a convalescent child, or a very old person. Peter hitched himself up in his chair.

"That would be nice," he said.

And his voice, his vibrant husky male voice, was suddenly thin and treble and weak, like that indeed of a five-year-old child, a timid little voice, odd to be heard coming from a tall male form. . . .

He must truly have been very far back in his past.

(20) May 25, 1937

Paris on a spring night! I had spent many evenings in the old city, but the magic of the place had never been smothered for me by repetition, and the call was never stronger than on that May night.

It was pleasantly cool as we left Arthur's apartment and headed west along the Seine, strolling under the leaf-patterned street lamps, past shadowed benches holding young lovers. Beside us the river ran silent and deep and black, with the glittering broken reflections of the lights probing its jet waters. Ahead of us the great twin-towered bulk of Notre Dame was haloed by white flood-lights, and far away we could see the top edge of the Arc de Triomphe, and the swinging beacon on the Eiffel Tower. The air had thickened from its morning quality of delicate wine; it was sensual and honeyed, a fit medium—like dark amber—to preserve the motionless figures on the benches, a boy with his mouth against a girl's neck, her dark hair half-concealing his white face . . . forever so caught, ever young, like the figures on a Grecian urn. . . .

We did not talk much. Arthur's hand had stolen silently down to Peter's, and the two walked pressed close together. I felt a little lonely and left out, but not annoyed. Neither of them, even if he had wanted, could admire as freely and openly as I could, when the youth of Paris passed. No ties, therefore no obligations—and the feeling of freedom was wonderful.

"The river runs much more swiftly than you would imagine," Arthur murmured at one point, and Peter asked "Is it deep?"

"About thirty-five feet here," I said, and then we lapsed into silence again.

Sometimes laughing or talking, sometimes silent, the people of Paris went by like shadows. There was the clattering of hard heels from some chattering students, with the chorus of their squeaking shoes riding noisily beneath their talk. A bent old man turned down a ramp toward the river level, clutching some newspapers—one of the *clochards* of Paris, the old and homeless poor who slept under the bridges of the Seine, moving their ragged bundles from one spot to the next. A handsome young gendarme swung his white baton as he came sauntering toward us. I let out a low whistle he could not hear and nudged Arthur with my elbow to whisper, *"Qu'il est beau, n'est-ce pas?"* and Arthur nodded.

Slowly walking, we came at last to the Louvre where the main lines of traffic cut through the Tuileries with outrageous racket and honking. We paused for a traffic light.

"Shall we wander to St. Germain for a spot of something?" Arthur asked.

Peter nodded. "I should like that." He looked very handsome and tall and broad shouldered in his uniform, standing under the streetlamp that picked out the planes and shadows in his fine face. Arthur was lucky in his choices, in some ways.

"Suits me fine," I said. We shifted our direction and crossed the Quai des Tuileries toward the gently sloping-upward bridge, the Pont du Carousel. The night excursion boat, the *bateau-mouche*, was heading down the Seine toward us, a moving brilliance of colored lights and violin music, its searchlight jerking along the bankside and catching startled lovers in its glare.

There was no warning when it happened. Peter dashed in front of me, put one hand on the balustrade of the bridge like a boy vaulting a fence, swung easily up and over, and fell from sight below the bridge level. A second later there was a splash. . . .

I was paralyzed. My memory photographed a still of the scene—all motion in the world seemed arrested. Arthur stood with his mouth open, one empty hand reaching out frozen in the air. I dug my fingers against the stone of the bridge. It seemed like minutes; it was hardly three seconds.

Then a loud cry from Arthur tore the air apart.

"Help!" And a moment later: *"Au secours! Au secours!"*

I found my voice and yelled too. A few people came running up the bridge. Before I knew what was happening, Arthur vaulted the bridge as well, and I heard a second splash. I redoubled my yelling. A gendarme came running. He blew his whistle. There was a furious churning from the river. For a split second I wondered how two persons could make such a racket. Then I knew. The *bateau-mouche* had reversed its engines and was stopping.

The gendarme was pounding my shoulder, asking what had happened. I pointed. I yelled something. Then I leaned over the bridge side. I saw Arthur vanish underneath the bridge, going downstream with the current. Careless of life I ran through the traffic—some cars were already stopping—to the other side. The *bateau-mouche* drifted through. Its spotlight picked up Arthur, swimming rapidly toward a dark something in the eerie light.

Then I saw Peter rise to the surface, throw back his head, gasp and sink again.

"To your right!" I shouted. Arthur had seen him too. He swam and then dived. When he came up he had hold of Peter's hair. I could not see plainly for all the threshing in the water. I heard a police wagon speed by behind me, its fearsome two-toned honking slitting the night apart. Without looking, I knew that it had turned down the ramp to the river side.

The *bateau-mouche* had stopped. All the passengers had crowded to the side rail. The boat leaned in the water. The searchlight moved with Arthur as he slowly pulled the limp body toward the right bank. All the noise was now up on the bridge. From the river below came not a sound except the splash of Arthur's arm against the water. The headlights of the police car appeared under the bridge and the gendarmes jumped out.

Suddenly I broke my own chain of paralysis. I turned and ran toward the stairs that led down to the water level. My tongue was a great swollen dry corncob in my mouth. My knees were trembling so that I could scarcely run. I slipped and stumbled down the last three darkened steps; and then I was at the river's edge, the light from the boat in my eyes, the black shadows of the policemen moving. And then suddenly everything was silent. There was no sound at all, not even from the people on the bridge.

Arthur had found the slanting steps cut in the retaining wall, and pulled himself up on the first one. He had Peter by the collar, and Peter's blond head hung down against his chest.

"Help!" he gasped in French. "I can't lift him out!"

The police were already on the way. Someone grabbed Arthur and guided him up the steps. Two others carefully, cautiously—for the steps were narrow—pulled Peter upward, slowly. They felt for the steps with their feet, mounting them backward, dragging Peter from the water.

I ran to Arthur. He was sitting on a stone bench trying to get his breath, gasping for air in great gulps, and shivering. He could not speak. I ran back to Peter. The police had stretched him out on his back and turned his head sidewise. A gendarme in shirtsleeves knelt beside his face and put his mouth to Peter's, pinching Peter's nostrils shut.

Suddenly my knees weakened under me so that for a moment I

thought I was going to faint. I staggered to the bench where Arthur was coughing and choking, and collapsed. I bent my face forward and put it between my knees until I felt the blood rush back to my head.

In a minute I was all right again. I looked at Arthur. He coughed and spat out water and then looked at me. He shook his head blankly. unbelievingly.

"In—God's name—why?" he gasped. "Why?"

I could do nothing except shake my own head. "I don't know," I said.

Arthur got up and half-lurched, dripping, to the knot of shadows. He was extremely agitated. "How is he?" he asked, mopping his face with a wet handkerchief. Then he asked it again in French.

The gendarmes wanted to know who the sailor was. And then who Sir Arthur was. He told them. He said that Peter was his cousin. Why had he jumped in? He had not jumped—he had fallen, Arthur said. I admired Arthur's presence of mind. He went on: Peter was feeling very lively—he had sprung to the railing of the bridge and was walking along it. He lost his balance. He fell. That was all there was to it. The gendarmes scowled. And why did the monsieur think the railing had been put on the bridge in the first place? It was to keep people from falling over, it was not to be walked on. It was a disturbance of the peace. Sir Arthur grew indignant. How could an accident be a disturbance of the peace? He mentioned a name—that of the prefect of the Paris police. The gendarmes grew respectful. He mentioned his own name again, with the full title. The gendarmes were even more respectful.

Suddenly there was a cough from Peter. Water and bile came from his mouth. His arm moved. The gendarme sprang up and lifted Peter at his waist. More water. He coughed several times. Arthur kneeled beside him. I stood by.

Peter's eyes fluttered several times and then opened. He looked at the lights and the people. A deep groan came out of him, ending in a choking cough.

"You'll be all right," Arthur said, clumsily trying to lift him. A gendarme helped, and Peter sat up, his head down, coughing. Arthur looked up at the circle around him.

"Will you take us home?" he said to the gendarmes.

"*Bien sûr, milord*," said one of them, and several others helped

Peter to his feet. With one of his arms around Arthur's shoulders and the other around those of a young *flic*, they walked unsteadily toward the police wagon, and Peter was hoisted in. Arthur looked around for me. "Come on," he said. *"C'est un ami,"* he explained to the police. I climbed in and sat down on one of the narrow leather benches. At any other time I would have enjoyed the experience of being taken home by the police in a guiltless ride, but the black humor of the situation did not impress me that evening. The possible complications worried me.

"Can you keep it out of the newspapers?" I whispered to Arthur. He nodded, and then spoke rapidly to the gendarme who had made the report in his notebook. At the end, the *flic* touched his cap and grinned. He was very young and blond and stalwart, sitting there.

"I understand completely, monsieur," he said. "I think it can be arranged with no trouble at all. I will, however, have to call upon you tomorrow to ask you to sign some papers, and to see that all goes well with the young sailor—with monsieur your cousin, that is." He smiled slowly. "But there is, *bien sûr*, no need to inform the journals—it was a small accident and no harm done— to no one, that is to say, except your friend—your cousin." Again the flicker of a certain smile, a wise one . . . "It is not worth the trouble . . ."

Arthur nodded and smiled at him through his down-dripping mustache. "How very amiable you are, monsieur, thus to keep us from a situation very tiresome." He looked at the young cop slowly, up and down. "What time may we expect you?"

"At four hours, the afternoon?" the cop said, with a grave twinkle.

"Is he not *gentil*?" Sir Arthur asked, turning to me.

"Bien sûr," I said, but I was not sure I liked what I saw happening.

Peter sat with his head on Arthur's shoulder. His face was winter white and the skin looked thin as paper. His eyes were closed. His uniform clung to his body like a black skin, and under the gray blanket that they had put around his shoulders I saw him shivering. The light from the streets flickered through the small high-barred windows as the wagon jolted along.

End of the dream, beginning of the nightmare. In a kind of imagined vision like that in a movie when the camera begins a slow withdrawal from a tragic scene, and on the screen the arrested figures are frozen in their melancholy grouping, I began to withdraw and ascend from the place until—with eyes shut—I felt myself looking down from a great height at a vehicle filled with little jostled marionettes, moving slightly, shifting with the ride.

Were these the ends to which "love" brought us? To the dripping trembling figures riding homeward over the streets of Paris in a black enclosed wagon? To the little men wet and huddled together? And at the end, what? Comfort, relaxation, the warmth of enfolding arms and happiness? Ah no—to the beginning of the end, to bickering and recrimination, and devotion treacherously betrayed, and blankets around bodies exhausted with their last efforts. . . .

I was half-sickened by my immature musings when the wagon stopped. The slim and handsome blond *flic* and two others helped Peter and Arthur to the door of the apartment, and I trailed on the fringe of the group. And at the door Arthur paused, and turned and thanked them once again.

"And you," he said to the one who smiled, "we will expect you at four."

The *flic* brought his hand smartly to his cap bill, clicked his heels, and smiled again. And I was certain that I saw his eye, turned partly from me, close in a large wink.

(21) June 15, 1937

I saw very little of Sir Arthur for the next three weeks. It was not that I particularly disapproved of anything he had done. I rarely used the word "disapproved" anymore; along with "normal" it had been discarded in a semantic housecleaning, for it contained a moral judgment. Further, I did not like to be involved in unpleasant situations in which I was not to blame.

There was no formal story in any of the newspapers. The young *flic* had done his job well. I never learned in what kind of coin Arthur paid him, but I suspected. After all, cops too like orgasms. Arthur himself undoubtedly told the story here and there. With his flair for the dramatic, he would hardly have missed such a chance as the story of Peter, retold with elaborate embroidery. Indeed, several years later Arthur referred to Peter as "the sailor who tried to commit suicide over me." In some of the gossip columns—in *Les Arts et les Spectacles*, and also in *France-Soir* in the column called *"Les Potins de la Commère"*—there were references to it. *France-Soir* was biting: the piece said that a young English milord, noted for his painting as well as the handsome young men attending him, had recently been involved in the suicide attempt of a young British sailor. The writer had asked bitterly why a title should protect a person entangled in *"une affaire rose,"* and had complained about the flagrant outrage of customs [*outrage des moeurs*] permitted by a Napoleonic law that had been designed by an admitted member of the "filthy club." The sharp-tongued writer, a woman, was answered with some fire by Henri Delarue in *Combat*, who held the thesis that the artist, any artist, existed outside the stodgy limits of bourgeois morality, and that Paris— with its reputation for allowing personal freedom—had traditionally not concerned itself with private lives.

It was a sorry little battle for ten days, ending when Delarue suggested that the author of *"Les Potins . . ."* examine her own association with one of the most notorious women of Paris, a chic lesbian noted for her exploits—among which was one in which she set razor blades into the handrails of her stairwell, then jimmied the elevator and blacked out the lights. The men invited to her party—on the third floor—arrived with deep-cut bleeding hands, much to the sadistic glee of the hostess and her amazon band.

Delarue's reference cut short the exchange of malice.

For me, the speed with which time was passing was heartbreaking. The eighteenth of June was only a few days off, my departure date, and the first shiploads of tourists were beginning to arrive in the city. And now, when Paris was rising to a height of excitement and gaiety, I had to leave for a dull summer in Chicago, and duller students. I had paid dearly for my April in Paris; it was a severe psychic shock to have to leave this early. Still, it had been a good ten weeks, and Rome a great experience. Through it all had run the thread of Arthur and his sailor like a continuing melodrama, and strung on the days were also the gratifying numerous encounters of my own. Thinking of them diminished my regret a good deal.

But I was not to leave Paris without seeing Arthur again. He had called once during the three weeks and talked mysteriously of an arrangement about to be made. I had firmly declined, giving an unbreakable excuse. And then about five days before I was to leave, he called again.

"I am going to see Peter," he said. "This afternoon. Would you like to come along?"

"Where in the world is he?" I asked, startled.

"The Navy has put him in the psychopathic ward at St. Mandé," he said.

"Good heavens! When did all this happen?"

"About two weeks ago. I tried to tell you, but you couldn't come over. And it's scarcely a story to be told over the phone, even in Paris, even in English. But the doctor will let me see him for a moment. He is a very gentle patient, I understand."

Curiosity overcame me. "I would like to very much," I said.

"Good," he said. "Come about two. You can see the new painting I've done."

When I arrived he was dressed and ready, without the usual half-hour wait. He was extremely nervous and pulled constantly at his black tie. I reached over to push down the pearl pin in his ascot more securely. "I want to hear all about this," I said.

"Tell you in the taxi," he said. "But come—I want to show you the painting."

He pulled me toward the studio door, and switched on a light that fell directly on a large canvas, about six feet high and eight feet long. It was the largest painting of his I had ever seen. "It's called *The Three Kings*," he said. "D'you like it?"

My gasp when the light went on should have told him I did. It was a tremendous thing. The canvas *glowed* with color—deep reds and purples and greens, startling accents of white and yellow light, riotous and rich. The three Kings of the Orient—but what a difference from the shabbily pious treatment usual in religious art! The three majestic figures filled the right half of the painting. From them—rising to the upper left-hand section in an adapted treatment of medieval perspective that took in great and improbable distances—ran a path that ended in a burst of radiance under a thatched roof.

And the kings themselves! Such young men, of such elegance and beauty! Two of them stood out boldly and the third was shadowed—and did not the third have the face of Peter Quint? And the first, if you took away the little anchor beard below the cruel lips—was it not Wally Herrick? Capes of ermine and velvet, rich glowing crowns heavy with garnet and purple jewels, slashed and skintight sleeves, legs in tight-clutching fabrics—yellow striped with green, white with golden fleur-de-lys, maroon with gray thigh designs. The three carried their gifts—all worked out in fantastic enameled detail, luminous and metallic, with an urn in porcelain white overlaid with blue and gold.

A kind of chill ran through me; the skin of my shoulders raised its pores. This was great art indeed. So must a patron's of Leonardo have felt when the painter pulled aside the curtain over one of his great canvases. It was a thrilling—almost holy—moment, and if there had been any lingering doubts about the genius of Arthur Lyly, they were dispelled forever. This was one of the greatest modern paintings I had ever seen.

I was considerably shaken. "Do you like it?" he repeated.

I could only nod my head and gulp noisily. "It is so great it—it makes me want to cry," I finally said.

"I am glad," he said, and his voice sounded humble.

"You must have worked very hard on it," I said.

"Day and night," he said, "all during the horrible experience of getting Peter lodged in the hospital. If it had not been for the painting I think I might have gone mad along with him. I kept painting so that I would not think of the tragedy that had come to him. So young, so handsome . . ." He sighed.

I followed him out of the studio reluctantly, glancing back for a final look at the jewel before it was extinguished by his turning off the light. Then I said, "I wonder if the painting is a result of your flight from the thought of Peter's illness, or whether it springs from the excitement of your being involved with him."

It was a cruel sentence and I tried to temper it. "I mean—both of us know that you work best when emotionally distraught, upset in your personal life."

He looked acutely embarrassed. "Perhaps," he said in a low tone. "Both, maybe." He looked down at the rug, tracing his toe in a circular pattern. "At least, it is done." He looked up, took a breath, and smiled strangely. "Shall we go?"

I followed him out the door.

Then suddenly—standing at the stairwell as he turned the lock—I was smitten with a dreadful idea. Could it have been that

Arthur had done all that he could to induce the madness in Peter deliberately? So that out of the terrible fear and tension and excitement he could have produced a great painting?

I almost lost my footing on the stairs. My head whirled. It was a horrid thought. I tried to suppress it, my eyes wide in a desperate unbelief. It was good that he was not looking at me directly.

But the thought would not fit back into its Pandora's box. The wickedness had escaped. As we rode through the streets of Paris in the warm and mellow afternoon, the contrast of that evil darkness in my mind with the golden patched sunlight on the sidewalks was sharp and upsetting. Arthur continued to talk of Peter and I answered automatically, enough to keep him going.

If this were true . . . I remembered that once I had had a fleeting image of Arthur as a sort of batlike monster who drew the blood for his painting from the throats of the young men he knew, hovering over their unconscious forms, their white thighs . . . and then the image altered: I saw him as a potbellied monster with a forked and phallic tongue, with a dozen umbilical cords writhing out of his gaping navel, each one of the snaky tentacles wrapping its suction cups around a young man, drawing nourishment from him, changing it in the dreadful alchemy of his belly into the beautiful colors that shimmered on his canvases. A vampire art . . .

Were those colors, that wonderful painting I had seen, produced by the breaking of Peter's mind? Was that moving conception sucked from the shattered synapses of a young sailor's brain? If true, it was probably a thing Arthur was unconscious of and could not admit to himself. He would be shocked and hurt if one asked him. And how could you phrase such a question? "Arthur, do you ruin young men to get the inspiration for your painting?" "Do you squeeze them dry to get the brilliant colors on your canvas?" Or more specifically: "Did you deliberately drive Peter mad—poor unbalanced uncertain Peter—just so you could paint *The Three Kings*?"

The artists of the world have used many things to inspire them—hashish, opium, beautiful men or women whom they have loved, alcohol, sex, nature, music, mythology—an endless list. But there was a difference here. It was not "inspiration" with Sir Arthur, although he might have indignantly claimed it was. It was a direct cannibal feeding of a psychic or mystic sort, the actual meal of the parasite upon the host, which died when its vitality was exhausted. And in a sense Peter was dead right now.

The taxi stopped. "We are here," said Sir Arthur.

"So we are," I said. My words sounded to me as if someone else had spoken them.

(22) June 15, 1937
Afternoon

"Just where are we?" I asked.

"The Bégin Military Hospital, near the Bois de Vincennes," he said. "On the Avenue de Paris, number 69, in the suburb of St. Mandé—the full address."

"But it's a French military hospital, not a British one!"

Arthur climbed out of the taxi, leaving me to pay the bill. I did, with a sigh. "They have an arrangement with our government," he said. "Besides, they have the best facilities in Paris for . . . uh . . . mental cases. I guess they are going to begin insulin shocks next week. Or electric ones." He shuddered. "Imagine poor Peter having to go through all that torture."

And all because of you, I thought, but did not say it.

There was a long leafy walk through pleasant and well-tended grounds up to the gray stone hospital. A few wheelchairs were on the lawn—some in sunlight, some in shade—and there were patient men in them. A good-looking boy sat close to the walk; his grave unsmiling eyes followed us from his wheelchair. His blanket was wrapped around an awful emptiness where his legs should have been. A few flowers bordered the gravel of the drive; an occasional bird sang from an overhanging tree. It was as genial as hospital grounds could be, but I suddenly wished that I had stayed at home.

Inside the hospital, all was a kind of green yellow gloom of window shades low drawn against the beating sun. The floors were rubber tiled, and there was a bitter-clean odor of carbolic antiseptic. Arthur asked at the information desk while I dawdled in the waiting room, and then came to say in a hushed voice that the doctor would be there in a moment, and why not sit down? We did, and said nothing. Hospitals induce a respectful silence. Two or three other persons were in the waiting room with us, turning the pages of magazines they were not reading. You could almost see the anxious thoughts ascending like smoke from a censer, to gather near the ceiling of the enameled room and curl oppressively back down upon the waiting ones.

Presently a doctor came in, a white-jacketed and intelligent-looking small man. He spoke to the nurse, who pointed to Arthur and myself. He came toward us.

"You are Sir Arthur Lyly?" he asked in French.

"Yes," said Arthur. "And this is a friend, Monsieur Mc-Andrews."

"*Enchanté*. I am Doctor Villemin," he said, and we all shook hands. "You have come then to see your cousin?"

"Yes." The doctor turned and we followed him. "How is he?"

"Monsieur Quint is very quiet and comfortable at the moment," the doctor said. "We have examined him thoroughly." And he launched into a rapid explanation of Peter's ailments. His was a case of catatonic dementia præcox—schizophrenia, the symptoms of which were the compulsive repetitions of certain acts. From observation they had found the acts themselves were few in number: he wrote certain words over and over, he rubbed two fingers in a small vertical motion up and down in his pubic hair, and he imitated the actions and speech of any person who entered the room alone. This last, the doctor said, was often associated with catatonic repetition, and was called echopraxia. Also, Peter would often maintain the same fixed position for hours. These were simple manifestations, nothing that a course of shock treatments would not cure, of a certainty. But the case was complicated by a hereditary factor—a very rare one. And here the doctor left me as he spoke of body chemistry, some inhibition of Peter's metabolism and a failure to oxidize a certain acid—it was too much for me to follow in technical French, and I imagine too much for Arthur as well. But suddenly I began to listen again when he started speaking of their discovery of an odor about Peter, an odor that led them to identify the rare factor. I heard him say "*acide phénylpyruvique*" and I nudged Arthur, who nodded comprehendingly. I was glad that I had stolen my grandfather's medical books.

"And the chances for a cure?" Arthur asked.

"They are fair," said Doctor Villemin with a bright birdlike stare at us, "save for the inherited biochemical disturbance resulting in the odor. Whether the metabolism can be readjusted no one knows. But we will try."

It was good to hear him talk freely about a patient's ailments, in contrast to the hedging generalizations given out by so many American doctors, delivered in inflections usually reserved for not-quite-bright children. I also liked the square set to his French jaw and his inflection as he said, "But we will try." You felt that all the Pasteurs and Curies, the Laënnecs and Parés of France were standing behind him with microscopes and magic powers, determined with bulldog stubbornness to restore health to a young British sailor, if for no other reason than to prove French medicine superior.

Doctor Villemin stopped before a closed door. He raised his hand to a small metal arrangement set in it, and motioned to be quiet. Then he looked into the peephole for a moment. He turned away, and signaled for Arthur to look. Arthur stared for a long moment, then pulled me to the door.

What I saw became another permanent still photograph in the files of my mind. The polished brass of the peephole narrowed to the scene within, held within sweeping circular brass lines like a miniature whirlpool. Peter sat at a table that held two piles of paper—an untidy one on the right on which I could see large black writing, and a neater one to the left, still blank. Between them lay some broken charcoal sticks.

Peter wore a maroon bathrobe and sat in a chair with arms—an old-fashioned "peacock" chair like a bishop's throne. He was pressed back against it, sitting erect and motionless. His hands clasped the ends of the chair arms, and his fine young profile was turned toward the window in an unwinking stare. He seemed carved in stone, motionless, finished. The flesh of his eye sockets was tinged with a faint powder blue, but that was the only physical change I noticed. The "V" opening of his bathrobe showed the edge of his hospital gown cutting white across his throat, and I thought for a sad moment of the way his undershirt had looked upon his chest many weeks ago. His curly yellow hair was neatly combed, his beauty undiminished. More than ever he looked like a Greek sculpture of an athlete who died young. Beauty . . . and youth . . . I felt old and dry.

An unexpected flood of pity washed through me, and the room

blurred. Ah, God—this silent lovely husk, unchanged except for the mysterious idle machinery of the brain—when again would those legs be moved in running, or the mouth opened in laughter, or light return to those empty eyes?

I turned my head away from the peephole and secretly brushed the tears aside. Sir Arthur looked at me curiously.

"We will all go in together," said the doctor. "So, he will not be forced into the mirror imitation of my gestures. His mind will recognize, wounded as it is, the impossibility of imitating all three of us."

For one moment as I stepped across the threshold I thought I might break wide open, but I kept control of myself. The doctor advanced toward Peter and touched his forearm, rigid on the chair. Only then did Peter turn his face to look at us with strange and vacant eyes.

The doctor spoke to him in English. "Peter," he said very gently, "I have brought some friends to see you."

"Fr-iends?" The word came out hesitantly, almost in two syllables.

"Friends," the doctor repeated. "Your cousin and Monsieur McAndrews."

"Friends," said Peter. He took his hands from the chair arms and crossed them in his lap. He looked down at them, and then up. "Friends," he said again. His mouth barely moved. The lips remained in a straight line. He did not smile. There was no recognition.

The doctor looked at us. Then he picked up the sheets of paper. "I see you have been working," he said. "What have you to tell us this afternoon?"

"Friends?" asked Peter.

"Yes, we're friends." The doctor turned to us. "Often we find important clues in these repeated words," he said, shuffling the papers. "Here—the top sheets are filled with 'underwear.' And below that, 'torpedo' on several pages. 'Kings' farther down." The doctor looked puzzled. "Does that mean anything?"

Arthur appeared confused. "The 'kings' might refer to a painting I was working on," he said, "called *The Three Kings*. I do not know what 'torpedo' means. The 'underwear'"—and here I thought he looked ashamed—"Well, someone left a pair of shorts in my apartment and Peter found them." He explained rapidly to me: "They belonged to Tony Midnight. Peter was terribly upset. I tried to explain that Tony had just taken a bath—" He stopped and looked at the floor.

"Friends," said Peter.

Doctor Villemin looked at Peter with narrowed eyes. "Is your cousin homosexual?" he asked Arthur.

Arthur continued to look at the floor. He nodded.

"Ah, well," said the doctor. "That is nothing. But we are happy to know it. We will have more to work on."

He turned to Peter who was staring at us. "Do you know these people, Peter?"

"Friends," said Peter.

The doctor looked at us soberly. "No recognition," he said. "You see how his mind is frozen." He put his hand to his forehead a bit wearily. "We know so little—my God, so little! We theorize that catatonia is a failure of the synapses—or rather, a kind of hysteric clutch of one synapse against another. He utters only the one word, until the feeble searching of his mind makes him clutch another burned-out connection—then he transfers to that word."

"Friends," said Peter.

The doctor glanced at his watch. "We have observed that he repeats at approximately twenty-second intervals, with one pattern lasting from four to five hours. Of course, he may be quite silent after we leave."

I felt again a kind of welling up in me, and turned nervously toward the door.

"Do you think the shocks will work?" Arthur asked.

The doctor shrugged, and spread his hands. "Who can say? If not, perhaps we will attempt an operation—a prefrontal lobotomy. One slices certain centers here—" he put his fingers to his forehead and moved them down to his eyebrows—"and leaves the early training in control of the patient, taking away all personal and emotional reaction. He will no longer be able to have—"

"Friends?" Peter interrupted. I shuddered at the timing.

"—many of the usual sensory motor reactions. But we will first try insulin, and perhaps *le choc éléctrique*."

"Have you told his family?" Arthur asked. We moved toward the door.

"The Ministry of the Navy has communicated with them," the

doctor said. Again he looked searchingly at Arthur. "Is he in truth your cousin?"

Once more Arthur was fussed. "Not truly," he said. "We were just—"

"Friends?" said Peter behind us.

It was too much for me. I moved rapidly toward the door and opened it myself. As I escaped into the corridor and turned to wait for them, I remembered in a delayed perception what I had seen hanging on the back of the door—its short straps jiggling violently as I wrenched the knob—a canvas garment with sleeves sewed shut, symbol of violence and agony—a straitjacket.

The doctor was closing the door. I caught a glimpse of Peter looking out after us questioningly, leaning forward a little. His gentle voice was clipped off as the door came shut upon his last word:

"Frien—?"

(23) July, 1937 to June, 1939

During the two-year interval while I was back in the States, I twice heard news of Arthur, about ten months apart. One was that he had married a girl named Genesa Wilkington—a commoner, he would have called her—and the other that he had "gone back" to the Catholic church. Both pieces of information left me speechless.

Word of the marriage came first from Alice Toklas. She wrote: "Arthur has surprised us all by marrying a Genesa Wilkington, who certainly is not much. But perhaps it will be good for him; it is time he settled himself. His painting, however, will probably suffer if his life becomes regular."

Trust Alice for a pointed analysis! I put the letter down on the desk and looked at it for quite a while. A marriage for Arthur was unbelievable. Male homosexuals frequently got married legitimately—that I knew. Often it was a case of a panicky youngster trying to "normalize" himself in a desperate gesture. But this was weird news about Arthur. Even more odd, I later learned from Jacques Guerre in Paris that Genesa Wilkington was actually a spiritualistic medium, and that her "control" was a Spanish dancer who continually warned Genesa—even after her marriage—against "Guess whom?" wrote Jacques. "Against Sir Arthur Lyly himself." I wondered if it were the same Spanish dancer whom Arthur had once known.

Although the news of the marriage was upsetting, I remembered my manners and sent a note of congratulation to Arthur, saying that I was surprised but pleased to hear of the wedding, and that I wished him all kinds of happiness. Back in a short time came a word from him thanking me, and saying that Genesa was perfectly aware of his shortcomings, and that "a very amicable understanding had been worked out." I angrily put the letter into a drawer and did not answer it for many months until my irritation had lessened.

The other news came from Fitzie, a friend of mine who had never met Arthur. He wrote: "All Paris has been astonished with the revelation that your old friend Sir Arthur has recently returned to the Church. Fact—he's been seen there almost *too* much. Goes every morning, takes communion regularly, more devout than the old ladies, and at present working on fourteen paintings for stations of the cross in a Normandy church—*those* I'd like to see, especially the scourging ones! Naturally no one thinks him sincere. There's all kinds of gossip—from saying he is doing penance for a recent murder to the fact that he has his eye on an altar boy in St. Sulpice. They say he's got a small shrine in his apartment, with a holy water cup at the door (I should be afraid to dip *my* finger in it!) and uses church incense. I can believe all this infatuation with ceremonials from what you have said of him. But I think he's really holding Black Masses (more like him!) and that he's found a renegade priest in the rat holes of this wicked city, and that wild orgies go on nightly in the Île St. Louis. At least, that's more in keeping with him. I heard he had his wife's wedding ring presented to the priest on a little purple pillow filled with the pubic hair that Sir Arthur had collected from his favorite tricks. . . ."

Fitzie's tongue was as sharp as ever, and I laughed at his letter. Still, I was puzzled. Arthur's "return" came ten months after his marriage, and Genesa was a Catholic (strange that she was a "medium" as well!). Before, Arthur had rarely gone to church, and I was not quite satisfied that he was in earnest about this new conversion. He would have to turn his life around completely. The Church never offered much to such as he, except the advice to work and pray—*ora et labora*. There was no provision for the homosexual in the Church except to be celibate in the priesthood, and that was certainly not for Arthur. Hypocritical Catholics always distressed me, and I had known many—who would rise dripping on a Sunday morning, go to Mass, and then return to the spotted sheets and the warm arms of their Saturday night lovers.

Like an old cow chewing her cud, I kept turning the news over and over. Another thought struck me, more in keeping with the subtle refinements of evil in Arthur's life. He might have returned to the Church to reinduce in himself a sense of sin. He could thus use his reawakened sense of guilt to give an added fillip of pleasure to his secret delights. He could dramatize and utilize the feeling of remorse and repentance and then go out to "sin" again, a great wicked sinner in the eyes of God. Thus he could open a whole new cabinet of emotions that had long been under lock.

I liked the last idea best, and was pleased to have thought of it. The more I speculated, the truer it seemed. I was positive his real nature had been revealed in the Peter Quint affair, and I felt I did him no discredit in his evil, in this "new" Sir Arthur.

Meanwhile his name and reputation continued to grow. Most of the art magazines managed to mention his name in almost every issue—what he was doing, the review of a show, or some remarks on a new project or canvas completed. He was rapidly becoming famous during those two years. I wondered if he would be able to be famous—as Gertrude once phrased it speaking of Saroyan—he "could not stand the weight of being great." But there would be no way of knowing that until I saw him again. Often those thrust into the public glare crumble in one way or another; more are destroyed than survive.

Much was made of the stations of the cross he had done in Normandy, and color photographs appeared in several journals. A show of his in Paris had the phenomenal result of selling every single painting three hours after the gallery was opened. The wallpaper that he had designed skyrocketed in price until only the very wealthy could afford it; he stopped that work, incidentally, about a year and a half after our last meeting. A portfolio of his Spanish sketches appeared in America under the Peristyle imprint—a large elegant book that retailed at an absurd price. In

England he was commissioned to create a church window for a Wessex cathedral. He also designed a set of playing cards for Hermès of Paris, the face cards of which were elaborate and richly fantastic. You had to search to find the tiny obscenities with which he had jokingly embroidered the clothing of the king and queen . . . and the knave! He seemed to have entered his ripest period. All was going well, and the world was his.

My life in Chicago was dull—heavy with drudge work and the unending piles of student reports to be graded. I sometimes wondered if Arthur would still know me when I went to Paris. He might be embarrassed that I knew so much about him, or perhaps I would too much remind him of his former life—if indeed he had renounced it. Guilt can break a friendship in such cases.

But I plodded on. I would know before long. I was sustained by the hope that I might get a fellowship for which I had applied— a whole year in Paris! So I read the themes, I cursed the days, I complained about the puritanism-optimism-and-hypocrisy of the country, and I graded the eternal papers. Had Dante included professors in his hell, I could have devised their punishment: they should be set at a table over a sulfurous pit, and compelled to grade papers forever. As the stack diminished, more would feed into it from beneath. There could be no worse hell.

But the days turned into weeks and the weeks months, and before I died in every part, the early months of the second year arrived. Once again there was the flurry over reservations and tickets and passport, and everything was sealed and stamped. Then came only the waiting until June, and the days grew lighter and longer. I throve on the jealous and admiring comments of colleagues, married with children to support, who could never afford the trip. I rubbed it in: "Wasn't it only a few months ago you were pitying me for not knowing the delights of wedded bliss?" or even more nastily: "Yes, I'm looking forward to it. Are you going over this year?"

The day came, the ship left, the wind was cool and the sun was warm. Within me the compass pointed and I followed—to magnetic North? Never. To France, *la belle France*, where my heart lay sealed in a little corner of Paris—any corner, dear God, no matter which one, so long as I could see it and go to it, and unseal the urn, and open my breast and return the heart to its empty matrix, and feel the blood once more begin to flow through the dried and shrunken channels of my veins. . . .

(24) June 6, 1939

With a certain nervousness I sat at the Royale St. Germain café, around the corner on the unpopular side where no one ever wanted to be. I tried to make myself as inconspicuous as possible. In a tight dark blue sweater and a pair of faded blue denim trousers called Levi's in the States, I would not have liked to be seen by even the moderately elegant element of the café's north side.

Sir Arthur had called in answer to my *pneumatique*. In it I told him I had mislaid his unlisted telephone number and could reach him only by this means. I had not really lost it, but I did not want the first greeting to be by phone. If he did not want to see me, he would have time to excuse himself without being caught unaware. But he was as cordial as ever over the telephone—perhaps even more than usual. "Let us have a frisk," he said. "Come in your very oldest clothes and we'll go to Montmartre and look into some of the bistros, eh? Perhaps we can have some *fun*."

No one could ever make the word "fun" carry such a weight of obscene meaning as could Sir Arthur. Hearing him pronounce it in the old way, I decided that perhaps he had not changed much at all.

I tried to shrink in upon myself as I sat there, conscious of my disreputable outfit and the blue worker's cap pushed to the back of my head. I had bought the *casquette* only that afternoon in the Bon Marché; it sat very well on me but the total effect could hardly have fooled anyone into thinking me one of the toughs of Paris, let alone Chicago. Arthur had once said it was not wise to overdo one's costume in either direction when on such excursions—so I had left my black leather jacket at the hotel.

Suddenly he was standing before me. I rose and we embraced. He smacked me loudly on each cheek, and I returned it, this time prepared.

"Jolly to see you again, Mac," he said, grinning widely. His big mouth spread over half his face. He had not changed much—his mustache still drooped, his face was still full and quite ruddy. I thought I noticed a thin network of broken red veins spreading over his cheekbones, but the color beneath was so fierce and Indian that it was hard to tell. He was getting a bit heavy around his lower middle.

And yet—and yet he still maintained the curiously appealing "little boy" quality that had sparkled in his eyes and his expression when we had first met four years ago. He seemed not really to have aged during that interval. His smile was still the same—not winsome perhaps, but very attractive, and his mobile eyebrows still announced—a millisecond earlier than his words—what extraordinary or delightful thought was about to spring from his active and image-filled mind. When he wanted to, he could be a real charmer—vibrantly warm and pleasant.

"And wonderful to see you," I said. "You're looking quite fit, as youthful and handsome as you did when we first met. Do you have a magic picture in your attic that grows old the way Dorian Gray's did? Your fame rests easily on you."

He chuckled. "There's no picture," he said. "And as for my fame—well yes, I am coming to be known a little. It is pleasing but at the same time rather terrifying, because the obscurity was very comfortable. I used to do a great many things I daren't do now—there might be reporters around. And I am always 'Mr. Pickett,' or 'Arthur Pickett,' when we go out like this. Just as you are 'Mr. Belvedere.' And you—*comment ça va?*"

I told him briefly of the boredom and hypocrisy and emptiness of American life compared with the Parisian, but I was short about it for his eyes were roaming, and I saw the hunter's look. I finished quickly with "—and so it is really only in Paris that I feel alive."

"Yes, I know," he said, drumming nervously on the tabletop. The waiter took his order for a *demi* of beer and mine for a *fine*, a brandy. Then he said, "I wonder if we shall have any luck tonight. I have got a feeling that you have a kind of magic about you. You bring me luck."

"How do you mean?"

"Every time we're together, I seem to meet some fascinating new person with whom I have an exciting adventure for a while. Perhaps your special kind of magic will be working again tonight. It was just a little over two years ago that you introduced me to that sailor who jumped into the Seine."

I could hardly see the good luck in that affair, or how any

magic was attached to it. And that was only one occasion—how could he say "every time we are together"? I thought of our various meetings and could remember only Wally Herrick; luckily neither I nor my "magic" was responsible for that encounter.

"Ah, yes . . . Peter," I said. "Whatever happened to him?"

Arthur made a vague wave of dismissal, unconcern, or lack of knowledge—I couldn't tell which. "Haven't the foggiest, dear boy, not a clue," he said. "I believe he was released from a hospital in England some months ago, but I've heard nothing." He passed the back of his hand over the light sweat on his forehead, a wetness that told me the beer he ordered was not his first drink of the day. "I really can't afford to know him or anything about him," he said. "And I prefer not to know. Hevvings . . . how I suffered over that boy!"

My mouth opened, then closed. I think he actually believed he had suffered over Peter. Perhaps he had—his mechanisms were mysterious.

"Let us speak of pleasant things," he said. The waiter brought our drinks. He downed half his beer in one tremendous gulping, and wiped the foam from his heavy upper lip. I noticed a small white scar that cut a short distance into his mustache.

"How did you get that scar?" I asked without thinking. "It's new, isn't it?"

He let out a high-pitched giggle. "Yes," he said. "I . . . er . . . got it some months ago in a strange little café for working men near the Gare de Lyon—called 'Chez Narcisse' improbably enough. But it certainly wasn't as delicate as it sounds." He rubbed the scar with his forefinger. "I deplore the use of certain American gangster tactics in Parisian life," he said, but his twinkle told me he was not serious. "Such things, for example, as brass knuckles."

"Oh, come now," I said. "They originated in Italy. They're merely a smoothed-out adaptation of the metal spikes that Roman boxers used to wear when they straddled a bench to fight each other."

"Reely?" he said. "What a bloody sport!" I could see that it amused him to be able to use the word "bloody" in a proper sense.

"I haven't seen you since your marriage," I said. "Let me congratulate you face to face. How is Lady Lyly?"

"Oh, quite well," he said. "She's in London now. Hates Paris.

Simply never comes over, and keeps wishing me in London more. But I don't mind, reely." He smiled and winked once at me. "One can have lots more *fun* here, alone." Then he grew more serious. "She's quite nice," he said, "and she understands all my whims and waywardness. She has a wonderful head for business—keeps the books and that sort of thing, which I can't do at all."

I hesitated to ask any real questions—but Arthur went on talking, as I had presumed he might.

"Actually," he said, rotating the beer glass on the table top, "I think she had a kind of mothering instinct about me at first. Thought of me as a poor, sick thing, y'know. She would marry me and 'cure' me of all my obliquities. And then too I think she was fascinated by the fact that I was an artist—something unusual and colorful in her rather unexciting life. And perhaps she had just enough of the snob in her to be attracted to my title, donchaknow . . . quite a step up for the gentry, after all. I find that she's helpful in many ways."

"An anchor in a stormy sea?" I suggested.

"No, not that. Good hevvings, if she anchored me down, I would probably be tempted to leave her the next day. And she understands me enough so that she will not show any jealousy, or probably even feel it."

"She . . . er . . . is not lesbian?" I said tentatively.

Arthur laughed. "Farthest thing from it," he said. "And anyway, one in the family's enough."

We finished our drinks. "Shall we go?" he said.

"Yes," I said. "Do I look all right?"

"Perfect," he said. He was wearing his usual striped sailor's undershirt beneath a faded gray workshirt, with sleeves rolled to the elbows. He had on a pair of sailor trousers.

"Where are we going?" I asked as he hailed a cab.

"Rue Lépic," he said to the driver. And to me: "Near the Place Blanche."

The Place Blanche was in the heart of Montmartre—a gaudy square filled with many people, garish neon signs, little clumps of wandering tourists. Like so many spots in Paris, it had lost its character when the tourists came. They had descended like locusts, mainly from America, upon places they had read of or seen Hollywood versions of—and with their coming the neon went up, prices rose, souvenir sellers opened shops, and all was ruined. In the Place Pigalle you were now almost as safe at midnight as you were in the Place de l'Opéra; the somber and shadowed alleys of mystery and terror were clean now and lighted with arc lamps. The underworld of Paris had been driven up the hill into the little dark side streets, into the small dark holes of furnished rooms and unlit alleys. The Arab runners who offered more francs for your money than did the legal exchange remained in the Place Blanche to approach the tourists. At night, however, you could see some of the real underworld—the whores with hard eyes and orange hair, the pimps in their pointed yellow shoes and their fantastic silhouettes borrowed from America—these ones came down from their tunnels deep in the darkened mysterious hill above, to link the real and hidden evil of Paris with the phony well-lighted show around the Place Blanche.

We got out in the middle of the crowd, but fled at once from the neon glare. I was somewhat nervous, but pleased that we passed six or seven money changers who did not once say "Change your dollars?" to either of us.

Once away from the Place, Arthur said in a low voice, "It's still dangerous as ever, beyond the lights. I wouldn't come here alone after midnight, or go into the bars alone."

It was hard to believe him, knowing his tastes and loves, and his ability to speak argot. He had mastered the Parisian argot completely, and spoke it like a true apache.

He guided the way to the Rue Lépic, a narrow street that rose sharply upward as it left the Place Blanche. There were not many people here. The street lamps threw circles of light on the upward-slanting cobblestones, rising in sharp perspective to the high end of the narrow street. Two French sailors passed us. Sir Arthur nudged me. The sight of one of them clutched at my heart. He was tall and blond. He wore his white hat tilted to the left side, and he had bent it so that it rose like a white flame in the night above his clear tanned face and inquiring glance. I felt his blue eyes pass intensely over my entire body, and then sensed a sudden rush of blood in my veins, so that I felt enclosed in an envelope of fire. The glance lasted just a second but it left me staggered. I put my hand on Arthur's arm and said weakly, "A moment—just a moment."

He paused and looked at me. "Whatever is the matter?" he asked.

"I have just had—what do the French call it?—a '*touche*,'" I said, "from the blond sailor—with a few thousand volts behind it."

"Ah, yes, I thought I saw him looking at you," Arthur said. "Some of the French develop a tremendous power behind the *touche*. Did you notice that in the middle of it—when the eyes make direct contact—the clothes are all whipped off and there is a very real physical sensation in the body?"

"I'm suffering from it right now," I said. I looked after the sailor. He turned his head and looked at me, then smiled and flicked his finger to the peak of his white hat in a kind of heart-breaking adieu. I would never see him again. But dead or living, drunk or dry, sailor, I wish you well. . . .

"There is a bar right there," Arthur said, pointing across the street, "that Genet has written about."

I reluctantly returned from my fantasy with the handsome sailor, astonished to find myself out of the rumpled bed, clothed, and walking on the street. Genet's name was just then beginning to be known. Criminal, thief, homosexual, masochist—the man by force of his literary power had compelled the world of the arts and the intellectual to notice him, and to read his sexual confessional, his analysis of the nature of his evil and his crimes. "Is he still in prison?" I asked.

"I believe he's out now," Arthur said. "He hides somewhere in these holes of Montmartre, and dashes out just long enough to drop a manuscript on his publisher's desk. Then he's back again to his *durs*—his tough boys—to sleep with them and go on writing. A fascinating man."

"You know him?"

"Quite well," said Arthur. "We've spent a lot of time to-gether."

We crossed the street and approached a bar. It was very small. There were posters on the windows that almost concealed the interior. Arthur laid his hand on my arm.

"Let me do most of the talking at first," he said.

"Willingly," I said. "And you may have to translate too, because my argot is limited. Tell them I'm from—from Scotland."

"Good," he said, "and remember, Mr. Belvedere, that I am Arthur Pickett."

We entered the little bar.

(25) June 6, 1939   Later

It was a small poorly lighted place. Toward the rear were three narrow booths covered in bright red imitation leather. A square French jukebox, lighted inside with flashing colored bulbs, stood against one wall. A young French tough was in front of it, studying the selections. Several other young men were in the booths with beer or wine in front of them; from the far corner came a clatter and shrieking where two boys and two young female tramps were crowded together. As Arthur and I entered a complete silence fell, except for the worn phonograph that went on grating "Madame la Marquise."

The elegant patronne of the place sat at her cash drawer at one end of the very short straight little bar. Her black hair was piled high in a glossy pompadour, and her plump face was heavily enameled with white powder. Her underlip was drawn in with a perpetual coy pout. Her eyebrows had been shaved off and a thin line penciled on, but the faint blue marks of the brows were still visible. Two enormous rhinestone earrings dangled almost to her shoulders and the edge of her black satin dress. She turned her head to look at us with cold sleepy eyes. The bartender, a thin and seedy-looking fellow, stopped drying the beer glass he was holding—the towel poked inside.

It was an uncomfortable moment. Arthur walked to the bar and ordered a beer, and I nodded for the same. "Two," he said to the bartender. Then, still in the silence, he stuck out his hand to the patronne.

"*Bon soir, Madame*," he said in French. "It is a long time since I have seen you, is it not so? It has been almost a year since I was here—do you not remember?—with Monsieur Genet."

The name was a talisman that erased the faint scowl on Madame's face. Her eyebrows rose, her eyes opened wide, and a smile appeared.

"*Voyons!*" she said, and pumped his hand up and down, far beyond the required quick jerk of greeting. "It is the anglais, Monsieur Peek-eet, not so?"

"Indeed it is," said Arthur and grinned hugely at her.

The silence around us fell to the floor like a dissolving wall. I could almost hear the sigh that marked the release of the room's tension. The talk began again in the booths, the young tough pressed his button on the jukebox, and the bartender put down the glass he was holding, picked up two others, and filled them from the beer tap. He cut off the foam and set them before us.

"And how have things been going for you?" the patronne asked. "Have you seen Monsieur Genet recently?"

"No, that I have not," Arthur said. "I was wondering if he is in Paris."

She shrugged. "He was here last week," she said. The ivory splendor of her shoulders moved up and down like a soft white wave. "He is in here much of the time. But where he lives, where he is, alas, that I do not know. He is very careful, you know . . . the gendarmes . . ." She sighed again.

"Ah, yes," said Arthur. He turned to me and mumbled an introduction to Madame, whose last name I could see he did not know. "May I present my friend, Monsieur Belvedere, from Scotland."

"Enchanted," said Madame. Her hand was warm and fat and faintly sweating. Then she peered around the side of the bar, down at my legs. "But Monsieur is not in his Scotch skirt."

The French expression for kilt always struck me as a bit irreverent. I meant to let out a baritone guffaw, but my nervousness turned it into an alto giggle. I plunged the whole way.

"Madame," I said, "in Paris I wear the very short one, underneath my trousers. It comes only to here —" and I indicated a point just below my crotch—"for to say true, I am afraid the Frenchmen of Montmartre might take advantage of me."

Madame bellowed heartily and Sir Arthur laughed. She wiped her eyes. "Ah, the Scots," she said, "they have the sense of the ridiculous as he is necessary."

There was now a pleasant and relaxed atmosphere in the place. A young tough pulled a girl to her feet, and they began to move slowly together on the tiny space of bare floor. Both his hands were behind her, pressing her buttocks close against his body, and her arms were around his neck. His eyes were closed, his heavy lips parted. Their feet moved slowly, in no dance-step pattern . . .

"There is a question I would like to demand of your friend, Monsieur Peek-ett," Madame said, leaning confidentially close.

"But I am not certain she is the kind of question to demand of a stranger. Will he then be angered?"

"But of course not," said Arthur. "Demand it then."

Madame lowered her voice and I leaned toward her. "Is it true or not," she said, "that the Scots wear a little something beneath the skirt—yes or no?"

Luckily, I had once known a young Scot in Paris—a stalwart fresh apple-cheeked lad smelling of heather, who had told me all. I spoke with authority.

"It is just as one desires, Madame," I said, "and as the . . . er . . . occasion demands. Some wear a dark brief swimming suit or *slip*, and others do not. I would hesitate to walk in Paris without something beneath, for the wind blows up from the subway stations most devilishly. But unless you are of the military you may do as you please. They, however, must always go unclothed. At the barracks threshold is a mirror on the floor, by which sits a guard when they go out on permission, to make sure they are naked. It is a tradition."

Madame's eyes grew wide and then crinkled with laughter. "*Ah ça!*" she said. "That, it is a job for myself in my old age—to be the inspector at the mirror in the barracks!"

Wherewith she fell into a fit of laughing that ended with her leaning her enormous breasts on the counter and burying her head in the crook of one arm, while she beat weakly with one plump fist upon the bar. Her rhinestones jiggled wildly. Arthur and I joined in the laughter, and the bartender as well. The young Frenchmen in the place were all looking with interest at us because of the uproar. Their attention was pleasing, and I tried to think of something else amusing, when suddenly I realized that no matter how sophisticated or intelligent we become, we are still at the mercy of our desire to show off, hoping that someone who sees us will think us attractive enough to be approached—more scintillating than the rest, broader shouldered, narrower hipped, with a stronger chin or whiter teeth.

A young man detached himself from the males at the back. He held a half-empty glass of beer in his hand. With studied indifference, stopping at the jukebox, watching the dancers with a frown—he slowly drew near to us like a scout advancing on ambush, or like the trees moving against Macbeth at Dunsinane castle. A small movement, unnoticed in the room—a pause and then another movement in our direction. He was an extremely husky young man with powerful shoulders and a good face, a young animal. His hair was brushed roughly back without a part, and stood fairly high—dark brown and shining.

He wore a sportcoat of a heavy gray brown material. Beneath it was a gray pullover jersey with a rounded collar attached, open on the strong brown column of his neck. The top button of the unpressed jacket was buttoned, and the width of his shoulders put such tension on it that the fabric was drawn in ridges toward it. His unpressed trousers were of a darker material, and the great bulge down the left side of his fly put small accordion pleats in the cloth above it. There was strength beneath the clothes that bursted to spring forth, so that I felt his fly would pop open, or his suit fly off him at any moment.

I set about the pleasant work of constructing the image of his body, a trick that my sessions in life-drawing classes had taught me. With the details of wrists, hands, neck, and ankles I could produce the whole image of the body concealed beneath the clothes. I saw that he had a giant chest with swelling plateaus of muscle, a ridged abdomen, and extraordinary development in thighs and arms. The definition of muscles was excellent, with no flabbiness; the waist was strong—a worker's body. And judging from his beardmark and the backs of his hands, there was only a medium amount of hair on legs, chest, and arms.

His forehead was wide and the brows set straight across it, not arched. Beneath them were clear dark brown eyes, a straight nose with wide-flared nostrils, a sensual mouth with full well-cut lips, and a cleft chin. Brutality and sex were there. You felt he would never tolerate light-fingered gentleness or dainty dalliance in caresses—it would be flame and force and violence, a hand in the hair forcing the head back, the mouth pried open, the heavy weight crushing down against the face . . .

I shook my head; the images of violence melted away. I continued to watch his approach in the mirror behind the bar. It reminded me somewhat of the courtship dance of the bees, or the nectar announcement, or the two combined.

Although Arthur went on talking with Madame, he had also become aware of the approach of the young David. And then the quarry, the hunter hunted (unknown to him), at last gained the bar. He rested his forearms on the edge of it, clasped his glass between his hands, and scowled straight ahead into the mirror, moody and unsmiling.

I saw his hands—large ruthless worker's hands with raised veins. They were hands for pick and shovel, not dexterity and skill. The nails were well shaped and short, but not bitten or ragged. Then I looked up into the mirror. He was looking directly at Arthur but when I raised my head he looked into my eyes and smiled—within his scowl, which did not completely vanish.

I smiled back and then turned to him at the same time he half-turned to face me. He spoke, and I saw that one of his perfect white teeth, right in front, had a small triangular chip off the lower corner. He was aware of it, and tried to draw down his lip a little.

"*Il fait beau*," he said.

"*Oui*," I said, "but it is perhaps going to rain."

It was the only remark that I got to make alone to him that evening. At that point Arthur turned to the bartender and said: "Drinks! Another beer for you?" he asked me, and then included the Frenchman. "And you—another?"

"Yes, thanks," said the young man.

The bartender set the three beers in front of us, and Arthur turned his back on Madame. He took out his snuffbox, tapped it, opened it, and inserted a pinch into each nostril. The young man was fascinated.

"What is it that you have there?" he asked.

"*Tabac prisé*—English," said Arthur, extending the box. "Try some."

"*Ah non, merci*," he said, gesturing it away with the flat of his palm. "That, that makes to sneeze."

"But it is excellent," said Sir Arthur. "It is well perfumed. Here, smell it," and he stuck the box under the young man's nose. "It is very good for the cold in the head, and it stimulates."

The boy inhaled. "It is good, that," he said. "I will try some." He stuck two fingers forward and took a considerable pinch. He applied it to one nostril and sniffed strongly upward. A tremendous look of astonishment came over his face. He opened his mouth wide, looked toward the ceiling, and sneezed mightily. A large clot of mucus burst from one nostril, and he turned quickly away, fumbling with lowered head for his handkerchief. We were all embarrassed.

When he recovered he turned back to us, his eyes watering.

"That, it is very strong," he said. "At least three times as strong as French snuff. Let me see it again." He took the box and inhaled cautiously. Then he took a very tiny pinch and sniffed it delicately up the other nostril. "Yes," he said. "Three—perhaps four times."

"It is very strong," Arthur admitted.

"It is not much used in France," said the young man.

"It is much used in England," Arthur said.

"Monsieur is British?"

"Yes," said Arthur—and the conversation rolled away. The preliminaries were done, the rapport established. Now all that remained was a few minutes of talk, perhaps two more drinks, and the inevitable suggestion that they return to Arthur's apartment. There were many advantages to having a place of one's own in Paris, rather than a hotel guarded by a watchdog concierge.

It had commenced to rain outside—gently, but enough to wet the passersby. A woman ran past the door, her head covered with an angled tent of newspaper. Another dashed by in the opposite direction, shrieking to someone to wait for her. I looked at the young people in the back of the room, but they all seemed to be paired off in one way or another. Perhaps it was true that I had a kind of magic for Arthur, but evidently it did not work for me. For a while I tried listening to the talk between Arthur and his new one, but it had fallen into argot and I could make little sense of it.

Then Arthur turned to me. "Did you hear that?" he said in English.

"Sorry, I wasn't listening."

"My dear chap, he knows Genet quite well—was even a member of his 'stable' for a time. He said that Genet put him in a book. I asked which one but he doesn't know—he's never read any of them."

The young man was listening, hunting for a word that he might know in the English Arthur was speaking. His right hand clasped the beer glass on the bar, and the wrist was turned in such a way that I could see an odd arrangement of black dots that seemed to be tattooed on the skin—four horizontal dots in a line, crossed vertically by three, rather like a division sign in arithmetic. I reached over to pick up the young man's wrist to look at it.

"Whatever in the world is that?" I said, peering closely at the markings.

"Oh, my God," said Arthur in English, and took my hand off

the boy's wrist. The young man was looking sidewise, down at the bar. "Oh, hevvings no—don't ask that!" Arthur said hurriedly in a low voice. "It's the criminal tattoo—he's been in prison for a felony, some act of violence."

"Oh, Lord—" I said, and then stammered to the boy, "Sorry . . . forgive me."

He shrugged his wide shoulders. "It's nothing." But he did not smile.

I had not blushed for years but I felt the heat begin to mount. I said, "I must go to the lavabo—" and looked around for it wildly. "Excuse me?"

I escaped into the smelly triangular hole and stood there breathing the foul air of deodorant crystals and old urine until I was more composed.

When I went back they were deep in conversation. Arthur turned to me. "André would like to see my sketches and photographs. Will you come along with us?"

"Not this evening," I said. I knew my cues.

"Well, we'll be going then," Arthur said. "Be careful around here."

"I will," I said. "Don't fear."

"Goodbye," said André. He shook my hand firmly, looking gravely at me.

They went out into the rain, which was now falling steadily. I yawned and looked at Madame. She was knitting but she looked up sympathetically. "The rain is very sad," she said.

"It is very sad," I agreed, "especially coming down outside the open door of a small bar in Montmartre. It comes down more sadly there than anywhere else."

In the mirror I saw one of the young men in a booth stand up. He bent over his companion, looked at me, and then took his glass and wandered slowly in the direction of the jukebox.

The evening's second quadrille of the bees had begun.

(26) June 7, 1939

"You can see for yourself!" Sir Arthur said. "But the red has faded by now." He stood up quickly, turned his back, and pulled off the old plaid shirt in which he had been painting. He was standing beside one of the windows in his apartment. The afternoon sun fell against the yellow parchment with its red and blue medieval insert, and put a hazy radiance around him.

His back was crisscrossed with sharp angry whip marks, thinly vicious. The red was still deep and violent. He had evidently been lashed from only one side, for the whip end had cut deeply into the skin over his right ribs, leaving small uneven cuts and crusts of dried blood.

"In the name of God," I muttered.

Slowly and painfully he put his shirt back on, stuffing the tails into his trousers. He turned to face me. "I am like that all over my back down to my ankles, and even the bottoms of my feet." His face was drawn and lined, and there was a deep scratch over his left eye.

"How in the world did you ever let him tie you to the bed?"

Arthur sank back gingerly into the large chair. "Took me completely by surprise," he said. "When we got home we looked at some of my photographs first, and he got quite excited over the group that is called the 'motorcycle series.'"

I nodded. They were crudely exaggerated but effective pornographic drawings that had been widely circulated in the States.

"'I like these,' he said several times," Arthur went on, "and then we decided to go to bed. We had undressed, and he was ready—oh, *so* ready!—when he asked where the bathroom was. I pointed it out to him, and he went. I was standing at the mantel when he came back. I don't remember what I was doing—setting up some postcards that had fallen over, I believe. Then suddenly I saw his face in the mirror beside mine. His eyebrows were drawn down, scowling—very ferocious. He seemed to be holding something behind his back. Then suddenly he grabbed both my elbows behind me—"

"Locking them, I suppose," I said.

"Yes," Arthur said. "Naturally I struggled. I am very strong, but he was stronger. He laughed—you could hear the devil in it—and then I saw what he was holding. Some lengths of rope he had found in the bathroom closet. He whipped a few turns around my elbows and then down around my wrists. I was helpless. 'In heaven's name, what are you doing?' I gasped at him. He laughed again. 'Voyons,' he said. 'We will try out one of the pictures, will we not?' and with that he pushed me so that I fell on the bed—"

"Face down?"

"Yes. He jumped on the bed and sat on me, facing my feet. He knotted a rope around one ankle, and then he jumped off me and tied that foot to the bedpost. All the time I was kicking with the other foot, but he grabbed that one and tied it too. My word, what strength he had!"

"Weren't you yelling for help?" I asked.

He shook his head. "I was talking to him all the time, telling him this was a mistake," he said, "but I wasn't shouting. Didn't want the neighbors . . . y'know. Besides, he threatened to gag me if I wasn't quiet—picked up his socks and began to stuff them in my mouth. I promised to be quiet. Then he pulled the rope on my wrists back and up and tied it to the head of the bed. The pain was terrible. I thought I might faint. And that position forced my head down into the pillow so that I was smothering. I had to turn my head sidewise and that nearly broke my neck."

I resisted a strong impulse to giggle, seeing Sir Arthur Lyly, baronet and peer of England, trussed up like a pig in a slaughter-house.

"I had a little plaited whip of black leather hanging inside the armoire door," Arthur said, "and André must have seen it when I was hanging up my clothes. He jerked the door open and got the whip. Then he came to the bed, cutting the air several times with sharp strokes so that I could hear that terrifying swish. 'You and that pig Genet,' he said bitterly. 'You're all alike, you swells, you—people with brains. I, I have no brains, but I got strong arms.' And with that he raised the whip and brought it down on my back so hard, so viciously that all my muscles contracted and I—I really thought I was going to die! 'Ah!' he said, 'you do not like the taste of leather? You will learn to like it by the time I am through with you.' And he really began to—how do you say in

America?—to lay it on. I writhed with each cut but he would not stop. Over and over again—I don't know how long it went on. I was certain I was bleeding all over the sheets. I felt wetness running down my sides, whether blood or sweat I couldn't tell. It was agony—dreadful burning agony all over me."

Sir Arthur's voice had become very low and intense, and his narrative had made me sweat.

"It was horrible," he said. "I really thought my last hour had come. Or that I'd die of a heart attack if he didn't kill me with whipping. I pleaded, I cried, I retched and pretended to vomit—but he wouldn't stop. I could twist my head and see him a little—legs apart, torso contracted violently, forehead beaded with sweat, huge erection . . . even with all that pain I couldn't help admiring the beauty of him—like a savage bull."

I took out my handkerchief and wiped my face. Sir Arthur went on.

"And then," he said, "then something mysterious happened inside me. It was like opening a door, almost—a black door against a warm black current that flowed out from my groin over me, as if I were standing in a dark tunnel and felt the warm black rush of a mysterious fluid first around my ankles, and mounting, mounting with a kind of sucking sensation against my flesh, mounting up my body until it passed my waist and then my arms and chest and was finally completely up over the top of my head. And through that warm blackness I still felt the whip cutting into my skin, but with what a difference now!"

He rose from his chair and hit his fist into his palm.

"Johnny," he said, "the blows no longer hurt! Instead, each cut set up an intense spasm of pleasure in me, each blow was the start of a lightninglike ripple of . . . of ecstasy that flashed over my whole body, sank, wavered, and flashed again as the whipping went on. It wasn't a biting pain now, but a stimulus, an intense thrill . . . a thousand little violent orgasms. I no longer struggled. Finally, he stopped, panting. I felt the warm black liquid begin to sink rapidly around my body—it left me exposed and cold and shivering. The pain came back to my arms, and I whimpered. He reached over to the bed and untied my hands. But he was not through. He—he had his way with me, and somehow it was enormously . . . right."

My hand was shaking as I lighted a cigarette. I dropped the

match into the ashtray. "Have you ever known before that you're a masochist?" I asked.

Arthur straightened. "I, a masochist? I am not one at all. Never have been the least bit interested in it."

"Well," I said, "you'd better begin to be, because you certainly are one."

He made an impatient gesture. "If anything I'm a sadist."

"It's a wavering line between the two," I said. "But don't you realize that you just perfectly described the masochistic reaction when you spoke of the black fluids? Sometimes even admitted masochists never get to that point in all their lives. You crossed the threshold of pain—into the pleasure principle, as Freud says."

"The threshold of pain," said Arthur musingly. "That's a pretty expression. Well, I'll take your word for it, but I'm not going to read Freud at this late date. I don't need to know *why* I feel the way I do—it's enough just to feel and enjoy."

"Or suffer," I said sardonically. "But how do you feel about the whole experience? I mean—aside from the pain or the pleasure."

"You mean my psychic reaction? I don't know. I guess I deserve to be beaten." He looked down at the dark blue carpet. "I am really a very great sinner in the eyes of God. It's time I began to be punished for my misdeeds." Then he looked at me. I was careful to keep my eyes empty. He had given a masochist's answer, but was there mockery in that rather pathetic expression on his face?

"I have heard," I said, feeling that this was a good moment, "that you have returned to the Church. Does that statement about 'being punished for my misdeeds' have anything to do with the pleasure you got from your beating?" Having gone that far, I decided to go on. "Could it be possible, Arthur—now please don't be offended—"

"At anything you say, Mac?" he murmured. "Of course not."

I was not sure how he meant that remark, but I continued. "Could you have returned to the Church just to reawaken your sense of sin, to give the added pleasure of remorse, or guilt feelings, to your encounters, so that you'd paint better?"

"Good heavens!" he said. "Johnny, you give me credit for more subtlety than I deserve. No—I honestly feel that I am wicked and weak. That's really rather outrageous, old chap. I am not so jaded that I would have to stimulate myself that way."

He seemed perfectly sincere. "Well, I'm glad—" I began.

Then a kind of evil twinkle returned to his heavy face. "But your question has been asked before by others," he said, "and you have just heard my *standard* answer. Not very often asked, it's true. So many trusting souls accept answers to such questions without doubting one's sincerity. But Johnny, smart Johnny—" and he leaned forward to put a hand on my knee—"I can tell you and you'll understand. My honest answer to your question is— that's exactly why I returned to the Church."

There was a long silence. I looked at his eyes. They were black and empty, like a merman's eyes or those of some strange wild half-human animal. He looked at me fixedly, without expression. Finally he leaned back in his chair.

"Do you understand?" he asked.

"I s-suppose so," I said.

"Don't sound so miserable," he said. "You know me thoroughly. You know that I must have sensuality and excitement. You know I can't paint unless I can feed on my own emotions, or those of others."

I rubbed my forehead wearily. "Yes, I know," I said. "But you are a little hard for me, Arthur. I suppose it's the early training I had, like your own. Grim, narrow. I'm just now learning to accept . . . these things in life. I've never known anyone exactly like you."

He laughed in the merry old way. "Good boy," he said, and I rather expected a pat on the head. "I'll paint you a picture."

"Are you going to see this André again?" I asked.

"Of course, my naive one. I gave him five thousand francs and that will bring him back. A week from last night. After all," he said, "I do have to give my poor back a chance to heal, don't I? And besides, I began to paint a new picture this morning. The jolt from last night probably won't carry me through for more than the next seven days."

(27) June 10, 1939

I am a dreamer.

Fantasy plays an important part in the life of every man. The extent and color of his dreams depend on the richness of his background and imagination. Yet the talent for fantasy is the only human ability not improved by constant exercise. An overuse ruins its delicate mechanism. When its fragile structure lies broken, no wisps of dreams arise from it. Amid remarkable situations, one can only sigh that this has been done or seen too many times before. In anticipation and retrospect lie the only pleasures left in life.

My dream mechanism sometimes carried me away, although it was usually well controlled. But Sir Arthur's story about André Vignot started an idea sparkling in my head. How nice it would be if I could carry off that savage young Parisian tough to the country for a few days—to a calm and isolated lake somewhere, so that the two of us could spend an exciting idyllic time in swimming and sunbathing and making love. Slim as my budget was, it could stand an interlude like that.

Bouncing my happy little idea before me, I walked into the café of La Reine Blanche—the White Queen—on the Saturday following Arthur's first Wednesday beating. La Reine Blanche was one of the most notorious cafés in Paris, filled with screaming shrieking young men, from the carefully marcelled and plucked ones to those in T-shirts and two-day stubble, cigarette a-dangle from the lips, waiting for someone to approach. When you went into La Reine Blanche or sat at one of its sidewalk tables, you were marked. Perhaps a stranger wandered in by mistake from time to time—but he never stayed long.

It was hard for me to enter the brilliantly lighted place alone, to push through the persons standing three or four deep at the bar. I hated the assayer's stare one had to undergo—what kind of ore is this? Is it worthwhile? How much gold per pound? Their razor glances sliced you, shredded you, as they weighed your potential in either money or muscle. I made myself as inconspicuous as possible and sidled around a rounded corner of the bar. Luckily a man suddenly gave up his stool, and I slid onto it, pulling it next to the wall.

It was a good seat. I could see everyone down the bar. And then with a startled surge of excitement I noticed the hazily familiar outlines of the back of a young man's head right beside me. He had crossed his arms and was resting his head upon them on the counter. Both Jean the bartender and Madame Alice, the patronne, were casting dark looks at him.

It was indeed André Vignot! Same coat, same jersey shirt— right beside me!

I looked around nervously, not knowing exactly why. A half-flash in my mind suggested that I move elsewhere—perhaps a small guilt reaction at finding my dream object suddenly quite close to me. But that was silly—no one else could have known what a part André played in my fantasies. I put a hand tentatively on his shoulder. The cloth was warm from his body.

"André!" I shook him gently. "Wake up!"

He raised his head and blinked. I shook him again and he looked at me, his eyes a little blurred. "Are you between two wines?" I asked.

He shook his head and focused his eyes. "Eh!" he said. "It is my good copain—the friend of Monsieur Peekeet! How is it that you call yourself again?"

I told him my name. "I, I am not drunk in the least," he said, by now quite awake. "I was taking the small nap. If one is sleepy, one naps, hein?"

"*Bien sûr*," I said, lighting his cigarette for him. "You want a brandy?"

"Brandy? Ah no, thanks. It costs too dear. I will have a beer."

"Have a brandy," I urged, seeing he was already a bit drunk. It was not mere sleepiness that had overcome him.

"*Bien alors*, I will," he said. I signaled Jean. "*Deux fines*," I said, and he set them in front of us.

"Have you been well?" I asked him.

"Yes, yes . . . *très bien*," he said, and then smiled rather crookedly, to hide his chipped tooth. "But *voyons*, I am disgusted with the life. It is the grand struggle. I, I am of a mind to join the Foreign Legion."

I pretended to believe him. "But that, it is the difficult existence," I said. "Sand, sun, work, no women—"

He raised one eyebrow. "That to me is equal," he said. "I would bed with men. I am tired of women."

"Well, the Legion uniforms *are* handsome," I admitted. "When they parade."

"I want to be in uniform," he said. "I have never been in uniform."

"It would make you feel important?"

He shrugged.

"What do you do in Paris?" I asked.

He smiled his crooked grin again. "I? I maintain myself. I have no profession except male whore. *Pédé.* I was a barman once. I did not like it. Got drunk and told the patron to kiss my ass. I had to listen to many sad stories. And all the *pédés* tried to make me. 'What time do you finish work?' they said. 'What are you doing then?' they said. 'Would you like to come home with me?' They were always after me."

"And did you object?"

He looked straight at me. "Yes. But it was the way I made my living. It made me angry. The anger followed me through the alleys. I hated the queers, hated 'em, hated their mouths on my cock, slobbering. I beat 'em up. I stole from them. But most of 'em had no money." He looked down at his wrist and rubbed the tattoo on it. "You asked about that the other night," he said. "I got that because I killed one of them. Five years only . . . there were circumstances . . ."

"I'm sorry if I embarrassed you," I said. "Do you want to tell me about it?"

"Why not? The world knows it." He rubbed his chin. "He was an old man. Nearly seventy. I was sixteen. I'd known him a year, maybe two. Used to take me home for tea and biscuits and then go down on me. That night I was broke. I asked for more money than he usually gave me. He said he didn't have it. All the time he kept fumbling with his tie. A red tie. Too tight on his neck. I got mad at him when he wouldn't give me more money. So I grabbed his tie and pulled it tighter. His eyes began to bulge. He looked like a fish. Then he died. I was scared—bad. I looked all over the apartment for money—couldn't find it. So I gave up. I thought I'd take some cognac from the bottle on the mantel, so I reached for it. But I knocked a vase over, see? It fell and broke. And among the pieces—twenty thousand francs. I took it and beat it. But the *flics* caught me and there was a trial. They knew why he'd picked me up. And I was under eighteen. So I got five years instead of my head chopped off. And they tattooed me." He rubbed his wrist.

His smile was mocking and sardonic. "Now that I've told you," he said. "Are you scared? Won't you run? They mostly do."

As he told his story I had begun to tremble. I recognized the details of the episode. But I had to ask two more questions.

"No, I'm not scared," I said. "It's an exciting story. But you— you haven't killed anyone since . . ." My sentence had the barest inflection of a question, and yet sounded calm enough.

"No," he said.

"Tell me—you say you know Monsieur Genet?"

"Yeah, I know him. I used to be one of his boys. He's a good guy. I used to beat the hell outa him. He liked it."

"Did you ever read any of his books?"

"*Merde*—no! I tried to once. I couldn't understand it. He's too brainy. I guess he wrote about me in one of them. Somebody said he did. I don't know what he said about me."

My mouth was dry. I took another swallow of brandy and said nothing. I knew what Genet had said about him. The episode made the story of Adrien Baillon. But Genet had not let Adrien escape; he had been executed in the novel.

"He used to call me Dédé," said André, looking off into the bar mirror.

And Genet had used that name, too, in the novel I had translated as a labor of love. An author picks from here and there, sews, patches, selects, quilts a thousand fragments together. Everything is adjusted—nothing in fiction is ever wholly true or untrue.

I was very excited, wondering if Arthur knew this story yet.

"Have you told our friend Arthur what you've just told me?" I asked.

"No," André said, finishing the brandy. I motioned to Jean to fill it again. André looked at me. "He's a good guy," he said. "He gave me some money. Did he tell you about it?"

"Yes," I said.

"All of what happened?"

"Yes," I admitted.

He took a swallow of the new drink. "*Fiotte!*" he muttered.

I did not know exactly how he meant the word—in argot it had the sense both of a passive pederast, and one who informed or denounced.

"But I don't care if he told you," he went on. "I'm seeing him next Wednesday. I'm gonna beat him again. Tell me," he said, and suddenly made a direct attack with his strong young thigh against my leg, so startling that I had a surge of panic. "Tell me—we are good buddies, hein? Can I get some money outa him? I mean, really a lot?"

"He is rich enough," I said, still disturbed by the sensual rubbing, and feeling vaguely like Judas kissing Christ. "If you are nice, he'll be generous."

"What do you mean—be 'nice'?"

"Do what he wants. You inspire him in his painting," I said.

"No joking? You think perhaps he'd paint me?"

"Hard to tell," I said. "Perhaps yes."

Gradually my courage was drawing itself together. Soon it would be strong enough for me to suggest the trip that was in my mind. The urgency of my dream overcame me as the desire swelled large—a kind of painful and watery edema in which my brain floated, aching. I knew the young man for what he was. That he had killed someone did not deter me at all, nor the knowledge that he wanted money. I had long since stopped trying to analyze the stain that drew me to the violent ones.

As for André's belonging to Arthur, I was not in the least concerned. If a week had to elapse between each visit from André, to give Arthur's beaten body a chance to recover, it would be simple to take the young man to the country, and be back before the next "appointment." Arthur would never know.

The moment was at hand. I called my courage and said, "André, I have a lit—"

At that he laid his hand on my arm. "Excuse me a minute," he said. "I see an old friend at one of the tables outside. I must speak to him. You will excuse me?" He got up, his hand squeezing my forearm, his eyes on mine.

"*Bien sûr*," I said. "You will return?"

"But certainly," he said. I watched him shoulder his way through the press of people at the entrance, and approach a table where a white-haired man was sitting. He shook hands. The man rose in delight and grasped the boy's elbow. Then they both sat down again.

I waited a long time. The fly-specked clock moved on from midnight to one, to one-thirty. André did not return. I switched to wine and drank slowly, one glass after another. The two were still talking, heads close together, laughing now and then. The crowd in the bar changed several times—grew noisier, then quiet, then noisy again. The weasel faces, the cherub faces, the plucked eyebrows, the rouged cheekbones, the large signet rings—amethyst and jade and silver, the bright metallic chatter in French and English and German and Italian, the high falsetto screams of laughter, the smoke of caporal cigarettes and Cravens, the sloshing of beer rags, the turtleneck sweaters, a French sailor or two, the Arabs, a boy in a kilt—all the impressions crowded heavily on me, and finally turned suffocating.

At two o'clock I left. André and the white-haired man were still talking. Their table was strewn with peanut shells. It had turned chilly, and André had raised his coat collar against the wind that blew coldly down the boulevard.

I crossed the inner street and reached the traffic island. There was a bench under the trees, and I sat down for a final cigarette, watching the two. The crowd had thinned; the street lamps burned with a harsher whiter light. The silvered leaves were cold.

André did not look around, nor wave, nor get up and come walking toward me. After a little while I got up and walked farther down the street. I could still look up toward the Reine Blanche and see them. A laughing crowd of happy drunks teetered noisily on the curb, waiting for the light, and then invaded the Royale café, filled with small knots of late talkers.

There was a half moon. Its light did not reach down into the naked hard light of the street. At last I put both my cold hands into my trouser pockets and strode off resolutely toward the Rue du Four, looking without interest at the few people still sitting at the tables of the Royale.

Monsieur Charles was a very long time pressing the release switch after I rang the night bell at the hotel. And my room seemed more than usually bare and cheerless and depressing as I closed my door and locked it against the world.

(28) June 23, 1939

Certainly I had spent enough time with Arthur to begin to understand him. We liked many of the same things, and disliked others, but curiously he was still an enigma to me. The sense of locked doors was as strong as ever. The episode of André Vignot, instead of answering an aspect of the riddle and opening a door, had merely added another locked room to the long line of them down the corridor of this strange and talented man. My understanding was more tangled than before. Arthur was indeed an experimentalist—but that was only naming another side of him. And the name did not explain the nature. Whether Arthur was a real masochist or whether this experience was merely another heading on his program of sensation hunting, I did not know.

After the conversation with André Vignot that ended so frustratingly for me, I tried to call Arthur to tell him that André was really Genet's Adrien. But either he was out or busy painting, for he did not answer the telephone. A week went by without my hearing from him. Other things occupied me but I was still conscious of my gnawing curiosity. Finally I called Gertrude and Alice one afternoon and asked if I could stop by for a moment.

Madeleine, the maid, let me in, and I entered the salon upon a very curious scene. Gertrude was standing in the middle of the room, solid and foursquare, with a look of intense exasperation upon her face, and Alice was sitting calmly, basting small stitchings of red thread into a pillowcase she was making, quite in control of herself.

But Gertrude was not. In her hands she held a square metal box about eight inches on each side, and four inches high. It had a curious oval opening, like a little tunnel, running clear through it. The box was plainly labeled "Ketch-All" and it was evidently a mousetrap of some sort, for from within it came a scrabbling scratching sort of sound.

In a tone that was almost a wail, Gertrude said, "Now that

we've caught them, what shall we do with them. What."

"Kill them," said Alice.

"I *can't!*"

"Certainly you can," Alice said calmly. "Take them out one at a time and slowly wring their little necks. There're just two of them."

"No, I can't, I won't," said Gertrude emphatically. "Isn't there a society somewhere in Paris that has someone who can do that for you."

Alice smiled and bit off a piece of thread, and went on basting the pillowcase. "No, there isn't," she said. "It's up to you. You might give them to the neighbor's cat, Sans Peur."

"Sans Purr?" said Gertrude. "I've heard him purring plenty."

"Ninny," said Alice, for Gertrude's French was sometimes not up to all the niceties and subtleties of the language. "'Sans Peur' doesn't mean without purring, but means instead 'Fearless.'"

"Oh," said Gertrude. "I can't do that either."

"Why not?" said Alice.

"Marie told me that he's already so stuffed with mice that he can't even look at another one."

"Well, I'll tell you what," said Alice. "You go out into the kitchen and get a big brown paper bag and put the trap down inside. Then you slide the top open and raise the trap out quickly. Then you fold the bag over and take it across the street, up to the Seine, and throw it in the river. The bag will dissolve and the mousies will drown . . ."

"Which time they will be chanting snatches of old mouse songs, like Ophelia," I could not help adding.

Alice giggled. "Or else they will swim to safety," she said, "but they will be so far downstream that they'll never bother us again."

"You mean really to kill them," said Gertrude in horror.

"That's the idea," said Alice.

"The poor little things. They're all alone in that dungeon there. They look at you with their little beady eyes so pitifully . . ."

"For heaven's sake," said Alice, "don't turn them into people so much!"

Gertrude didn't hear her. ". . . and they're hungry and thirsty," she went on.

Alice in some irritation put down the pillowcase. "It's the survival of the fittest," she said. "Let Jehovah take care of things. You don't have to kill them. Jehovah and Charles Darwin will solve your problem."

"But they're alive," said Gertrude.

Meanwhile, as I listened to this colloquy between two of the best minds of our generation, I thought perhaps I was going to break in pieces.

"Look at it this way, Lovey," Alice said. "They have broken the law. They have entered our house without permission. They are trespassers. They have invaded our privacy, and stolen things that belonged to us. They are thieves. They have left mouse tracks in my skillet and little turds on the floor. They *must* be punished!"

"But why by me," wailed Gertrude. "Can't I call the gendarmes."

"God, no!" said Alice. "They'd run *you* in then."

"I heard them scratching," said Gertrude, "one of them, and then I heard a bang, when the trapdoor smacked the second one into the dungeon, but I didn't go into the kitchen last night because I knew I wouldn't be able to sleep for thinking of them if I saw them."

"Well, you just take the paper bag . . ." said Alice.

I was doubled over with silent laughter.

"I could do it on the back porch," said Gertrude, "with Sans Peur sitting beside me so he could get one if it got away."

"*Now* who's being bloodthirsty?" asked Alice. "Just fold them in the bag together and throw it in the Seine. Then it's all in God's hands."

"Maybe I should feed them if they're hungry," said Gertrude.

"They'll eat each other," said Alice, "if they get hungry enough. You eat meat, don't you?"

"Yes," said Gertrude, "but not mouse meat. If I had to kill a cow I'd never eat beefsteak."

"Well," said Alice, "neither would I, for that matter. All that blood . . ."

"It just isn't right," said Gertrude.

"You're wrong, Lovey," said Alice. "It is right. They're invaders of the night. Burglars. You trapped them in your own home. You're an American, aren't you? Doesn't the second amendment give you the right to bear arms? That silly trap you're holding is your 'arms.'"

"That horrible amendment," said Gertrude.

"Well," said Alice. "You've got 'em, now you've gotta kill 'em."

"Don't you know *anybody*," said Gertrude plaintively, "who might come do it."

At that point I was about to offer my services, and said tentatively, "Well, I . . . uh . . ."

"No," said Alice. "Johnny doesn't want to do it either. And I don't want anyone to think *I'm* crazy by asking them to do such a thing. You just go ahead, Lovey, and do it. Be brave. God is on your side. They are not really animals. They are vile intruding rodents with only two thoughts in their heads—food and sex. Any good orthodox fundamentalist like yourself should know that Jehovah's vengeance will eventually overtake the evildoer. The mice are evildoers. They *must* be punished."

"Well," said Gertrude, "since you put it that way . . ."

"That's my Lovey! Go to it. And let me know what happens."

Gertrude disappeared into the kitchen. I heard a great noise of paper bags being opened. In a moment she reappeared holding a bag from the bottom of which came the same faint scufflings and scrabblings.

"Well, I'm going," she said. "And then I'm going on some errands. I'll be back soon."

"Goodbye," I said.

"Goodbye Johnny," she said, "come see us again shortly."

"I will, don't fear," I said.

After Gertrude had left, Alice let out a tremendous sigh. "Oh dear," she said. "Sometimes I just don't know what to do with her. She's so tenderhearted in some ways and so fierce in others."

Then she put the pillowcase aside while she surveyed me narrowly and read my mind and conscience to see if I had been a good boy. Finally I approached the subject directly.

"Have you seen Arthur lately?" I asked, as casually as I could.

"Have I seen him! Humph!" It was more a little explosion through her nostrils than a word. I thought I saw a glint of yellow flame. "Have *you* seen him lately yourself?" I shook my head. "He was here yesterday for a moment," she said. "He looked as if the kitchen cupboard had fallen on him. He had a black eye and a cut behind one ear and scratches on his hand and red marks all over his neck. His turtleneck sweater did not hide them at all."

I wanted to titter. That was a Friday. Evidently Arthur had seen André for the second Wednesday night as planned. But I kept a straight face and asked innocently enough: "Whatever in the world happened to him?"

She picked up the pillowcase again and bit off a piece of the red basting thread. "The chances are you know more about that than I," she said, and looked sternly at me. "But he had a wild tale of being beaten up by four blacks who pulled him out of a taxi and hit him and stole all of his money."

"For goodness' sake," I said.

"For anything but that, probably," Alice said. "I must say that I can't even look at him anymore when he tells such tales. Usually there's a hard center somewhere in the fancies he hands out, but this one seems completely false."

"Did he mention a young man named André Vignot?" I asked.

Alice put down her sewing and looked at me with something close to exasperation. "Of course then you know all about it, you silly boy," she said, while I began to turn red. "And you make a fool of me. Well, he did tell the story about *les hommes du couleur* first, and I was only trying to protect him a little. You know I would have done the same thing for you. But—*Dieu merci*—you don't get into such scrapes as he does." She bit off a few centimeters of thread.

"Oh no, my dear," I said quickly. "I knew about the *first* time he met André because I was with him. Honestly, I don't know a thing about this last."

Alice was calmed. "Well, he got beat up by this André Vignot whoever he is," she said. "Who is he anyway?"

I told her what I knew, adding the story about Genet, the vase, and the twenty thousand francs. Alice nodded. "Yes," she said, "he knows about the Genet affair. He heard of it for the first time Wednesday night."

"I've been trying to telephone him all week to tell him about it," I said, "but I haven't had any answer."

"Ah, well," said Alice, "he's been working. Feverishly, I guess. He finished one large painting last week and is beginning another right away. In a sense it's very good for him to get beat up if it makes him want to paint again. He is the laziest person I know. His escapades and his life have always got in the way of his work. And yet if he didn't have these hair-raising adventures he would never get anything done at all."

"Very strange," I said, and shook my head.

"It's a mystery," said Alice.

There was a pause. "Do you understand him at all?" I asked.

"I used to think I did," Alice said, "but nowadays I'm not so sure. He is the only person I've ever known who has what you might call *absolute* courage. He is not afraid to do anything, if he wants to do it and thinks it will bring him pleasure. When I was younger I used to think he was evil. But now I believe he's just a sexual animal—a very great and talented one, of course, but wholly sexual and wholly animal. And yet I don't mean that as condemnation."

"Could you slant it otherwise and say he's wholly free and wholly 'natural'?"

"I suppose you could, if by 'natural' you mean true to his own nature."

I nodded. "That's what I meant."

"Gertrude and I have got him out of countless difficulties," Alice said. "I suppose you know how Gertrude even went to the British Embassy to keep that American—what was his name? Herrick?—out of England after he'd stolen practically everything Arthur had. We've scolded him, sometimes refused to see him for weeks until he came to his senses, but Gertrude has always taken him back and so have I." She put the pillowcase in her lap with a helpless and rather old gesture. "But what can you do with one who has genius? You have to put up with the cart that brings the vegetables. Especially if you admire genius and love it as both Gertrude and I do. But these affairs he gets involved in are certainly exasperating now and again."

"Do you think he's as great as Picasso?"

"Not I," she said. "Gertrude does—perhaps. She says he's as great right now—perhaps—if not greater . . . perhaps. But I think not. I don't feel the short hairs on my neck rise when I look at Arthur's work. Not yet, at any rate. But they still rise when I see Pablo's. It's an infallible test with me." She smiled.

"It is true that genius lives outside of ordinary patterns," I said, "usually—but not always," I added hastily. "You two don't."

"Not today perhaps," Alice said, "but when we were younger and first came to France—well, even *that* was extremely unconventional. And when we drove a Red Cross ambulance during the war—oh, I guess both of us have lived outside the pattern enough in our day." She smiled again with a certain satisfaction.

"Arthur had an affair with a woman once, didn't he?" I asked. "A Spanish girl, daughter of a dancer, I believe? Wasn't her name Ramirez, or something like?"

"Yes," Alice said, "Juanita Ramirez, I think—and I believe there's a child somewhere. Juanita was a great beauty. I think Arthur offered to give some fabulous sum to her, fabulous in those days, five thousand pounds maybe, but she refused to take it. Or rather her mother made her refuse to accept it. Gypsy pride. Let's see—how old would the child be now?" She made a rapid calculation against the ceiling. "Oh, seventeen or eighteen, I suppose. It seems a long time ago."

"I would really like to see Arthur soon," I said. "I'll call him again this evening, but if I can't get him will you ask him to call me the next time you see him?"

"Certainly," Alice said. I rose. "Must you be going? Gertrude will soon be back." She squinted at me. "Whatever kind of material is that in those trousers you have on? They're so tight."

"Denim," I said.

"Oh," said Alice. "Hemingway had a pair of those once. Did you knew he used to go to those notorious Penthièvre Baths behind the Élysée palace near the Place de la Concorde?"

"No, really? My God."

"Yes, the gossip is that he met Arthur there once and they had a little fling, neither knowing who the other was. But Hemingway is rumored to have really preferred pretty little boys who were in—what is it called?—drag? Like the Chevalier d'Éon, only lots younger."

"Yes—in drag."

"But as I said, it's only gossip. Not true, as far as I know. By the way," she said, "those trousers of yours are really almost too tight. Why are they lighter colored in certain spots?"

I blushed furiously. "S-sandpapered," I managed to get out.

Alice nodded sagely. "Ah yes," she said. "Like a girl's decolleté. If you can't really show the whole thing, you can at least point to it."

"I must run," I said in great embarrassment, strangling. "My love to you both." I took her frail hand and kissed it. Sweating, I let myself out the front door and went down the worn oak steps. I had learned nothing new, aside from the tidbit about Hemingway, save that Arthur's whackings went on, and André was studding at good prices, probably.

Do not interrupt Arthur, something said inside. Let him continue. Violent as this affair is, it cannot last long. A fever fled upward to my brain as I thought of them together. In a constricting vision I saw them in their room—naked with spines humped like goats, and black hooves beneath shaggy thighs. I heard their obscene bleatings as they possessed each other like two satyrs in rut. The world turned red and burst with flames. Knives cut into white marble that bled. Whips sang and whistled and bit deep into flesh. And out of the room arose a golden mist that wavered and hung over the two beasts beneath, and I saw the haze form itself into a painting. . . .

The puzzle of genius, the Gordian knot . . . All the pluckings of my fingers left it tighter than ever before.

(29) June, 1939

Excerpts from Sir Arthur's journal:

Stopped painting this afternoon about three, deciding to take *un petit proménade*. Crossed over to the Île de la Cité. Troop of Boy Scouts from the provinces was just preparing to go into Notre Dame. Decided that I should also go in to *meditate*. The children were very well behaved, didn't stay long. One small beauty (face of a seraphim, *big* basket) winked at me. But actually pleased they left so I would not be *distracted*, because I had intended even before I saw them to go to the cathedral as a *penance* for my sins, and in preparation for the *punishment* I will receive this evening when André comes (2nd time). He will probably be *severe* with me and with *good reason*. I am a *very great sinner* . . . Tried to concentrate on the number & character of my sins, but all was cold within. Looked at main altar, saw instead a vision of André white and naked, rising up—filling whole nave—head brushing ceiling, *vast thighs* larger than the columns. He scowled—the church filled with *thunders & lightnings*. He raised his arm in a *threatening* gesture—the columns tottered. As I looked up, the vision's perspective drew together sharply, making his tremendous genitals hang down like an *obscene chandelier* above me. Woke from this trance state in a sweat and left church hurriedly. Outside all was bright, and usual.

Later: André more than an hour *en retard*. A *complete wreck* by time he arrived, having torn up *two* handkerchiefs. He isn't wise enough to be late deliberately, to give me time to think ahead, let *anticipando & terror* grow. Or is he? Pretended to be furious at the delay, saying *nasty* things to *inflame* him, goading him as a picador *infuriates* a bull. He grew quite angry—brows together, shoulders hunched forward & inward, lower lip drawn down to show his teeth, hands clenching & unclenching. Finally told him the first thing a *male whore* should learn was to be *on time*. Then turned away. Unprepared for what happened. He grabbed my shoulder, swung me around, hit me in eye with his fist. I hit back, pleased to see *blood spurt* from his nose. Then he hit me on chin & knocked me unconscious. Awoke to find myself spread-eagled on bed again, tied face down, both hands & feet to corners. He was standing beside me, holding large corkscrew from kitchen. Jabbed it into me several times, thighs & buttocks. I fainted, he poured water on me. Then he inserted two fingers into me, greased with butter, then two more, and finally his *whole hand*. Agony terrible. Sweat poured off me. He laughed, twisted hand around, made fist. Horrible. Wonderful.

My eye looks *dreadful*, swollen & already turning greenish yellow at edges of bruise that is dark blue. Could scarcely walk or stand, & sat only with difficulty. Hobbled to studio to paint some more. *Alarmed* to discover no response in fingers, which still seemed numb. But after exercise they loosened (still painful to write this). André went through my wallet last night, I watching. Took out ten thousand franc note I'd put there for him. Threatened greater harm if I didn't have *twenty thousand* next week. While I was still tied, slapped me *viciously* until I wept. I said I would have the money. Certainly not *too much* to pay for *all my sins* & I more than deserve the horrid beating he gave me. His *brutality* made me feel better *physically*—cleansed & *purified* me. Felt almost as I did when a child after First Communion. Despite pain, my mind *clear & limpid* this morning so that when I began to paint, my sense of color & line was excellent & there was no *wavering* or *uncertainty*. Worked feverishly, & accomplished much.

*   *   *

My eye nearly well. Wanted to go to Gertrude and Alice today but they refused to see me. Alice says I must not call or visit for thirty days. Tried to explain but Alice rang off. Most dismaying, though this has happened before. After all, artists must live *alone*. Great art must be *torn from the soul* in solitude.

Tuesday. From two in the afternoon until midnight—despair.

Saw Johnny McAndrews this evening at the Royale. Talked of André being Adrien in Genet's novel. Thanked J. for exercising his magic for me. He inclined to be rather snappish. Intimated I was a *fool* in trying to make him think I considered André's brutality a punishment for my sins. I maintained it was & that I deserved it. Pretended to become irritated. Parted rather annoyed with each other—he at my *determination* to keep up my pretense, I at him because he was *clever* enough to guess the truth & at myself because I was not *skillful* enough to deceive him as I have the others. Perhaps I've made a mistake in letting him know me so well. But he is a nice chap & it does no harm to have one discreet *confidant*. He is *trustworthy* enough but sometimes I *pity* him because he *tortures* himself so much in trying to *understand*. Should just *accept*, as I do.

Have been having fearful dreams, *intense* & *frightful*. On waking, sometimes fear for my sanity. I find myself almost *smothered* in bed linens that are wrapped around my neck & arms while the rest of my body lies naked in *cold sweat*. Last night, thought for a moment I was back *within* my mother, head & shoulders, while rest of my body *outside* on a *frozen lake*. Hopelessly trapped. Could neither *crawl back* nor *leave* . . . Often dream of flying & wings break suddenly, plummeting me downward. Several nights ago dreamed that André, armed with red-hot pincers, was *extracting* my teeth. Those he couldn't pull he *smashed* with a hammer. Then choked me by sticking his *big fist* in my mouth, *squeezing* gums until all teeth fragments popped out. These dreams highly colored, terrible & beautiful. I believe that as *inhibitions* vanish, color comes to dreams. But these nights *dreadful & exhausting*. Frequently can't paint next day. *Disas-*

(157)

trous. Will see Jean Lalongue tomorrow and ask for *something* from chemist's to make me sleep without dreaming.

Saw Jean Lalongue today. The man is extremely *irritating* although I do not doubt a good doctor. Told him of my nightmares & detailed some of them. He *laughed!* Asked me what I'd been doing to stir up my conscience. Told him nothing had happened, then remembered my return to the Church. He laughed even more. Said that in seven/eight years we'd known each other, had never seen a sign that my conscience even *existed*, and that I was deliberately trying to *revive* it or *resurrect* it. Must admit that the man is very *keen*, though *annoying*. Then told him about André. He grew quite interested. Asked me all the details, &c. Told him. His interest sank below *professional* level, grew *personal*. Recognized all the signs of erotic arousal in him—eye sparkle, short breath, nervous gestures, one foot tapping/twisting. Finally he got control & became doctor again. Told me there was no prescription for what ailed me, save *penis normalis, pro re nata* (as need arises), that roots of *everything* were *inside* me. Suggested if I wanted dreams to stop, should a) forget my reconversion, & b) find a playmate not so violent as André. Then he gave me a lecture on *playing with fire*, how inexperienced sadists sometimes inflict *grave damage*, even *kill*. Pointed out that human mechanism contains many *mysterious phenomena* & emotions that should often be left alone. Said *lust to cause pain* one of these. Perhaps I should *get rid* of André. But how? *Must think* about all this.

Another horrible session with André. He burned his initials on the inside of my thigh with cigarettes. *Wrenched* my spine horribly. This must end.

Sudden clever idea occurred to me today while painting. Remembered the blond *flic*, Edouard Rameau, the one I met the night that sailor jumped into the Seine. Have not seen Edouard for a year. Looked up his address and sent him a *pneumatique*. He called, said he would come to apt. tomorrow. Remembered *fondly* the size of his *bitte*. . . .

Edouard & I have conceived a wonderful plan to get rid of André. Will cost a few thousand francs, but well worth it—Edouard will have to give a *recompense* to two of his friends, also gendarmes. They will *assist*. Next Wednesday when André is here, Edouard will arrange to arrive at ten o'clock, evening, with his friends and a police van downstairs. They will break down my door—or rather merely open it because I will leave it *unlocked* when André comes. Will say they called because of neighbor's complaints (must remember to make *some noise*). I to arrange to be tied to kitchen chair when they come in & André will be *torturing* me. They will *arrest* him because I will say A. is torturing me to find where my money is hidden. Edouard will then *recognize* A. as the felon who was tried for murder of old man. One *flic* will see A's tattoo. All will be settled; A. must be arrested. Of course, no real arrest, no trial. They will take him down to van & *frighten* him, say he *faces prison* for rest of his life. Or *la Veuve*—the guillotine. This the *delicate* part. Edouard assures me he can handle it so A. will never bother me again. But says I should send A. a discreetly worded letter, saying that what I said about *torturing* me was really the only possible excuse. Edouard pointed out I must arrange for A. to be standing over me *fully dressed*. Naked would turn situation against me, esp. with initials burned on my leg. Edouard suggests I *irritate* the burns until they look fresh. This will be *painful*, but *necessary*. Oh, how I *love* these *little games!* They are *exciting!* They are *fun!*

All went well with one small exception. André locked the door after I had turned away from it & I had no chance to unlock it. Edouard and his friends resourcefully broke lock open. André went absolutely *white! Terror* made him look *strange*—eyes wide, mouth open & moving soundlessly at first, then *babbling* incoherently. They caught him with long bread knife in hand. He had just given me one slight cut on shoulder, small slice, not deep, but much blood. They had to half carry him out of apt. because he was *trembling*, could not walk alone. He was sick on the stairs.

Later: cleaned up the mess. Concierge heard nothing. Edouard returned about midnight. Gave him fifty thousand francs. Everything is quite all right. André promised never to see me again, will not have to write letter. Edouard in state of *smouldering* excitement on his return. Gave him brandy—he was *hot*, intense, his face very beautiful beneath his tan. The muscles worked in his cheeks, his eyes *burned*. Very nervous. After a while he rubbed crotch, suggested another payment if I were truly grateful. I was only too glad to *oblige*, on my knees. A monster cock! Leaving, said with *evil grin* that this *second payment* was first of many . . . Hevvings! Rid of one blackmailer, and have another! However, enjoy this one no end.

Door around lock splintered. Shall have to call carpenter. This a dreadful bore.

(30) July 16, 1939

André swung down from the train ahead of me and turned to put out his hand to help, since I was carrying a suitcase, a fat portfolio of sketches, and a bottle of wine. I looked at his face turned up toward me, at the wonderful planes of his cheeks, his chipped tooth in the center of his gleaming smile, and the ten days' tan of the sun of Finistère in old Brittany upon his face and hands. I did not need his help but I took it, and landed upon the uneven cement of Paris once again.

The ugly old Gare Montparnasse had seen odder arrivals and partings. I looked at the streaming crowds, the queues waiting in the dinginess. I shut my eyes for a moment, letting spread over me the concentrated flood of sunlight and black water, white clouds and gray black cliffs, that we had had for ten memorable days. The dream had ended but the memories were strong.

"We are back again," André said simply, taking the bag from my hand.

I protested. "Let's find a porter."

"No," he said, "it's not worthwhile."

I walked beside him into the hideous station with its dirty glass-paned roof. He was heading for a taxi when I stopped him.

"Here," I said, and pulled an envelope from my coat pocket. "It's been fun, André. Here's what I said I'd give you—twenty thousand." It was hard to be direct about the transaction, but it was what we arranged two weeks before. He took it and put it into his pocket without opening it.

"*Merci bien*," he said, and his hot brown eyes looked into

mine. He smiled and winked. "What are you going to do now?"

"Taxi, hotel, bath, and bed," I said. "And you?"

He shrugged. "Back to Montmartre," he said. "To my little room with bedbugs. We will see each other again?"

"Perhaps," I said. "You have my address. You will call me?"

"I may," he said. There was an awkward pause. On a sudden impulse I thrust the bottle of wine into his hand. He took it, looking up from the bottle to me without saying anything. There are golden gestures that speak to the soul without words. He shifted the bottle to his left hand and reached for my right hand. His firm fingers closed tightly around mine. He gave one sharp short jerk. *"Merci,"* he said, "and *au revoir."*

Then he turned and left, heading for the subway entrance. I watched him; he did not turn again. Then I picked up my bag and started for the taxi stand.

It had all worked out as naturally as the sun's rising and with no more fuss. When Arthur had called me about two weeks before, he told me in highly excited tones how he had frightened André away—the story that many years later I found in his journal. I listened and made appropriate responses. At the end of his monologue he had asked when we could see each other. Not immediately, I told him calmly, since I was leaving for Brest the next day and would be gone for about two weeks. Before his call I had no idea of going away. But while we talked, I knew that I would— and not alone.

After he finished talking, I opened the door to the booth and walked downstairs to the street, without hat or coat, only feeling in my pocket to see that I had money with me. Quiet and determined, I stood on the curb and hailed a cab. I gave the driver the address of the Bar Lépic in Montmartre.

It had taken me almost a day to find André but I succeeded. And then—again calmly—I offered to take him to Finistère for a few days—all expenses paid and twenty thousand francs as well. He was suspicious and surly at first. My association with Arthur did not help my case. He asked me again if I were not afraid of him, if I did not think he would kill me. It was a stormy scene for a few minutes, but I finally convinced him that Arthur meant nothing to me. The invitation was for himself alone. He suddenly grinned and said yes.

After I returned to the hotel from finding young Ganymede,

my motives began to trouble me. I could not analyze them without seeming stuffy to myself. But I hated the trick Arthur had played on the young man, the kind of trick that money can arrange against those without money. Mixed with distaste for Arthur's plot was a sympathy I had always had for the underdog, a feeling of kinship for those who *can not* and *have not*, a kind of sentimentality that had always been with me. Once I found it crystalized in a poem to the "little creatures"—the cony, rabbit and the hare—"all trapped and frightened little things" suffering in silence and despair. And the situation between Arthur and André also took on a symbolic quality—on one side the power of the hunter and his gold, on the other the "little things that quailed." Perhaps I could help the victim, and enjoy myself in the bargain; and perhaps my own enjoyment was the real reason. . . .

But André had not been exactly terrified, nor plunged in silence and despair. He had been raging. For the first two days he had been sullen and snarling, threatening all kinds of harm to Arthur, chilling projects of revenge, some quite ingenious. Gradually I helped him grow calm about it all, and even finally dismiss it from his mind . . . or so I hoped.

Nonetheless I made a mental note to suggest to Arthur he forage elsewhere than in Montmartre for a while. Actually there was no need to warn him. For a long time he was never alone. Several times I saw him in the company of the handsome blond *flic* who had helped pull Peter from the Seine, and again with young huskies who were strangers to me.

Finistère had been a few days of actual paradise. André and I became completely compatible. We went on from Brest to the coast itself, and in a small village found an inn where we lived as I at least would have liked to live always.

Every day we would climb down the black cliffs to the yellow sand to swim and sunbathe, lolling in the heat, going into the water and returning to lie naked on the hot golden grains and clutch them as if they were a woman—or a man. It was one of the most sensuous and sensual vacations I had ever spent. I sketched the young animal over and over in all positions—lying on the beach, a leg up, a leg down, flat, staring at the sky, standing with legs apart, sitting, digging in the sand. And all parts of him as well—thighs, feet, shoulders, face, belly—sometimes putting them together, sometimes separating them. I was happy to see my line relax, grow expressive, and begin to suggest roundness where before it had been stiff and academic. And in the cool nights when the wind blew fresh from the Atlantic and whistled in the eaves, we would be alone in the room, returned from a few drinks in the town's only café, happy in each other, or seeming to be.

André unfolded like a flower. The toughness and meanness of the young Parisian hoodlum dropped away from him like a garment. He laughed and joked with everyone. And everyone liked him. Perhaps the people of Brittany knew why we were there and what was between us, but never by word, look, or greasy snigger did they show disapproval, and I was certain they did not care.

As for the brutality with which André had handled Arthur—well, there was not much of that—just enough for my tastes. He stood over me one night as I lay naked on the bed, holding in his big square hands the wide black brass-studded belt of which he was so fond.

"And do you like it too, like the dirty English *tapette*?" he said, and viciously whacked the belt down on the bed, missing my leg by a couple of centimeters. I did not flinch, but wondered why I did not.

"Not particularly," I said. "A little perhaps, but it is not a speciality."

And a little was all I got.

Several times during those golden perfect days, I wondered if what I had done was treacherous or unethical. But reason helped me decide. If you live in a world where black is the only color, how can one thing be blacker than another? Arthur's world—and mine too—was a world of take-what-you-wanted, with only two concerns: do not get caught by the police, and do nothing to harm yourself. We were victims of anomia, bragging that we were natural, free, and uninhibited. We rejected the narrow codes of our social matrix, for beside the skillful and silent American persecution of the homosexual, the whole history of anti-Semitism was almost amateurish. Arthur could hardly confront me with such a "sin" as betrayal. I comforted myself with old proverbs about pots calling kettles black, and bricks thrown at glass houses, and all cats being gray at night.

All that summer I had been hoping for word of a project on which I had been working—a fellowship that would give me a full year in

Paris. But so far—nothing. And September seventh, my sailing date, drew closer.

But the realization of my departure did not get me out of bed any more quickly on the morning after my return from Brest. I lay looking at the ceiling and at the green-painted underside of the bookshelf that hung like a Damoclean sword just above my pillow. Someone had scratched some dates and names into the paint—a memorialist leaving a record of conquests wherever he went.

A sudden tapping at the door brought me out of the pleasant half land between sleeping and waking. "*Qui est-ce?*" I asked.

"It's Arthur."

"Oh," I said and reached for my dressing gown. "Come in," I said, opening the door for him. He stood there grinning widely, his mustache somewhat scrambled and full of tiny nuggets of snuff, a red handkerchief tied at his throat above an old blue sweater.

"Good morning," he said, "and welcome back." We shook hands. "Did you have a good time in Brest?"

"Perfect," I said.

"Lots of new tricks? Sailors?"

"Enough," I said, lighting a cigarette. He plopped on my happy-go-lucky bed.

"I was just passing this way," he said, "and thought I'd stop to see if you had got back yet. Someone has given me two tickets for the ballet at the Opéra tonight. Would you care to go along?"

I had a pure guilt reaction, and thought of refusing. My fondness for André turned me away from the idea of spending an evening so soon with the man who had hurt and frightened him. At that moment I did not like Arthur at all.

Then I remembered that it had been three years since I had seen Leon Danelian dance in Chicago with the old Ballets Russes de Monte Carlo. He had left that group to join the French company, or so the papers said. The prospect of seeing his lithe Armenian grace and his electric body once more in action was too much a temptation to resist. I gave way.

"I'd be delighted," I said.

"I won't be able to have dinner with you," Arthur said, "but I'll meet you at the Opéra." He raised his sweater from the bottom and extracted a large white ticket from his shirt pocket. "Here. Let's meet inside? At the stairs. It begins at a quarter of nine."

"Fine," I said. "I'll be there."

He shook hands and waddled away. I folded the ticket and stuck it in my wallet. For exactly five seconds I felt like a cad.

But it was all gone by the time I walked across the room to the washbowl.

(31) July 16, 1939   Night

Perhaps if I were to live to be a hundred—may God forbid it!—and went every evening for the rest of my life to an entertainment in the Paris Opéra, the building might come to lose some of the charm it held for me. I adored the old structure passionately. It elevated my heart and senses until I felt dazzled, almost drunk. It was a marvel of elegance with its marble floors and dramatic white marble stairway, its gilt, its gleaming irised chandeliers, the lustrous glitter of its mirrors and the breathtaking height of its stairs and balconies, rising like a rococo tiered palace of Cellini's to rapturous ceilings. Everything about it was just right.

The evening itself was rather a failure, however. Sir Arthur, somber in a black suit and tie, was nervously smoking a cigarette when I stepped into the great foyer. We shook hands and went at once to our red plush seats. The Opéra ballet was not renowned for its precision and delicacy. For the first number, *Swan Lake*, the orchestra set up a tempo like that of a Sousa march. The corps de ballet gallumphed onto the sloping stage like chargers of the Light Brigade, arms flailing and cues missed. The footwork was slovenly, and there were three or four pratfalls that would have sent more sensitive dancers offstage and kept them there. Even Leon as the prince was forced by the tempo into erratic and staccato gestures, like a marionette. The other numbers were no better. Lifar himself was in one of them, hamming impossibly but evidently much loved by the audience. The *Phèdre* of Cocteau was fascinatingly filled with handsome young men, but it was much too long.

The intermissions also left me somewhat miserable. For the first one Arthur and I joined the coffee-mill procession in the grand salon, marching around and around like the others, looking at people and hoping to be seen by the right ones. The languages made the salon a tower of Babel—you heard fragments of German, French, English, Italian, Greek, Danish, and Dutch. During the second intermission I stood beside Arthur, ill at ease while he chatted with some friends about persons unknown to me; and for the third, I drifted away by myself. But I saw nothing spectacular save a young East Indian with the purest cut of profile and lips I had yet to see except on Greek cameos. Alas, he was with his dark-skinned princess in her purple gilt-edged sari.

The long program did not end until nearly midnight. Afterward, Arthur and I paused on the steps outside. The night air felt good. The stars were shining. We lighted cigarettes.

"How did you like it?" asked Arthur, puffing at the match.

"Not much," I said.

"Nor I," he said. We watched the traffic moving around the square of the Opéra, dividing around the métro entrances, noisy, brilliant, bustling. Two Frenchmen passed us on their way to join the crowd, one speaking loudly and excitedly to the other. Sir Arthur giggled.

"Did you hear them?" he asked.

"No," I said. "I wasn't listening. What did they say?"

"They were talking about the *Phèdre*. One of them said, 'It is a ballet by *pédés*, about *pédés*, and for *pédés* . . .' Oh, I must tell Jean!"

"And they were right, weren't they?" I asked. I was still looking at the stars and thinking back a week to a time when André and I had gone swimming in the sea at night, and then lain on the faintly gleaming sand while I tried to tell him the French names of constellations for which I knew only the English terms. The memory of that evening sank me into a kind of gray melancholy, threaded with a weakening sentimentality.

"What shall we do?" Arthur asked.

"I have no suggestions whatever," I said.

"We might walk back to St. Germain," Arthur said, "and have a drink."

"Oh no—not walk," I said. "Too far, too tired—and a little depressed."

"We'll take a taxi then," he said. I awakened sufficiently from my mood to sense the sudden presence in him of the hunter—the dozen small signs—a darting eye, a quick flare of the nostrils as if he had caught the scent of game, the slightly raised inflection, the faster speech . . . He was out to prey. Ho, my lads! A-hunting we will go!

We stood at the top of the steps outside the Opéra, just under the shelter of the roofed columns. Below us the tide of people moved together, flowed along, and then parted. My glance fell on a young man with hair so black that a blue glint showed in it. He was standing at the foot of the steps. He was poorly dressed, and in one hand carried a small cheap suitcase scarcely large enough for a typewriter. But his was the second good face I had seen that evening—the first the Indian cameo, and now this one, as white skinned as the other had been blue-gray-brown in its almost metallic luster.

The young man stood hesitant and undecided in the midst of the crowd, in a small space all to himself, uncertain which way to go or turn. A stranger in town undoubtedly, a boy from the provinces. His clothes had a kind of archaic country cut. He looked Italian or Portuguese, perhaps Spanish. I almost nudged Arthur to direct his attention to the young man, but something restrained me.

A kid in Paris. A kid with a face like that. He would discover soon enough what kind of life Paris had to offer a good-looking young man with black hair, smooth white skin, and a firm body. The vision of what he might be like in ten years crossed my mind—pouches under his hardened eyes and lines down his cheeks, shabbier still—or elegantly dressed and prosperous?

"Shall we go then?" asked Arthur a trifle impatiently.

"Yes," I said. We walked slowly down the steps and passed within five feet of the young man. His face was even more wonderful than it had seemed from the steps, the eyes dark and gleaming, and a little puzzled frown between his full black eyebrows. I looked directly at him. Sir Arthur was looking the other way for a taxi. Our eyes caught and held for a brief moment in a clinging gentle caress. I smiled ever so slightly at him, and the barest flicker of a return moved his lips; then he looked modestly down, and up and away in another direction. My heart chugged four or five times and my throat contracted a little.

Then we passed him and Arthur was opening the door of a taxi. He spoke to the driver and climbed in after me.

"I told him to go by way of the Place de la Concorde," Arthur said. "The lights will at least give the illusion of being cheerful."

"Good," I said, and settled back in silence for the ride.

We said nothing during the trip. As we crossed the Concorde we were sprayed with the fantastic illumination of the great square. But even as we went by the obelisk of Luxor, the springing columns of water in the fountains jerked higher once and then subsided quickly, and the floodlights went off. Almost at once thereafter the other floodlights on the buildings around the Place were extinguished. From the blinding whiteness we were thrust into a comparative darkness that made me blink. Now only the pale circles of the ordinary streetlights gleamed with a pallid yellow glow as the harsh white floodlights faded to a greenish afterimage in my eyes.

When we got to the Royale St. Germain I paid the driver his doubled fare, since it was then after midnight. Arthur hopped quickly to an empty table, brushed some peanut shells from a chair and sat down, tilting the other chair to knock more shells away. I sat down with a sigh.

"What's wrong with me this evening?" I said petulantly. "I am thoroughly depressed. Usually the ballet leaves me stimulated, but tonight I'll be damned if I don't wonder if suicide isn't the best solution after all."

"Well, it's the ultimate one," Arthur said, grinning, "and we must be careful, for many men are dying this year who have never died before. Cheer up, old thing. If you will just look around a bit you might find a cure for your vapors. Pick out a pretty josser from the passing fair."

His last phrase gave me a horrible moment. I saw the human fair passing in all its vanity, a kind of apocalyptic flash in which the glamor of the city winked out, and the human spirit lay naked before me in all its bitter ugliness. The passersby seemed no longer attractive, alluring, or amusing. Their flirting glances turned to leers, their clothes became ill-fitting covers for acned and pimpled skins, their necks grew scrawny and their hair needed trimming. In their dirty eyes I saw cold calculation. I saw the furtive sneaky hoodlums of Paris passing in the marketplace of flesh, in a kind of Dantesque vision of hell. An old copy of the *Divine Comedy* had terrified me when I was young, and Gustave Doré's illustrations of the lost souls had stayed with me for many years. And here they were, those souls, all of them, lost and damned, selling themselves for the transient flutter of pleasure that bank notes can buy. A dirty stairway, a filthy room with a spotted bed, the universal odor of the unwashed crotch—you came so close, you reached out for an ineffable secret, and then, and then . . . the captains and the kings departed, the flesh relaxed into the "little death," sly fingers stole into the wallet or knotted themselves into iron knuckles to smash into your teeth, or the icy edge of steel jumped from a sweating hand. . . .

Good lord, I thought—I have indeed worked myself into a bleak and empty mood. It was never good to pause to think. Sustain yourself on sex or sensation—but *never* think! Taste the cigarette, sip the brandy, take lemonade or a coke when you are hot, accept the enfolding arms and the nuzzling mouth when you are lonely—but heavens! never *think*.

I shook myself mentally and sat up very straight in my chair. "I feel better now," I said to Arthur. "I want a double brandy."

"Good," he said. "You were having quite a turn through the lower depths." He waved to the trickle of persons walking past the tables. "Perhaps your old magic will work again for me this evening. Remember? Every time I am with you . . ."

"Perhaps," I said sourly. "But it's already worked once this summer."

Our drinks arrived. We sat at the table talking idly for a half hour, commenting on those around us. The crowd was not distinguished nor exciting and there were few who pleased us. Arthur's interest rose slightly when three American sailors sat down—but two of them, as he said, were "dogs," and with them was a French friend their own age who was doing the translating for them.

Then suddenly I saw him, the young man with the suitcase, the black-haired youth who had smiled in front of the Opéra. I forgot my resolution not to call him to the attention of my huntsman friend, and tugged at Arthur's coat.

"Look!" I said. "That boy—I saw him earlier near the Opéra. Evidently he has walked all the way here. Isn't he extraordinarily handsome?"

Arthur raised his forelock and squinted at him. "Charming," he said. "How did I ever miss that one?" Involuntarily he ran his tongue across his upper lip. "Looks a little Italian, or Spanish."

Suddenly I laughed. "Well," I said, "you wanted some of the magic—how's that? Shall I get him for you?"

My question irritated him a little. He gave a huffy small female twisting of his shoulders and said, "I'm quite capable, myself." He looked at the boy who was slowly passing. "H-m-m . . . I see he has one button open on his fly."

"I suppose that will be something to break the ice," I said.

"Of course," said Arthur, grinning hugely. "I will say what the French do on such occasions—"Ah, the door of the grocery is open, and the vegetables are in view!'"

"You'll embarrass him," I said. "Can't you see he's just off the farm?"

"So young, so shy, so unsophisticated," Arthur sighed. He rose quickly. "I'll get him at the island while he waits for the traffic light." And he took off rapidly after the young man.

I was too far away to hear what was said, but I watched them as one would a peep-show pantomime. The downbearing light from the street lamp fell on their shoulders and put a long curving ribbon of blue shine across the boy's black hair. I saw the gestures: Arthur's touching him on the shoulder, a few words, the boy's involuntary glance at his fly. He shifted his small case to his left hand and rather clumsily fumbled at the fly button with his fingers. I half-expected Arthur to help him. Then the young man looked up into Arthur's face and smiled shyly, much embarrassed. Arthur's hand rested on his shoulder; he gestured toward the café. The boy shook his head, looked in my direction, and then at Arthur again. But Arthur persisted. The boy looked at his watch. Then with a small shrug he turned under Arthur's guiding hand, and both of them walked toward our table.

"*Mon ami,*" Arthur said as they approached. "This is—how is it that you call yourself?" he asked the boy in French.

"Juan Berlingot," the young man said, smiling nervously.

"—my friend John Belvedere," said Arthur. "And my name is Pickett—it is easy, is it not? In French it means to 'stick it,' as you would with a needle." Then he looked at me. "Juan does not speak a word of English," he said. "Spanish, yes—and a little French. He has just arrived from Marseilles."

"Enchanted," I murmured and shook his firm-fingered hand. "Sit down."

"For a moment," Arthur said. "But Juan has left his other valise over at the Gare d'Orléans and we must go to get it. Will you wait until we get back?" He turned to Juan. "Will you have a drink now or shall we return for one?"

The young man shrugged. "As you wish," he said. "I am a little hungry too."

Arthur turned to me. "Promise you'll wait, Mac," he said in English. "This young man is completely charming—and so well mannered. Your magic is working well tonight."

"But not for me," I said sulkily. "All right, I'll wait. But not more than an hour. I'm tired and sleepy."

"We'll be back before then," Arthur said. "If we're not, it will mean I'm putting Juan up for the night. He has no place to stay in Paris." He grinned again.

"An hour, no more," I said, and yawned. We all shook hands and they got into a taxi standing in the waiting line, and drove off.

It was probably much to my credit that as soon as the taxi disappeared around the corner I got up, stretched a little, buttoned my jacket, and went home.

(32) **July 19, 1939**

The privileges of beauty are enormous. By its mysterious alchemy the truck driver becomes a king, the delivery boy an emperor. We are the willing subjects of the one to whom it is given. He can trample us with his boots, demand outrageous tribute, and we forgive him everything. We voluntarily blind ourselves so that we can no longer see our ruler's arrogance or treachery or inadequacy. He is baffled to see us prostrate before him. Come, he says—rise and look into my face. We turn our blinded eyes upon him and feel the warmth and radiance of his presence, and in our trancelike mindless state we do his bidding like a captive Trilby before her master.

The beauty of Juan Berlingot was of such a quality. The dark-haired peasant boy, simple and naive, openhearted and childishly charming—he was only seventeen—entered quickly through the wide-flung doors of all our hearts, he of the intense and smoldering black eyes, the frank trust, and the embarrassed reception of the homage of all who met him.

For three or four days after the first encounter, the only word I had of Juan and Sir Arthur was a telephone call. Arthur was a little hysterical, or perhaps in high euphoria; and he told me once again that this time was really *it*—that he had found the one he had been looking for all his life long. He asked if I thought people would talk if he made Juan his *valet de chambre*. He spoke of the boy's honesty and forthrightness. Hearing the emotion in Arthur's voice, I did not remind him of the many times I had heard him say such things, and ask such a question. I soothed him, and said I thought Juan a fine young man from what I had seen of him. Arthur's admiration was perhaps genuine (but was it not always, at first?). Two days after the first meeting he wrote in his journal:

"Juan was talking about his parents this evening. I sat on floor and watched him, listened to his husky young male voice tell the *sad* & often *sordid* story of his childhood. Told me of the scar that still pains: *bastardy*. Spoke of his mother's cruelty & of the police-man-father his mother later married—to get a name for Juan. Grandmother the only one to treat him well. Scorned, buffeted, he still grew up, seems *unspoiled* by the *mistreatment*. He is frank and honest & open . . . Gradually grew silent & I asked no more questions. His fine young head sunk on his chest, eyes lowered. Table lamp caught *exciting* pattern of shadow & light on high cheekbones and firm jaw. Hands covered with fine thin straight black hair, folded between thighs. Sat silent for some minutes, I drinking in beauty, he lost in thought. Feel a strange *attraction* to my pure young peasant, stronger than I've felt for many years. He is *gentle & unaffected*. Almost as if he were really the other ½ of me of which Plato speaks, the ½ cloven from me long ago, which I have vainly pursued until now. Very sensitive to his aura. It falls on me & enfolds me like a fountain's spray."

Arthur had told me to come over soon, and I promised that I would. But even before I got there I heard of Juan again from Alice, one day when I stopped to see the two of them. Gertrude was out on an errand again. The time limit of prohibition against Arthur's visits had evidently run out. I was bursting with a piece of news of my own that I wanted to tell Gertrude and her, but she got onto the subject of Arthur first, and my news had to wait.

"Arthur brought his new young friend around the other day," Alice said, lighting her own cigarette. She had long ago stopped me from jumping up to hold a match for her, saying that if a woman were going to smoke, she ought at least be able to handle the fire.

"What do you think of him?"

"A nice boy," said Alice. "A very nice boy. Well mannered—beautiful manners indeed when you consider his rather unfortunate background. He has a kind of nobility in him that is not unpleasant."

This was the highest sort of praise from Alice.

"But really quite young," she went on. "Good heavens, he's only seventeen and Arthur's thirty-six, or thereabouts. A thing like that can't last very long. Arthur seems quiet for the first time in years. He sat there and simply exuded peace—really, it came out of his pores! But I shudder to think what Arthur may do to the boy if he's around long. He has an uncanny effect on many of his 'protégés'"—Alice clearly pronounced the quotation marks "—and they end by being completely ruined. Destroyed. He rots their fibers—moral, spiritual, even physical. There was one of them who looked ten years older after he had been with Arthur for only six months."

"Arthur said he was going to hire him as a *valet de chambre*," I said.

Alice made a small impatient noise. "Oh, of course. He fools no one—absolutely no one. But that is the wonderful thing about Paris. Everyone knows, no one cares. Juan should make an excellent valet. Poor boy, he has a kind of servant mentality, what with a waitress mother and a policeman father."

"You couldn't say that if you were in Chicago," I said. "Our waitresses and policemen are anything but servants."

"Yes," said Alice. "Well, here things are a little different. A gendarme's cap here marks him as a public servant and he is conscious of it. From what I hear your Chicago ones think their caps are designed like papal miters."

I laughed. "Well, at any rate, in the home Juan's father must have been the anointed sovereign."

"Yes," Alice said, "a frightful childhood, I guess. But I have a feeling that Juan will be very good for Arthur. He has been utterly wild of late."

"Sorry, I don't think Juan will help much," I said bluntly. "I'd be afraid to tell Arthur, but I really feel very uneasy about what may lie ahead for them."

There was a long pause while Alice carefully rolled a bit of ash from her cigarette into the silver tray. "Do you know," she said, "I had the same feeling, Johnny, at one point. I felt a cold wind blowing over me when I saw the boy for the first time. Even spoke to Gertrude about it. She said bosh, I was silly. But I'm not so sure. Why do you feel that way?"

"Honestly," I said, shaking my head. "I have no idea. Perhaps it's because of the difference in ages. But that couldn't be it. There have been other young men with Arthur. It's something deeper. They don't seem to—to *dovetail*, if that means anything to you. I'm not sure it does to me."

She nodded. "Yes, I think it does. Are you going to tell Arthur how you feel?"

"No," I said. "Or do you think I should?"

She nodded again. "I think I would. He is really very fond of you, I believe. But of course he probably wouldn't listen to you at all—just call you Cassandra again. He will have to go on the way he is and see it out to the end." She sighed. "Maybe we will all be surprised. Perhaps it will last a long time and keep Arthur quiet and happy."

"Maybe," I said reluctantly. "But I have my doubts, I really do."

"Well," she said, "he will ask you what you think. He's bound to. He asked Gertrude and me at least a dozen times. We reassured him. We said we approved of Juan, though we made it clear that the approval did not necessarily extend to the relationship between them." She suddenly looked old and tired. "Good heavens," she said, "we've seen so much of this sort of thing in our lives that we have got dreadfully bored with it. Just worn out with all these tales, I guess."

"I know," I said. "I've been bothered about what will become of Juan after a while."

"Well, at least he'll know how to make one kind of living after Arthur gets through with him," Alice said cynically.

"The difference in their ages is too marked," I said. "I've never been able to adjust to that without a mild shock. We see a lot of it at home, but perhaps not so much as in Europe. Very often you'll see what you take to be a father and son sitting quietly in a restaurant—all very natural. Then if you watch you'll get a sudden sign—a clasp of a hand lying on the table, a quick look or secret smile exchanged over the rim of a wine glass, a high little giggle from the older man . . . and then you know it's something else."

"Ah yes," Alice said. "The difference between Arthur and Juan is quite wrong. It should be either fifty years or three years, not a horrible eighteen or twenty—that's the most indecent of all."

I had a fleeting vision of myself grown old, darkening the gray hair along the temples, clipping the long hairs from nostrils and ears, rubbing eye cream into the pockets beneath my eyes, wearing a male girdle of some sort—doing all the things that are presumed to delay the dreadful slackening of the flesh, to postpone the death of youth—but never do. I hoped to be spared such panic activity. When I was seventeen I knew I was going to be seventy, and busily—sometimes hysterically—I had been storing up memories, tangible objects and souvenirs to sustain me after I "retired." When the day of renunciation came, I would stop as a good man should, and live among the memories. Yet I wondered if my resolve to renounce it all would be firm when the time came.

"What are you thinking about?" Alice asked.

I stretched my legs in front of me. "The best time to give it all up," I said.

"That's easy," she said. "When you find yourself straining to meet your monthly quota." She laughed charmingly, delighted with herself. I blushed, remembering I had once told her of my keeping statistics about Eros.

I turned the topic another way. "If you are, as you say," I remarked, "worn out with all these tales and confusions, here's a bright little change of subject. I heard yesterday that my fellowship for a year in Paris has come through."

Alice's mouth opened and then she extended her arms. "Why, you dear *boy!*" she exclaimed. "Come here this instant and let me buss you soundly!" In some confusion I received a smack from her on both cheeks and then sat down again. My face was scarlet and hot.

"And you so modest with this grand piece of news, while I went on chattering about Arthur and his mignon," she said. "All my best to you. Now we shall see a lot of our dear shy Johnny for a year, and nothing could be nicer, no nothing not ever, as Gertrude might say."

I felt like a schoolgirl in her first formal dress. We chatted a few minutes longer and then I left. Alice made me promise to return soon because—as she pointed out—it was the second time I had come when Gertrude was away, and Gertrude would begin to think I was avoiding her. A third time, said Alice, and it would be like my avoidance of Italy—it would amount almost to a criticism. I assured her I would come soon again.

I could not analyze the deep feeling of uneasiness that suddenly came over me when I left Alice. I wandered up the Rue Dauphine to the Seine, and looked over the side of the Pont Neuf for a while, down at the triangular point of green and trees that formed the west end of the Île de la Cité. It seemed cool in the July sun, so I left the bridge level and went down the green steps through the small tunnel and out again, almost at the river level. The usual crowd of young sunbathers was lolling on the narrow path, or lying at the edge of the stone embankment's steep slope. I walked self-consciously among them to the end of the point, stepping over several sunburned chests, edging around tanned legs spread carelessly across the path, and feeling out of place since I was fully dressed. A boy of fourteen looked at me with wise black eyes and asked what time it was. A few steps farther, a *type* with sideburns asked me for a cigarette. He had an anchor tattooed on his shoulder, and his smoky eyes were full of daggers and rumpled beds. I saw him stick his tongue-point into his cheek, a well-known sign in Paris, but I went on.

At last I reached an empty bench and sat down. The Seine stretched ahead of me, and I felt almost as if I were at the prow of a boat surrounded on two sides by water. The sun was hot on my back; I took off my shirt and let the light fall on my shoulders. I sat and dozed a little, and wakened with a start, thinking of the year in Paris that lay ahead. There were no creative thoughts, just the slow intertwining that we call daydreaming. And the end product of nearly an hour of such profitless but pleasant golden pondering was merely this, an adolescent conclusion of which I was somewhat ashamed:

We all grow old and wither. And it is the greatest tragedy. . . .

(33) July 20, 1939

Late the next afternoon I came out of the métro station of the Pont Marie, reluctant to leave the cool and stuffy mustiness of the subway for the heat outside. It had been a scorcher, one of the few hot days of the summer. I slipped the wrist strap of my small camera over my hand, and then fitted the camera into my palm to conceal it, for I hated carrying the "sign of the tourist." But Arthur had called that morning and said that Juan would like to have his picture taken, and would I mind taking a few of Juan and him? Delighted, I said. And then, said Arthur, you can stay to have dinner with Juan; he will cook for you, because I have to go out with the Comte d'Aiguy and his wife, and it will be jolly for you to get better acquainted. I asked him if he trusted me; he laughed and said not exactly, but that he trusted Juan, which was something else.

The heat struck between the eyes when I reached the street level, and I began to sweat at once. I crossed the Pont Marie slowly, and there was welcome shade as I turned down the Quai d'Anjou.

When I rang Arthur's bell I heard him shout inside, muffled through the heavy oak door. After a moment, Juan himself opened it.

"*Entrez, Monsieur,*" he said and smiled a wide and friendly greeting. I stepped in. He looked different from the shabby urchin of several nights before. His hair had been freshly cut and lay in a gleaming straight black thickness upon his head. He wore a spotless white shirt of coarse-woven linen, with white trousers to match. They fitted him well and tightly, and I saw that he was quite a man . . . They accented the black of his hair and eyes, and repeated the whiteness of his skin. Seen close and studied with attention, I realized that he was even more young and handsome than he had seemed at first.

"Arthur will be here in a moment," he said in French. I noted that they were already on a first-name basis. His French was not very good; it had a heavy peasant accent that made it difficult for me. "May I take your jacket?"

"*Non merci*," I said. "It is quite comfortable in here." I sat down in a chair. Juan brought an ashtray for me with a kind of nervous semiproprietary air, as if he had been told that all this was his and he could not quite believe it.

"How have you been?" I asked.

"Oh, very well," he said. "This is the first time I have ever been in Paris. It is big—and strange. I have never seen a city so big before."

"Yes, it is," I said. I could think of nothing more to say, not wanting to ask how he liked it with Arthur or what he thought of the apartment, because it might embarrass him. There was already a certain enigmatic look in his eyes; here is one, he seemed to be thinking, who knows everything that is going on with me. I felt that he might be naively ashamed of his little "sin."

Luckily Arthur came into the room at that moment. He was in his undershirt and was drying his face with a towel. He shook my hand in a water-wet clasp. "Nice to see you, Mac," he said. "I do hope this isn't a bore for you."

"On the contrary," I said. "I'm delighted to take a few pictures of you and Juan. It'll be a souvenir for me as well."

"I'll slip on a shirt and we'll go out," Arthur said. "Is there still light?"

"Plenty," I said. "Sun's still up."

"Be with you in a jiff," he said and disappeared. When he returned he had on an old plaid shirt, in great contrast to Juan's spotlessness. "Shall we go?"

For the next half hour we took pictures down on the street, perhaps twenty of them. The two were like children together, and Juan's youth became more and more apparent. "Take one of me like this," he said, springing to the embankment wall. Then he jumped down and thrust his arm through a huge mooring ring. "Now one like this," he pleaded, "with Arthur beside me."

After taking a great many I said, "Let's go down to the river. There should be some good angles there."

"Isn't it too shaded?" Arthur asked.

"Oh, no," I said. We walked down the steps. Something of their infectious gaiety struck fire in me, and we were all laughing like little girls on their way from school. I took them in all sorts of poses—on the sloping wall, seated on a wooden pier, arms around shoulders—and even broke out the timing device (a great mystery to Juan) to enable me to get in the picture myself.

We came back in high spirits. Juan's eyes were shining and Arthur was excited. "Isn't he wonderful?" Arthur whispered in English. "Pure gold—one of the most simple and delightful young animals ever. But he's so timid. And conventional. Would you believe it—" and Arthur lowered his voice even more, although he was speaking in English "—it is actually the first time the boy has had any experience of this sort."

"You don't mean you got his—" Try as I would the word would not come out. I took another step away semantically and substituted the French *pucelage*.

"But of course," said Arthur. He grinned evilly. "And by now he thinks it all great *fun*." Again the horrible inflection that Arthur could give the simple term. "I do always, however, seem to meet someone whose demands on me are . . . shall we say, often excessive and even irrational now and then. Well—" and he danced away from me a step or two, "I really must run, old chap—do make yourself quite at home—look at the books . . . dinner will be ready shortly. Juan can't cook many dishes but he does a few rather well."

Arthur vanished and made noises in the dressing room while he finished. Twice he called to Juan in the kitchen. And then he was ready to leave, drawing on thin gray silk gloves, looking very proper in black suit and tie, carrying his bowler hat.

"I'll be back about eleven," he said. "Will you stay that long?"

"I doubt it," I said. "I have a date at St. Germain about ten."

"Why don't you take Juan sunbathing tomorrow?" he asked. "He would like very much to get some sun, and I'll be busy all day."

"I don't mind," I said. In a way I did, for I liked being solitary on the Quai Branly near the Eiffel Tower, to play the little games with the passersby. Something had already told me there would never be any intimate encounter with Juan while Arthur was having his fling. But I owed Arthur a good deal.

"You make the arrangements then. *Au revoir*," he said and shook my hand. "*Au 'voir*, Juan!" he called to the kitchen. Juan appeared, wiping his hands. He and Arthur gravely shook hands and Juan bowed slightly from the waist. It was like the parting of diplomats rather than lovers.

When the door closed, I asked Juan: "Do you need any help in the kitchen?"

"*Non merci*," he said. "Sit down or read. I will call you soon."

I was left alone in the great blue and white room. I walked to the windows and looked down into the convent garden. It shimmered in a kind of golden light of plum and rose tones, and the green of the shrubs and trees had turned almost black in the evening light, which did not strike directly into the enclosure. One solitary nun, the white wings on her wimple moving slowly and evenly down the path, looked like the guardian spirit of the flower plots, which were now faded into a dusky gray black through which a few dark flower tones of red and yellow showed. It was a magic hour.

The tiny clock on the mantel chimed seven-thirty, a small tinkling treble sound. I walked to the ceiling-high bookcases and looked with vague interest at the titles. They were both British and French—Burke's *Peerage*, of course, and some genealogies, Gibbon, Lamartine, de Vigny, Mallarmé, Baudelaire, Rimbaud, and Hugo. After that I went silently opening drawers and looking at their messy contents—Arthur was not a tidy housekeeper. There was a kind of larcenous curiosity in me. I was not really a thief; I was merely a fetishist and a collector, and stole objects only for their emotional value. Who, for instance, if he wanted to thieve for money would steal a pair of soiled white athletic socks from a basketball player, or an unwashed *cache-sexe* from a ballet dancer?

That evening I found nothing to take except a postcard from Spain, one of a large collection, and I stuck it in my pocket only because of the fantastic codpiece on a young medieval man.

I had just closed the postcard drawer when Juan said behind me, "*Monsieur est servi.*" I turned slowly to avoid making a guilty start. Juan had put on a white serving jacket, and was standing behind a chair at the table ready to pull it out for me. He had a napkin carefully folded over one arm. He had lighted two candles and put white placemats down. The dark cherry wood of the table gleamed red under the white islands, the bone china, and the polished silver. A large bowl of salad was on one side of the table, with a wooden fork and spoon crossed on top of the greenery. A small decanter of *pastis* was next to a larger cut-glass one in which the red wine was lustrous as a garnet.

"How nice!" I said to Juan, letting him push the chair under me. "You should not have taken all this trouble."

"It was no trouble," he said politely, and sat down himself. Then he ladled out a dishful of thin soup with rice in it, and handed it to me, filling one for himself. "Good soup," he said before I had tasted it. "It has rice in it. I am very fond of rice," he said. "Rice, he is good for you."

"Indeed yes," I said and tasted it. It was—alas!—as thin as it looked. There was scarcely any taste at all and the rice kernels were hard inside. "It is delicious," I said, lying with grave politeness.

"I love rice," he said.

It was a strange meal, odd in two ways. It was filled with long silences, with the only noise the sound of silver against a plate or ice against the side of the glass, or the crackle of bread crust as one of us broke off another piece. And during the silences he would suddenly look up to catch me staring at him, or I would look at him to see him quickly lower his eyes from observing me. Once we both looked at each other at the same time, and smiled and then laughed in a rip of embarrassment that I tried to sew together by saying something about how looking at him took my mind off my meal.

The other strange thing was the meal itself. Arthur had been extremely charitable when he spoke of Juan's powers as chef. The second course was an egg in a silver cup. Juan slid it on the plate apologetically.

"It may be a little too hard," he said. "I forgot about them."

I attacked it with the egg spoon. The top did not come off. Then, trying as best I could, I attempted to break through the tough membrane inside the shell. Juan was watching me with anxious eyes. Finally I picked up the egg and tapped it all over with the flat of the knife.

"What a shame!" he said, half-rising. "I will cook two more."

"Nonsense," I said. "The egg is hard-boiled. I like hard-boiled eggs. It's perfectly all right."

"I left them too long," he muttered.

I did not know quite how to react, whether to be charmed with his shyness and embarrassment, or to be thoroughly annoyed with a wretched meal. But I continued to smile and ask for more bread, and to let my water tumbler be filled again, and to watch him drink his red wine in peasant gulps.

The next course was rice on a plate, with lemon juice over it. When Juan brought it in he once more explained that rice was a good food, rich in vitamins, and very good for one to eat. I took a spoonful or two and found myself growing very tired, and wondering how the Chinese stood it. The dish was not a great success but I complimented him on its taste, and said how very original I thought it was to put lemon juice on rice. Where had he learned such a trick?

"From my grandmother," he said proudly. "I learned all that I know about cooking from her. Especially how to cook sweets. Wait until we have dessert—ah, there will be the grand surprise!"

More rice, I thought.

The fourth course—I could scarcely believe my eyes when he entered after a little delay in the kitchen—was two fried eggs for each of us.

"In the country on my grandmother's farm," he explained. "we ate lots of eggs. My grandmother always said that eggs and rice were the two best foods in the world. She was very healthy. She lived a long time."

I was so annoyed with the eggs that I listened no further to what he said about his sainted grandmother. She was some kind of famous person, I guess, but the again-overcooked eggs were on the point of forcing my small appetite to leave me for the rest of the day. I managed to eat most of them, however, mentally shaking my head in a blind speculation about what would come next.

After the eggs he was gone several minutes in the kitchen, and there was a loud noise of something frying rapidly. Soon he was back, his face flushed and a platter of something in his hand. Ah, I thought—lamb chops perhaps, or small steaks.

It was eggplant cut lengthwise in long strips and fried, dripping with olive oil. He seemed so pleased with his efforts that I managed to swallow my gorge just as it was rising. "Very good for you," he said and put the platter down. "Very rich in minerals. And now some salad too?" he asked.

"Of course," I said. I looked in great dismay at the bent and twisted curls of eggplant on my plate. They reminded me of night crawlers blasted by sudden lightning. He filled my plate beside them with lettuce and romaine. I tasted the salad. He had sprinkled grated Italian cheese over the green stuff, and made the garlic dressing heavy with sugar. "Delicious," I said, aware that there were new jewels in my crown for the night's performance. Angels were busily pasting gold stars after my name, and I could hear the excited humming of their wings as they flew about the streets of heaven in pure joy over my conduct—or was it just my blood pressure beating in my ears?

The last course—but naturally! was a thick gummy concoction of rice. Laid over it—or injected into it—was a great deal of strawberry jam, the whole soaked with a cup of kirsch, making the hard kernels of rice swim in a pink bath around the edges of the mound.

"Rice—" he began.

"—is very good for you," I finished.

He blushed. "There was not much food in the house," he said. "Arthur forgot to bring any home. I thought there was some meat in the *frigo*, even some American bacon. But there was nothing." He looked miserably down at his plate, and for one harried moment I thought he was going to cry.

I put my hand over his. "Never mind, Juan," I said. "It was a very nice dinner, and I've eaten so much I'm stuffed. There's no more space for dessert. Let's eat some a little later. I love rice, really. We'll do the dishes and then we'll have a bit of your sweet in the living room, and—" a sudden idea came to me "—and you'll let me make a little sketch of you, hein?"

He looked at me with glistening eyes. "You really did like my poor meal?" he said. "I wanted it to be nice, but it is hard to cook out of nothing."

"Indeed I did," I said, all irritation gone. "Come, we'll wash the things."

Together we carried the dishes into the tiny kitchen. He washed, I dried, and stacked them neatly on the table. When it was done he turned and said, "And now the dessert?" with a little-boy eagerness in his voice.

"Later, Juan," I said. "Let's go in and sit down. I'll find a pencil and paper, and you'll pretend to read a book while I make the *petit dessin*, hein?"

"I will get the pencil and paper," he said eagerly, and vanished into the bedroom. I went into the salon, pulled a table lamp close to the chair he would sit in, and sat down beside it. He came back with a broken stub of soft pencil and a sheet of letter paper.

"It was all I could find," he said.

"It will do very well."

"My grandmother could draw and paint," he said, "as well as dance."

"I am just an amateur," I said, scarcely listening to him. "But Sir Arthur is a very good painter, Juan. He is already known everywhere. You are fortunate to know him."

"Do you think he really likes me?" Juan asked. His eyes were bright again.

"I am sure of it. Do you like him?"

Juan was suddenly embarrassed. "It—it is all very new to me. But I like him well. He said perhaps he was too old for me, but I told him that twenty-five was not really much older than I was."

I swallowed. One could not blame Arthur for trimming his age. But this was a considerable lopping.

"Ah, yes," I said. "Now—will you take off your shirt and trousers?"

The look of horror on his face startled me. "Oh no!" he said with vehemence. "Oh no—that is not nice! I would be embarrassed."

"Well, then—perhaps just your shirt?"

"Can't you draw me just like this?" he begged.

I shook my head. "No point in it," I said, and started to put the paper down.

"All right, then," he said reluctantly, and took off his shirt.

"Now sit and relax," I said. "Cross your ankle over your knee if you want."

He had a nice torso, a boy's torso. The tone of his body skin was darker than that of his face. The muscles were still undeveloped, but smooth and clean flowing and clear with their youth. The formation of his shoulders was a little strange. They sloped abruptly down from his neck, leaving it to rise from his body like an ivory column, and making me think of a few lines from the *Song of Solomon*. He settled himself and I began to draw.

The sketch was not good at all. The night had come outside. It was wholly black and we sat in the small circle of light from the table lamp. I was somehow not in the mood, and as I sketched I grew more and more annoyed with the "untouchableness" of this lad. I knew better than to suggest any dalliance with him. He would report it to Arthur, and Arthur would turn against me.

It was nine-thirty when I finished. I showed it to him. Charitably, he said that he liked it but I could see that he did not. Nor did I; it was another rice dinner. It lacked the life of the sketches I had made of André, in whom I was truly interested.

"Now I must go," I said.

"You do not want the dessert?" he asked anxiously.

"Not this evening," I said. "You really fed me very well. I will eat some of your sweets another time."

He went with me to the door and opened it. I could see that there was something on his mind but I did not help him express it. He made a timid start.

"I would like—" he said.

"Yes?" I looked at him a trifle archly, impatiently.

Suddenly he pushed the door nearly shut and reached over quickly. He kissed me on the cheek and then stepped back, his face scarlet, looking down.

I was completely astonished. "Juan—" I began.

He spoke rapidly in a low voice. "You are very nice," he said. "You are very kind. If I were not with Arthur, I would like very much to be with you." Then he pulled the door open.

I was staggered. I muttered something about liking him too, and then escaped into the corridor.

I am not quite certain how I reached St. Germain in my heart-singing daze, but for all the rest of the evening I felt that somehow life was very rewarding.

(34) July 21, 1939

To some extent all men are victims of "gestures." But especially so are we who build on the filmy foundations of impossible dreams. Since our lives are broken time after time in human relationships, we want a tangible memory of those encounters. And so we collect a handkerchief, a little hair, a love note, the label of a wine bottle, a water glass (because *his* lips had touched it once), a broken shoe-lace, a sock, a corporal's stripes (he ripped them off to sew his sergeant's on).

But mostly we collect gestures to paste in our mental scrapbook. Juan's gesture colored my dreams that night. The irritation of the wretched rice meal, the childishness of the boy and his limitations in conversation—these had undermined my interest. He could not be mine; he was Arthur's—and I had to admit that was the basic reason that helped me find him not really desirable. Then at the last, when all was dead and done, he had enchanted me once again with the parting kiss on my cheek.

I called the next morning to arrange the sunbathing. Juan answered; Arthur had gone to town. I suggested that Juan come to my hotel at noon; we could eat a bite and then set off for the Seine. No, he said firmly—I should come to get him. I protested—it was out of the way, a mile in the wrong direction. We would have to retrace. No, he said. He did not know Paris. He would get lost. If I did not come he would not go.

At last I said I would. But when I hung up the receiver I was furious with him again. It was a great inconvenience, an extra métro ride, a time waster when the sun was out in full hot ball. But I went for him, peevish to the core.

Everything was wrong. He had on his white shirt and trousers. I pointed out that they would get soiled on the dusty banks near the Eiffel Tower. He had nothing to lie on save a square of figured silk out of which he had made a sport ascot. It was enough, he said, and I was finally quiet, thinking he would soon find out; his clothes would get soiled. He took pen, ink, and paper along; he wanted to write a letter. In vain I told him that he could not write on the uneven ground in the dust. He took them anyway. He wanted to stop at a restaurant to get a full meal. I said a sandwich when we got there would be enough, since I never ate lunch myself. I hoped that the one bar where we could get sandwiches would be out of ham and hard-boiled eggs on that particular day.

During the subway ride I grew ashamed of myself.' When the train rose from the great nest of tunnels beneath Paris to become an elevated, my mood had completely changed, helped along by the admiring glances that Juan drew from everyone.

We got off the train at Bir-Hakheim, and went downstairs to the asphalt circle nestling under the straddling ironwork of the elevated tracks. It was a dangerous spot, a meeting of seven streets pouring in from five directions. The French had evidently tried to devise a system of traffic lights to guide the flow, but then with characteristic Gallic abandon had at last thrown hands into the air, and decided to let the autos work it out as best they could among themselves.

We skipped hurriedly across to the bar, and Juan munched at a foot-long length of French bread while I drank a glass of white wine. Then we tried the crossing again, and by some minor miracle made it to the safety of the Quai Branly, and the shaded mouth of the ramp that led down to the Seine.

As we started down the cobblestoned incline, the traffic noise began to fade. By some acoustic trick, there was a space on the ramp where the world grew completely silent. You heard neither traffic nor the small river sounds from the Seine below. It was a bubble of ear-breaking silence. And then once again came sound— the lapping of water, a child's cry of joy, the noise of an oar lock as an oar pulled, small sounds spaced far apart in the drowsy hum of the summer afternoon.

"It is very nice here," Juan said. He walked straight and young beside me.

"Rather dirty when you get close to the river," I said. "Let's walk under the bridge and beyond. There's a good flat place in the ground." Besides, I thought, it will take us past the great stone cube on which the muscle boys lie in the sun. I always chose a spot beyond them, never having the courage to lie down among them. For they were the weight lifters, the brown and rippling peacocks mapped with muscles, strutting and flexing and exhibiting their steely charms.

We walked under the bridge, feeling the cool air from the lapping water, and then we came into the sun again, near the cube of the Apollos.

"Look," I said to Juan. "Aren't they handsome?" One was flat on his back, holding his arms straight up; another clasped the extended hands and arced his body upward until he stood straight on his hands on the other's quivering support. Then the upper one lost balance and somersaulted to the ground, landing gracefully on his feet with no scramble.

Juan looked at them briefly, then turned his face straight ahead. "Yes, they are handsome enough," he said, "but they do not wear enough clothes. Their bathing trunks are too short."

The inflection sounded as prim and prudish as that of a spinster from the American Bible Belt. "Don't you think the human body is beautiful?" I asked. "The great Michelangelo said that the highest form of art is man. In motion the body is lovelier than anything that man has ever made."

"Just the same," he said. "They are too naked."

The shut-mind conviction of his tone exasperated me again. I nearly said something malicious about his taking his clothes off in front of Arthur, but didn't. His prudery was that of the farmers in Minnesota, Kansas, Nebraska, setting square-jawed about the indecent but necessary task of making future farmhands—lights out, under the bedclothes, with the wife in her nightgown (pulled just high enough) and the husband in long flannel underwear—no touching, no caressing, no kissing—a dirty job, this business of sex. Juan sounded on the same level. Before you can like nakedness, you have to reach a certain point of intelligence, or in mores. Juan had not reached it.

Youth has no conversation until the key is found; until it is, youth is sealed and secret. We quickly forget what fascinated us in the early years. Many times in Chicago I wore myself out in poking around the younger minds. It was like going through the contents of a young boy's pockets—a string, a broken knife, marbles, an eraser, a coat button—and holding each up to say "What is this?" and "What does it mean to you?" The young simply can not talk until the touchstone is found.

I arranged my towel on the dusty ground amid the dead grass, and Juan spread his pitifully small scarf. Then we undressed and composed ourselves. He lay half on my towel, squeezing me to the edge. He had a good body, quite muscular in the leg, and it was covered with the same aligned thin black hair I had seen on his arms.

Suddenly he raised to fumble in his trouser pocket. He pulled out a large blue-flowered silk handkerchief. He unfolded it and lay back, spreading it over his face.

"*Mon dieu,*" I said, exasperated. "Why that? I thought you wanted sun."

He lifted a corner of the handkerchief and peeked at me with a dark eye. "My face gets so dark," he said, "I become like a black man."

"And why not?" I asked. "It is the mode. You want to look healthy, don't you?" I pulled the handkerchief from his face. "All the young men of Paris are tanned if they can manage it. It is very chic this year. You want that, don't you?"

"Perhaps," he said, and let the handkerchief lie beside him. I began to probe for Juan's key. I asked him if he liked to fish; he gave me a monosyllabic no. Sports? A little, not much. Which ones? Swimming, from time to time. Did he like to go to the theater? Once in a while—a movie. His favorite stars? He had none. Did he read—novels, yes? No. Did he like music? Violin music . . .

My attempts wavered and began to collapse in the idle languor of the afternoon. The sun was hot on my skin and I stretched lazily and sensually in it. There were no flies to bother us. Then I heard Juan turn over, and a faint rustle of paper. I sat up and looked. He was beginning to write his letter. I shrugged and said nothing, starting to lie down again. But I looked down the long dusty bank beyond the bridge and saw one of my favorite strollers approaching, one with whom I daily played eye games.

I liked to think of the stranger as a boxer. He certainly looked like one. Every day at one-thirty he walked past with his dog, which he was training. The man wore loose trousers tightly gathered by a belt in apache fashion, with an old gray sweatshirt on his upper body. Sometimes during the course of his stroll he took off his sweatshirt to let the sun fall on a magnificent torso—powerful, muscled, cruel. Above it his face mocked the world. His nose had been broken several times. His lips were heavy and sardonic, his hair clipped almost to the scalp, and he swung the whip-leash with authority. A broad and exciting sensuality rolled in waves about him. The police dog loped at his heels, carrying a rubber ball in its mouth.

I touched Juan and motioned toward the man. "Do you like dogs?" I asked.

Juan looked briefly over his shoulder, shrugged, and went back to his letter. "Not too much," he said.

I flung myself flat. "Oh, *merde!*" I said, and put my forearm over my eyes.

Juan sucked in a little air. "That, it is not a nice word," he said gravely.

I did not trust myself to answer. My irritation was thorough. I silently marshaled some nasty words in both French and English, and then I gradually relaxed, thinking oh what the hell, he's just a kid. The basic cause of my annoyance was now crystalline: I couldn't have him but I still had to be nice to him . . . all of which made me a class A son of a bitch.

Presently I found that I could look at him again. He was having difficulty with his letter. The breeze blew the corners of his paper, and the ground was uneven. He lay on his stomach, raised on his elbows, and had the top of the pen in his mouth. When he saw me watching him, he sighed.

"It is a little difficult to write this letter," he said.

"Ah, well," I said, "what did I tell you? The ground is too rough, there is too much dust, too much sunlight. You'll go blind."

"No, it is not that," he said. "I meant—it is hard to think of the right thing to say." He paused a moment, then said, "Do you have a needle?"

I laughed ironically. "Oh certainly," I said. "I always carry needles with me. You'll find a whole package of them right down there in my crotch, in my briefs. Just reach over for them."

Juan looked at my trunks and then realized my sarcasm. His throat turned red and he looked down at the letter again.

"What in the world do you want a needle for?" I asked, somewhat ashamed. "Will a pin do?"

He nodded his handsome head and did not look at me.

"What do you want it for, Juan?" I persisted, and pulled one out of a belt loop where it had been guarding a split waiting to be repaired. "Here's a safety pin."

"*Merci*," he said. He took it and stuck it into his forefinger so that a bright bead of blood appeared on the skin. Then he extended his finger as if it were a pen, and drew a diagonal line carefully at the bottom of the letter, a line that passed through his signature and ended in a small red-filled circular dot. The whole thing was about an inch and a half long.

"*Ciel*—what are you doing there?" I asked. He shook his head and said nothing, blowing gently on the blood mark. Then he folded the letter and stuck it into the envelope. My curiosity soared.

"Juan, tell me," I said authoritatively. "If you don't tell me at once, I'll—I'll go off and leave you to walk home! If you can find your way."

Juan looked at me and said slowly, "It is a letter to the girl I was supposed to marry. I have told her that she is free to marry someone else, and I have sent back the mark of my blood so that she can burn it and be free and pick another man to be her husband."

A little trail of gooseflesh flickered briefly across my shoulder blades and then was gone in the sun. "You mean you have broken your engagement to her?" I asked in astonishment. "But why, Juan—why?"

"It is not honorable now," he said, "since I am with Arthur, and I think that perhaps I am not meant for women."

"Oh, for—Juan, you oughtn't to do a thing like that! You don't even know how long you will be with Arthur. You don't know if you want to be. Listen, Juan," I said, "you are very young. You must not make such decisions quickly. You should talk this over with Arthur first. Have you told him about it?"

"No," said Juan, eyes lowered, "This, it is my affair, is it not?"

"Yes," I admitted, "it is your affair. But even so you should not do this hastily. Do not send the letter yet. Think it over for a little moment. Will you do that, Juan? Promise me you'll think about it."

Juan was silent for a long moment. "Please," I said again. Finally he looked up.

"*D'accord*," he said. "I will think about it for a while."

"Fine," I said, much relieved.

He handed me the safety pin. "Thank you for it," he said soberly. I refastened the belt loop. I was still filled with curiosity.

"What kind of blood vow was that, Juan?" I asked. "I thought only gypsies made a marriage vow in blood."

Juan looked very confused. He turned on one side and stared out over the Seine. "If I tell you," he said slowly, "will you keep it secret from Arthur?"

"Certainly," I said.

"I—I am gypsy," he said.

"But I thought you said your grandmother had a farm on which you ate eggs and rice and learned to cook?"

Juan shook his head. "That, it was a dream. I am not a good one of the Old People—the gypsies. I dream of *gorgio*, the ones who live in one place on the land. We all have dreams. But I have always been gypsy. Life—it has been very hard," he said, and lay back on his scarf.

"Tell me about it, Juan."

At first the words came haltingly. He did not know who his real father was. His grandmother had been a terror. She had beaten him. His mother hated him. She had not wanted him. She had got

him by a *gorgio*. His earliest memories were of campfires and rabbit stew and rice and open wagons creaking through the mountains
of Spain and southwest France, and the king of the caravan telling
the story of the Old People while he plucked his lutelike *bosh*. All
the world hated and feared the gypsies. Signs on the road told
them the *gorgio* did not want them and that their campsites were
forbidden. Villagers thought them thieves and baby stealers.
Farmers shot at them and locked up livestock and chickens when
the gypsies passed. And still the gypsies lived, telling fortunes in
carnivals, pilfering from trees and vineyards, somehow making a
living from nothing. Outcasts.

When Juan was ten, he worked on the docks in Marseilles.
There he stole some peanuts and the agents of the police caught
him. His grandmother was sick with fever at the time. The police
put him in a naval reform school since he had no papers and would
not tell where his mother and the rest of the gypsies were. After a
year he broke out and stole a bicycle and fled. He wrecked the
bicycle and escaped on foot to the mountains. For a while he
worked on *gorgio* farms, always hoping his people would pass his
way. Finally he went to Toulon and learned how to work in a
garage. Toulon was full of sailors, bad, wicked sailors. One of them
captured him and took him to a room and tied him to a bed and
kept him prisoner for a week. [Ah, there Arthur! I thought; you
were not the first!] After that he felt disgraced. When he finally
escaped from the sailor he left Toulon and started through the
countryside once more, looking for his family again.

Finally he found them in a forest just outside Avignon. What
kind of reception after years of wandering? Embraces, tears, happy
kisses? Ah, no—his grandmother seized a firebrand and threw it at
him, his mother cursed and kicked and slapped him. The king told
him he was dead to the Romany because he had lived with a
gorgio. But he took the blood vow again and stayed and lived the
nomad's life, until the *gorgio* dreams wakened again. One night he
put his few possessions into a bag and slipped away into the dark
and hitchhiked his way to Paris.

"And so," he finished, "I met Arthur and you and that is all."

He had told the story simply. It was not a long recital but it
took me far away from the banks of the Seine. It moved me
strangely, told in his husky voice warm with the tones of Midi
sunlight and Mediterranean blue. I had not interrupted him at all.

But at one point—which point precisely?—something vague and dark rustled in the background shadows of my mind. I could not capture the fleeting sensation to analyze it. I only knew that it had been there, somewhere along the line of his narration.

"You will not tell Arthur?" he said.

"You do not want me to tell?" I asked. "Of course I will not, if you ask. But if I were you I would tell him myself. It will make no difference. Probably he will like you even more. Why not tell it to him?"

Juan rolled his head negatively on his blue-flowered scarf. "I have shame of it," he said. "Perhaps some day I will tell him but not now. Now, it is all too new," he said. He turned to look at me, his eyes six inches away from mine, great black wells of hurt and warmth. "You will promise?" he asked again.

"*Bien sûr*—it is safe with me," I said.

Juan took his hand from his belly where it had been lying and put it down to the side, where he found mine. He collected my fingers into its heat and pressed them once.

"You are *bon ami*," he said, and smiled at me.

We lay there quietly sweating palm to palm. I felt happy and foolish and old and young and quite content, all at the same time.

(35) August 22, 1939

One evening about nine-thirty Witold, Fitzie, and I sat at the Royale talking. The hot weather had brought out streams of people, and none of us was listening very much to what the others said— our eyes were busy on the passersby. I was more than a little bored. I liked Fitzie well enough—my skull-faced American friend who always wore the tightest pants in Paris, light colored to show off his *grand armement*. But Witold was another matter.

He and I had been acquainted for many years. He was an expatriate Pole who had lived in Paris a long time, a kind of drifter doing this and that, some writing, some import-export business, living a life without purpose or aim, except to make money—and boys.

But the affair of the Belgian hitchhiker had almost turned me against him. One evening, strangled with desire, I approached a young blond tough and offered him two thousand francs for an encounter. He said yes. But it was late; my hotel with its dragon concierge was closed to visitors. Along came Witold—who had an apartment that was not supervised. And off they went—unaware of the knife-cut of jealousy, the red murder-fury that ran through me as I watched Witold and Jean Renard, my boy, my hitchhiker, move off into the darkness. I had never forgiven him.

At any rate, there we were talking. I had told them about my year in Paris, and they made the proper noises. Fitzie had then gone on to tell how he had spent the last weekend at a small hideaway in the country with six others, sleeping in two beds. Or rather—not sleeping.

"It was incredible what went on," said Fitzie in his recently acquired and excellent French. "No one closed his eyes all night, or if he did, was awakened in a few minutes by a dark shadow straddling him. The next day I felt like a whore on Sunday morning. And about three A.M. one of the boys dressed and went out looking for new blood. He came back with a young curly-black-haired motorcyclist with red boots and fawn-colored trousers. So of course we all had to wake up to be friendly and hospitable."

Fitzie paused. "I wish the boy had told us what it was like to have six mouths on you at the same time—"

"—like being with an octopus," I said.

"—but all he said," Fitzie went on, "was 'Mon dieu, to think that I had always wanted to be the center of attention!'"

We laughed.

Suddenly I saw Sir Arthur come around the corner of the café from the Rue de Rennes. He walked with a decided starboard list. He was dressed in his old dirty sailor's sweater with the horizontal blue lines, and the sleeves pushed up to his elbows on his workingman's forearms. He had on a pair of faded navy dungarees that flopped around his ankles. His thick waist was pulled in sharply by a narrow belt, above and below which he bulged. On his feet were blue and white canvas shoes. His hair was mussed; he looked thoroughly disreputable.

"Oh my god," I said to Witold and Fitzie, shifting my chair so that I could turn my face aside. "Here comes Arthur Pickett, tight. I hope he doesn't see me."

Fitzie muttered through unmoving lips, "Headed straight for you."

Then I felt Arthur's hands on my shoulders. "So glad to find you, Mac," he said, slurred. He pulled up a chair.

I made introductions that he barely acknowledged. He was very drunk, and smelled of anise and beer. He sat down and drew his chair confidentially close. I glanced at Witold and Fitzie and made a sign of apology with eyes and eyebrows. They were looking at Arthur with a kind of wondering unbelief at his rudeness, and then after a moment they began talking to each other. Arthur paid no attention to them whatever.

"There had been the most terrible scene with Juan," he began.

"Is that why you're so drunk?" I asked sharply.

"I *am* drunk, aren't I?" he said, giggling. "I've been drinking steadily for hours. But there was a dreadful fight with Juan. Tell me, what do you actually think of him? I mean, do you think he is a good person? He is very fond of you. He spoke very warmly of you after you took him sunbathing."

"He's a nice boy," I said, repeating the old formula. "Nice— but very young."

"Tell me—don't you think him worthwhile? With very good breeding?"

"Quite satisfactory." If Arthur had asked the questions once, he had asked them twenty times in the past few days.

"Don't you think we can make a go of it?"

I turned and faced him directly. "I've told you a dozen times, Arthur," I said, "that I think you can't. What are you trying to do anyway? The boy is seventeen—you're more than twice that. It's ludicrous. It's even a little disgusting."

Arthur looked at the tabletop. "Don't be so cruel, Mac," he said. "I'm really terribly fond of Juan. He is so gentle. So loyal. I think it will all really work out this time."

"Lord," I said, annoyed. "How impractical can you be? You're well known in Paris—what will your friends say about you behind your back when they find out? What about your wife? No one will think for a minute that you've just hired a new *valet de chambre*. What silly kind of fake romantic idea is in your head?"

"Oh, it will work out all right," Arthur said. He was not listening at all, as usual. Logic can never quite reach the drunk or lovesick, and he was both.

"What was the fight about?" I asked. Arthur's continuing rudeness was annoying me more and more. He could have been tolerated for sitting down to exchange a few personal remarks, but the moment had come when he should have sat back and spoken to the others, making the talk general.

"It was terrible," Arthur said vaguely.

"Yes, I know," I said. "But tell me exactly what happened."

"There was a dreadful fight," Arthur said. "I hit Juan and cut his nose and gave him a black eye. And he never knew it." He giggled again.

"He never knew it?" I said. "How could that be?" There seemed to be no getting an orderly narration out of him. "What was the fight about?"

"Oh well," Arthur said, "he wanted to go with me to dinner at the Chesikovs' home, and of course it was impossible to take him, and then he spilled water on my suit, and—"

"Arthur," I said and dug my fingers into his arm, "tell me the full story. Don't jump around so much. I haven't the foggiest notion what you're talking about. Can't you tell it straight so that I can understand?"

"Well, he was beginning to resent my going out so much in the evening to parties, and after all I do have to go, not only clients but friends, you know, from the world I live in, and though there are certain ones of them to whom I could take Juan as a friend, good heavens, I couldn't take him to the Chesikovs, imagine introducing one's *valet de chambre* at a formal dinner—and anyway Irita had already seen him at my place and she would know at once, and more than that she'd be horrified at my bringing a *valet de chambre* into her house, so I tried to make Juan understand all that before I left this afternoon and I told him to go out to the pressing shop to get my formal suit that I had left to be cleaned, and to have it there when I got back at six-thirty, and it was there all right, and Juan asleep in the armchair with a half-empty bottle of Pernod beside him, snoring, and do you know what he had done—he had taken a glass or more of water and very carefully poured it all over my suit, which he had left out on the bed, and poured water into my patent-leather shoes too, and he had done it carefully on the suit, not even wetting the bedspread around it, so that I didn't know until I came out of the shower and put on my underwear and shirt, and then I picked up the suit and it was sopping, simply sopping wet, and so were my shoes, full of water, and I went right into the living room and grabbed him by the shirt and hit him twice in the face, once on the eye and nose and once on the chin, and my ring cut his nose, and then I just dropped him in the chair and left him there and changed into these clothes and began to get drunk and then I came over here."

It was the longest speech I had ever heard Arthur make.

"I'd hardly call that a fight," I said. "And he's still knocked out?"

"For all I know."

"Good heavens, I'd be afraid to go home tonight," I said. "He will probably be waiting for you with a butcher knife in hand."

"Oh, he wouldn't do that. He might not even know what hit him or how it happened, he was so drunk. He will certainly be wondering how his nose got cut and his eye blacked when he looks in the mirror, won't he?" Arthur giggled, then inched his chair closer. "But tell me," he said, lowering his voice, "what do you *reely* think of Juan? I mean, do you think he is a *worthwhile* person? He is very fond of you. He spoke very warmly of you after you took him sunbathing."

There is nothing more tiresome than a repetitious drunk. Those who have had experience with drunks will not be surprised that for the next fifteen minutes Arthur said over and over the same things about Juan, always returning endlessly to the question of his breeding, the innate goodness of the boy, and his fondness for me after we went sunbathing. My chest grew so tight with irritation that I found it hard to breathe. I looked constantly at Fitzie and Witold who seemed immersed in talk, but I could feel their irritation with Arthur reaching me in hot waves. The situation was almost intolerable. I knew the only way to get rid of Arthur was for either himself or me to leave. I did not want to, for I had planned to spend the evening together with Fitzie and Witold.

At last I leaned very close to Arthur and said, "Arthur, please talk to my friends a little, won't you? It is not polite."

He seemed suddenly to spiral upward out of his repetitions. "Oh," he said, "I am reely being very rude, aren't I?" He looked at Fitzie and Witold. "But I have nothing to say to them," he whispered. "They do not look at all interesting." Then he looked around. His eye caught a young Arab just entering the bar side of the Royale. "Excuse me," he said, standing unsteadily. He shook hands with Fitzie and Witold. "Delightful to meet you," he said wispily. "I must toddle along now. Just saw a friend go into the bar." He turned to shake hands with me. "G'bye, Mac old boy. I'll see you soon."

He lurched off down the sidewalk. There was a long moment of silence. Witold and Fitzie stopped talking and looked after him. I took out my handkerchief and mopped my face.

"*Well!*" said Fitzie at last.

"You know such charming people," said Witold ironically.

"The goddamned ass," I muttered.

We set about trying to repair the gaping hole in the evening that Arthur had left for us. He had almost killed everything, and our conversation was dulled. After a few minutes I saw his striped sweater emerge from the bar. He was clutching the young Arab and talking closely into his ear. They walked across to the traffic light and disappeared into the crowds moving down the Boulevard St. Germain.

"I hope he doesn't have too much money with him," said Fitzie.

"Why?" I asked.

"That Arab is dirt—one of the most notorious jackrollers in the quarter."

"But he has a face like one of the seraphim," I protested.

"And the soul of a pig," Fitzie said sardonically. "He'd think nothing of sticking a knife into your 'friend.'" By his inflection Fitzie made it clear that Arthur was no friend of his.

"He's old enough to take care of himself, I suppose," I said.

But to be quite truthful, at the moment I felt that it would have been rather pleasant to see a headline in the paper the next day telling how the body of a titled British painter had been found cut in four pieces, wrapped in old newspapers, and stuffed under a stairway near the central markets.

(36) August 23, 1939

"A *pneumatique* has arrived for Monsieur," said little Monsieur Charles as I came up the stairs in the Hôtel Ste.-Marie Gallia. He leaned coyly around the corner waving the gray envelope at me, his lids half closed on his smiling black eyes. His inflections were always flirtatious, even when he was commenting on the weather. "It is, without doubt, from one of Monsieur's young lovers?"

"Charles, you should have been a madame in a brothel," I said, laughing.

"And does Monsieur think he lives here in a convent?" Charles said, twinkling.

I made a low clutch at his crotch, but missed. He skipped gaily aside, tending the *pneumatique* to me with the tips of his fingers, and bending in an exaggerated willowy bow. "May Monsieur have always the good luck in his many conquests," he said.

Still laughing, I opened the *pneumatique*. It was from Arthur, scrawled in great haste: "Come at once, please, no matter what you are doing. A dreadful tragedy. Juan is in jail. I am thinking of suicide." The last word was so heavily underlined that the pen had torn through the paper.

My first reaction was disgust at the dramatics. I had heard Arthur cry wolf too many times to be alarmed, and I knew his love for overacting. Still, this did look serious. Arthur could not simply have made up a story about Juan in jail—you could too easily check. But why was he in jail? What had happened?

Monsieur Charles spoke. "But what is it that Monsieur has?" he asked in some concern. "Monsieur has become as white as the lilies of Easter."

"I must get a taxi at once," I said, stuffing the *pneumatique* in my pocket.

"It is not serious?" said Charles in alarm. "Is there anything I can do?"

"*Non merci,*" I said. "I am quite all right. A friend is in trouble." I turned and hurried down the stairs, and out into the street to hail a taxi.

I was completely baffled during the ride. I could see no reason—or rather, perhaps, I could see too many possibilities. Arthur lived on the edge of violence. He liked his house built on a trembling cliff. Perhaps the trouble came with the Arab of last night? No, nothing was said of that. Perhaps Juan in a jealous fit had tried to kill him? Possibly. But that would hardly account for the thought of suicide. It must indeed be a first-class event to force such a statement from him. I read the crumpled *pneumatique* again. There was no further clue.

My hands were sweating as I paid the taxi driver, overtipping him. I walked rapidly through the cool tunnel of the entryway and ran up the oak stairs two at a time. I put my finger on the bell and rang long and hard. There was no response. I put my ear against the door and heard nothing. I sniffed to see if there was an odor of gas. Suddenly I rapped my knuckles on the door and at the same time pushed the bell again. My impulse was to call the police.

Then I thought I heard a soft shuffling inside, and a board creaked. "Arthur!" I called loudly. "It's Mac—Johnny! Let me in."

The bolt slid with a faint screech and the door opened a crack. Arthur stuck his head around the edge. "C-come in," he said in a strangled voice. "Be quick!"

I slipped in "Arthur—" I began, and then stopped.

His face was horrible, ravaged. It seemed to have fallen apart. The eyes were red and swollen almost shut, and there was a stubble of beard on his face. He shut the door and looked at me with little pig eyes for a second. Then with a choking wail he fell against me, his head on my shoulder, sobbing as if his world had come to an end. His heavy body weight almost knocked me over. I staggered and then reached up and undid his arms from around my neck.

"Arthur, in God's name—what's the matter?"

He let go of me. With lowered head he stumbled into the blue and white living room, collapsing on the divan. His shoulders shook and he buried his face in the dark red cushion. I looked around for something, feeling helpless. Then I hurried to the brandy decanter and poured cognac into a glass. I brought it back to him. His face was still buried in the cushion.

"Arthur," I said. I took him by the shoulder and shook him. "Here—stop crying and drink this. For heaven's sake, calm down and tell me what's wrong. You're going to be hysterical."

The sobbing gradually began to stop. After two or three minutes he turned around and raised up a little on one elbow. His hand was shaking so that he could not hold the glass. I put it to his lips and he sipped, then choked, and finally drank it all. Then with a gasp he lay back face upward, and put his forearm across his eyes.

I felt totally helpless, the same feeling I had once had when I had tried to rescue a drunk who had fallen on the street late at night. In such emergency moments one would like to be cool, practical, and efficient—loosen collars, put pillows under the head, cold towels on the neck, and remain calm. But in moments of stress all I seemed able to do was pluck aimlessly here and there and wonder what to do next. Finally I put my hand on his arm.

"Arthur," I said as quietly as I could, but my voice caught and choked. I had to try again. "Arthur—can't you tell me what happened?"

"Oh, Mac," he said with a long pause between the two words, and the last one a kind of desperate whisper. "How—right—you were."

"About what, Arthur?" Somehow I felt I had to call him by name, as if he were a child or an idiot, else he might vanish from the room completely.

"When—you said . . . there was nothing but—disaster ahead."

"Well, now," I said, trying to be cheerful but not feeling that way at all. "It can't be as bad as all that. But you will have to tell me what happened, you know. I'm completely in the dark."

"Y-yes, I know." He sat up weakly and looked at me out of his tear-swollen face. There was a long pause. I waited. At last he began to speak in a slow disjointed monotone. His voice was hollow and uncertain.

"Juan did not come home last night. I was—frantic. I thought he had left me because—because of the fight. Or gone out and got lost. Then . . . the police called me—early this morning. They had Juan. They asked me to come, to bring his—papers. It seems—he had gone up to the flea market yesterday afternoon and bought a jacket in a secondhand shop . . . oh, it is all so mixed up!" He bent his head down for a moment and then looked up. He went on, still sounding like an automaton, a dull mechanical voice without inflection.

"The jacket had been stolen—a sportjacket. The owner recognized it and called the police. They took Juan. He told them where he had bought it but he could not find the shop again. So I went to the police with Juan's papers. I found them in his suitcase. They were—not right, either for Spain or France. So they put Juan in jail—" His voice trailed off.

"Well now," I said nervously, "that's nothing serious. We can find the shop again and—"

He silenced me with a nervous gesture. "Wait. You haven't heard it all. I looked at his papers in the taxi before I got there. I had never seen them. His mother's maiden name was there. It was . . . Juanita—Juanita Ramirez."

"Juanita—" I began, and then stopped. The world shook.

Sir Arthur looked straight ahead. He said five words, spaced about three seconds apart:

"Yes. Juan . . . is . . . my . . . son."

I have never known exactly what vertigo is, but I think I felt it then. The room seemed to whirl around once, rapidly, and then turn wavery and misty so that I had to lie back on the sofa and close my eyes for a moment. My heart pounded. Then I opened my eyes, feeling rather sick, and ran my tongue over my lips.

Arthur had not moved. He stared unblinkingly into the far distance, through the wall of the living room and beyond, into I know not what.

The whole perspective of the room seemed to be altered for me. The ceiling was higher, the lines sharper. The floor seemed to be at a curious angle. I got up and went to the decanter. The rim of it clattered noisily, like castanets, against the glass in my other hand. I was shaking now, shaking so badly that I had to take the glass in both hands to raise it to my mouth. I drank two great gulps and then sank into an armchair.

Sir Arthur still had not moved. The ticking of the clock was loud.

". . . Oh . . . my," I whispered. My voice rustled in the room and ended in a faint echo somewhere near the ceiling.

Moments of shock paralyze the brain. I sat there leaning back for a while until my head stopped whirling. At first the whole weight of my discarded morality descended on me in a dreadful flood. I could not credit the fact. I seemed to be standing aside from myself, watching a flight of hawks over the gray valleys of my brain.

And then acceptance gradually came, and with it a hundred milling ideas tumbling over it in great confusion. Here it was—one perfect working-out of the classical situation of Œdipus—except reversed, or perhaps upended. And was I not partly responsible? How many weeks had they been together? How long had Œdipus lain with his mother? Did the length of time make it a greater "sin"? What was sin anyway? Was the taboo against incest a man-created thing devised by Moses to save his race? Who were the wives of Cain and Abel—their sisters? The narrow training I had had throttled me at first, and then I gradually worked loose from it.

I had known several brothers who had been lovers, and also fathers and sons. Such arrangements were juicy tidbits for party gossip—why the fuss now? I had never been shocked by such information—and why was Arthur so upset? I seemed to have forgotten that persons such as Arthur and myself had a different kind of morality—how then could this be shocking? What other reason within Arthur had made him react this violently?

My shoelace was untied. I bent down to fix it. What would be the best thing to say to Arthur? I considered a few, and decided on one.

"Arthur," I said, putting my hand on his knee. "There is nothing really wrong about this. You surprise me. You are not really going to be bothered about this. He's your son—what of it? Think how it will all work out. You can tell everyone that the long lost is found. You will 'recognize' him and everything will be quite all right. And what's to prevent you from going on just as you have been? You've done worse things than this."

He looked at me; I could not interpret his glance. "I know . . . I have," he said slowly. "But I can't do this." He shifted his position and I stood up.

"There's really nothing to it," I said. "There won't be any trouble. Does Juan know?"

He nodded. "*That* is a main part of the trouble," he said. "Juan screamed and fainted. When they brought him around he looked at me as if I were a snake. He wouldn't speak to me." He ran his fingers through his rumpled untidy hair. "No, Mac—" he said. "It's all over. Too many people know. I could not face them."

Suddenly I understood. It was not that he minded copulating with his son—he had done worse things, and more amoral ones; the "morality" of the question had no meaning for him. But I

(203)

knew, I saw quite certainly in that sudden flash, the combination of elements that had ruined and shocked him—the pride and snobbishness, the sense of what was "done" and tolerated in his world, and what was not. Why had a cold and amoral sensualist like Cleopatra committed suicide? Answer: she could not stand the idea of being driven captive in a cage through the streets of Rome. And Arthur's pride, his snobbism, his sense of breeding and nobility—all these would be destroyed if he had to face his friends in this situation. It had gone beyond the limits of the liberated spirit and sophistication and "smartness." He was right. "Too many people know." It was, *enfin*, the utter destruction of his ego before the laughing throngs. They would be merciless.

"What are you going to do?" I asked.

He shook his head. "I have written to London, saying I'll be there on the twenty-ninth," he said, "and I am packing now."

"Are you going back there? Closing the flat here?"

"I am closing the flat, yes," he said, "but I am not going to London." He stood up and leaned heavily against the side of the divan.

"Where are you going?"

He looked at me with an expression I could not comprehend. At last he said, "Mac—good friend that you are, I won't tell you. I can only say—and hope that you will keep my secret and tell no one—that I am going to . . . disappear."

Then suddenly he was wildly sobbing again, and threw himself against me. I found myself clumsily patting his shoulder. But it was not Juan for whom he wept, nor anyone else in the world. His tears were for himself alone.

After a few moments the brief storm of self-pity passed and he looked at me with wet eyes. And then, of all wonders, he managed a strange little smile. He sank into a chair, his hands clasped and pressed tightly between his knees, rocking a little, and looking through the windows to the west.

There was nothing more I could do. I walked to the door, opened it, and closed it quietly behind me.

(37) **August, 1948**

The wheel has come full circle, the story of Sir Arthur Lyly almost told—save for two loose ends remaining . . .

The nine-year interval interrupting my regular trips to Paris had been caused, of course, by a war. My year-long fellowship had been canceled. My own fortunes during that time were varied. There was a hitch in the Navy as a Shore Patrol bullyboy, a fantastic and amusing experience taking me many places in a rough-and-tumble life, and learning to trade freedom from the brig—for our drunken sailors—for a little service that we talked them into providing for us.

During those nine years many things happened to me—and one left a deep unhealing wound. Gertrude died in the American hospital in Paris before I could get to see her again, and for many months my world was darkened. I thought of her dying alone, attended only by Alice—Gertrude, who loved life and people, she of the great heart and large mind, the unsubmissive one forced at last to bow. And with her death an era seemed to come to a desolate and whimpering close.

After the war I did some hack writing for a while, reluctant to return to university life. And then—and then—there occurred an event of such shattering impact that—coupled with a growing kind of hot restlessness, a feeling of disorientation and dislocation—I felt I had to get back to Paris at once to see Alice and talk with her. I could not write about the event, not knowing how it would affect her in her growing frailty, nor could I telephone her, for the same reason. The shock might have been too great for her.

But not only that. The blood was calling. I heard my heart complain incessantly, and felt its uneasy murmuring for the banks of the Seine.

So back I went to Paris after those nine long years, carrying my dreadful secret. I called Alice at once and arranged to see her. And it was then that she told me of Arthur's two trunks waiting for me, his books of sketches, and his journals. I accepted them scarcely hearing what I was saying, for there was a singing in my ears. Yet I calmed myself, waiting for the best moment.

We sat in the great high-ceilinged room while the sky deepened into the lyric purple of the Paris night. Finally Alice reached over and switched on the tiny tulip light beside her chair. It made a yellow hole in the dusk.

"Well," she said. "Is there any other news to report?"

I could not tell her yet. "N-no," I said hesitantly.

She looked at me narrowly. "*Bien*," she said, "but you're not telling the truth, are you? I suppose it will come out in good time. By the way, that new American writer, James somebody or other, sent me a book he'd written. Such cheek—even though he said Carl Van Vechten asked him to give it to me. He also said he was a friend of yours."

"Yes, I've known him for a long time," I said, grinning. "But he's no particular friend. I must confess I have somewhat of the 'Dr. Fell reaction'—you know, 'and why it is I cannot tell, I only know so very well, I do not like thee, Doctor Fell.'"

"Ah, well," said Alice. "His work bores me. I find it in bad taste. It's not even *purty* good—" said Alice, who rarely made a pun, chuckled at the aptness of that one. "Anyway," she said, "I'll be glad to get rid of Arthur's stuff and stop paying the storage charges on it."

I knew then that I could not delay much longer. The postcard in my inner pocket was actually generating a kind of heat. At last with a single quick movement I pulled it out and handed it to her.

"Please read it," I said.

My movement startled her a little. "Oh, dear," she said taking the card and feeling on the tabletop beside her. "Where are my glasses?"

I saw them on top of the big Spanish table behind the horsehair sofa. "Here they are," I said, handing them to her. She put them on and peered at the card.

"What a vile print," she said. "Where is the scene? Arizona? Such an impossibly vulgar blue in the sky, and those phallic cacti . . . or do they look more like railroad semaphores?"

I felt I might explode if she did not look at the other side of the card. But there was no hurrying her. At last she turned it over, readjusted her spectacles, and began to read. I knew the curl of each letter and the length of each line, and I followed her eyes intently, watching her expression. "Dear Mr. Belvedere," it read. "I am well and happy and have gone from here by the time you get this. Please tell no one except maybe Alice. Perhaps we shall meet some day."

And it was signed—Arthur Pickett.

She looked at the card a long time, holding it motionless. Her eyes had stopped their little reading movements. At last she sighed deeply and put the card on the table beside her. It lay there with the writing upward and the light reflected from it made a small white rectangle of shine in her glasses. She looked at me.

"So you got one too," she said in a low voice.

"Y-yes," I said. A great burning lump of bile and acid was rising in me.

"When did it come?"

"One afternoon last October," I said. "Ten months ago. I remember so well, because it was very hot and the arrival of the thing chilled me completely. I wanted to yell or shout or do some such idiotic thing. I was so upset I almost telephoned you from Chicago."

"When mine came I was upset too," Alice said. "I felt I had to tell someone, but there was no one to tell, with Gertrude gone. And he asked me also to keep the secret. Mine came about the same time yours did."

"Do you suppose he told anyone else?"

Alice spread her hands and lifted her shoulders ever so little. "Who knows? I presume not. He was declared legally dead last year."

"Just a few months prematurely," I managed to say.

"What!?"

There it was. "Arthur is dead," I said.

The room seemed suddenly more quiet than ever. I heard a faucet dripping in the kitchen.

"O-oh," Alice said. She fumbled for a cigarette and lighted it, her hand trembling slightly. "Do you have the details?"

Then I told her of the finding of a derelict's body in the Chicago river. I spared her the grisly parts—the bloated white flesh of the body, what was left of it, knocking against the pilings of the Wrigley Tower, floating amid the dead cats and unrolled condoms. I told her of the police finding on his body the penciled letter from someone named Wally, of the deep gash in his skull and the extruded brain, of the small address book (again in pencil—had it been ink it would have vanished in the water) with my name and address in it. I told her how the police had called on me to identify the body—but I omitted telling her how I fainted in the morgue.

After I finished, the silence in the room extended itself for several minutes. Finally she spoke.

"He was very tired of the life he had been leading," she said. "I know that is true. It is quite possible that he deliberately closed the door on his gifts and painted no more. I imagine that in a kind of perverse way it might have been amusing to him to watch his 'posthumous' reputation grow, if indeed he knew about it. Moreover, he always had a business sense. He might have felt that his continuing presence would hinder his reputation, whereas the glamor and drama of a 'disappearance' . . . well . . ." She finished with an expressive gesture of her hand.

"There are really many things he could have done in America," I murmured. My mind filled with small pictures. I saw him among the cowboys of Arizona sketching their lean tanned faces, watching the curve of their tight western jeans, listening to their noisy spurs. I saw him among the sailors and dockhands of San Francisco, staying in the Embarcadero in a small spotted hotel, or talking in the waterfront bars in his sly way with his innocent baited grin below his drooping mustache—and offering a young swabbie a pinch of snuff . . . and there the image broke down. I could not go on with *that* picture.

"What pleases you so much?" Alice asked.

I laughed a little. "I just had a vision of Arthur offering an American sailor a pinch of snuff."

Alice smiled. "He would have had to change his ways a great deal. Do they have any idea what happened?"

"Murder most foul," I said. "Possibly done by someone who hated queers. He may have picked the wrong person. But murder—at the hands of person or persons unknown, the coroner said. No case like that is ever closed—but it has been abandoned."

Suddenly another thought occurred to me. "Have you ever heard anything of—er . . . of his son?" The word came out with difficulty.

"He came to see me about a year and a half ago," Alice said. "He is now—oh, very grandly!—Don Juan Piedro de Lille. He sent in a cheap little calling card and I guessed who it was so I decided not to see him. Madeleine told him that I was not at home, that I had gone to Madagascar or some such, but he left the card. He penciled his address on it, although why on earth he should think I would ever go calling on him is more than I know."

"I wonder if you still have it," I said.

"Do you want to see him?" Alice asked.

I nodded. "Frankly, I'm curious, very curious. I want to see what's happened to him in all these years. I had an idea how his life would go, and I'd like to know whether it was right or wrong."

Alice pulled a small enameled box toward her and opened it on a collection of calling cards. "It must be in here," she said. "I'm just like Gertrude—I never throw anything away." She hunted busily and at last extracted one and held it up. "There," she said, peering at it. "He was at the Hôtel du Dragon," she said. "Number thirty-six. Third floor."

"Good heavens," I said, startled. "Just around the corner from me."

"You're bound to run into him then," Alice said, "even if you don't call on him." She held out the card to me. "Do you want it?"

"No, thank you," I said. "I can remember it."

Alice looked at the card thoughtfully. "I think I can make an exception to my magpie nature," she said at last. She tore the pasteboard into small pieces and dropped them into the ashtray. They fell on the lighted end of her cigarette and began to smolder. Both of us watched the smoke of her symbolic gesture.

Then she looked at me quickly. "You won't tell him about Arthur. . . ?"

"Have no fear."

Then we sat quietly watching the threads of smoke ascend straight in the motionless air and lose themselves in the upper shadows of the room.

(38) **August 21, 1948**

The next afternoon about three o'clock I went into the Hôtel du Dragon, eager to tie up the last loose end. The vestibule was dingy and dreary.

At the left of the entrance was a glass door through which I looked into an equally dingy and disordered waiting room. An upright piano stood at one side with a vase of dry and dusty straw flowers on top of it. A strip of olive-colored material was spread the length of the keys. There was a table in the center of the room, and around it some chairs with dirty tasteless coverings. A torn lace curtain hung like a slattern's petticoat against the window that looked out on the street. The room was empty.

A sign said "Concierge. Sonnez." I pressed the button below it. There was at once a fearful clamor from a huge bell somewhere in the hotel above me. Then there were footsteps and a voice called down the rickety stairwell.

"What is it there?" A man's voice.

"I search Don Juan de Lille," I said into the dark nothingness overhead.

"Mount, then," said the voice. "He inhabits number thirty-six."

I started up the stair treads that were carpeted with patched and threadbare material from which the roses had faded, and I was soon—like Orpheus—lost in the gloom. At the first landing a grimy little window opened on an airshaft, letting in enough light for me to see the gleam of the banister under my hand.

At the third floor a man stood waiting. His face was heavily powdered and rouged, and his black eyebrows plucked. He stood with one hand on a hip, and a broom in the other. I knew what was in his mind; his eyes ate away at me.

"Monsieur searches our Spanish friend?" he asked simperingly.

"*Mais oui,*" I said. "It is many years since I have seen him."

The man winked at me. "He is still beautiful," he said and tittered. Some of my revulsion must have showed in my face for his smile quickly disappeared. He turned and walked down a black corridor, and said over his shoulder, "His room is at the front," and vanished through a bedroom door.

I went on and found the room. For a moment I hesitated and then knocked.

"*Qui est-ce?*" came a sleepy voice from within.

"An old friend," I said. "John McAndrews, from America."

"Oh—*mon dieu!*"

There was a sudden creak of springs as a bed gave up its weight, the sound of a closet door opened, and bare feet moving toward the door. And then the panel opened into a gloom of curtains drawn against the afternoon sun, and Juan stood there.

We looked at each other for a second. He had thrown an old maroon dressing gown around himself and was knotting the cord. His feet were bare and his legs naked to the knee.

"*Mon ami!*" he said and opened his arms, tilting his head sidewise like a bird. I stuck out my hand, not wishing to embrace him. A little hurt, he seized it and pulled me in. "I am enchanted to see you again," he said.

His hair was mussed and I could not see his face very well in the gloom. "Come in and sit down," he said, picking up a towel from the one chair and then throwing the covers of the low sleeping couch into a semblance of order. He darted here and there busily tidying up, but he did not open the window curtains. And all the while he was chattering rapidly in his bad French, which in nine years had not improved a bit.

"How absolutely *wonderful* to see you, my dear! It has been *very* long indeed—eight, nine years, has it not? And what have you been *doing* all this time? I have often thought of you and wondered how you were, ever since my father disappeared." There was no hesitation in his use of the words "my father."

"Life in Paris was *absolute* hell for quite a while, very shitty, really it was. We have never yet *really* fully recovered from the Occupation. And then the American *soldiers* here—oh, my dear, it *really* has been gay *once* in a while! And in a way there has always been something to do. Or someone." He giggled, picking up a magazine and throwing it on the disordered table. "You *really* must excuse me for being in bed at such an hour—most of my work is at night. And how *frightful* that you should see me not shaved or dressed! I am *really* a lot better looking than I may seem to you now. Why don't you just make yourself comfortable there and wait until I clean up a little?"

I had expected something like this but the intensity of it left me numb. I sat down and crossed my ankles and waited. He drew some water in the dirty washbowl and took a washcloth to his face, continuing to talk.

"We went to the most *fabulous* party last night," he said, "over at François Reich's—do you know him? He's *frightfully* literary and artistic and knows all sorts of persons, and there were several Americans there. François is *terribly* rich. I guess all the Americans were too." He scrubbed at his armpits, lifting each arm high above his head. "Why is it that all Americans are *so* rich?" He sighed and pulled the plug from the bowl. The water ran out with a desperate strangled sound. Then Juan seized a comb and ran it through his black hair, not so thick as it once was. He spent a good deal of time getting the part straight, while the chattering continued.

"I suppose there is *really nothing* to making money in America," he said, "or is it hard? Have you been to any of the operas yet? They're extending the season just for the tourists.. Oh, I had *such* a dream boy making eyes at me last night at the party—he asked me to go to the opera tonight, which is why I thought of it. He's from California—simply *tons* of money—and he's handsome enough to be in the movies, although he says he *really* isn't interested. He even brought his car over this summer—simply a *fantastic* automobile—a wonderful big black Cadillac. It has *every* gadget imaginable on it, really! It has one of those things that automatically puts the lights dim, an electric eye I guess it is, and it knows enough to roll up the windows if it begins to rain. Simply *fantastic*! What will they think of next?"

I already had the answer to the question that had aroused my curiosity. It was quite easy to see what Juan had become, exactly what I had seen for him nine years before. A feeling of being stifled began to grow inside of me. I wanted to get out of the cheap hole with its artificial gloom and its strong odor of urine near the washbowl, away from the stained towels that drooped crustily from the rack beneath the basin, with the chipped and cracked bidet huddled behind them.

My eyes grew accustomed to the semidarkness. Juan had slipped off his dressing gown to wash his face, and he stood there

in the imperfect dusk, a white shadow in a tiny black *cache-sexe*.
His belly had grown, and his shoulders sloped as much as ever,
but he had retained a fair amount of attractiveness in his milk
white body. I remembered ironically how he had refused to look at
the nakedness of the weight lifters the afternoon we had gone sunbathing, and how he had almost refused to remove his shirt when I
wanted to sketch him. Now he seemed completely unconcerned
over his near-nakedness. Ah, well, I thought—experience teaches.
He had come far.

I began to cast around for an excuse to leave. "I really cannot
stay very long," I said, just as he reached up to throw back the
drapes to let in the light.

He seemed dismayed. "Oh, but—" he began, and then turned
to finish pushing the drapes. The afternoon sun fell in a hot triangular patch on the floor.

I looked at his face. It had hardened and grown old. Around
the eyes were fine wrinkles; two lines were strong down beside his
mouth. His eyebrows were plucked. The eyes themselves fascinated and repelled me at the same time. They were calculating
and cold, and yet sensual. They moved over me in small flickings
of appraisal like the glances of a pawnshop broker. I saw them rest
on my wristwatch and almost heard the estimate of eighty dollars.
On my suit, a hundred. On the shoes . . . Something inside me
turned over. Juan was no longer an enigma. His innocence and
naiveté had completely vanished, and his profession was as clearly
marked as the avarice in his eyes.

"But you must not go so soon," he said. "Would you like a
drink?" He looked around in the dirt and confusion. "I believe,
however, that a . . . a friend and I finished the bottle yesterday."

"Oh, but we'll see each other again soon," I said, and rose.

Suddenly Juan turned to the drapes and with a gesture pulled
them together again. He stood in front of them for a moment, and
then began to walk toward me.

"But first there is something to do," he said, "that we should
have done many years ago." He stuck his fingers under the side
edges of his brief black *slip* and pushed it down and stepped out of
it. Then he walked to the cot and sat on the edge of it with one
white hairless leg tucked underneath the other. He stretched out
his thin white arms to me. "Come," he said.

Everything sickened inside. I felt a quick desire for something cool and clean, a shower of spring rain with the black dirt fresh under foot. I wanted sunlight.

I shook my head in the dusk, stifled with the odors of stale powder and old cologne that hung over the bed. "No, Juan," I said.

He lay back on his elbows on the bed, and arched his hips out and up toward me, moving them lasciviously with a circular rotation. I had a sudden angry surge of blood to my eyes. "Besides," I said slowly and cruelly, "I haven't any money with me today."

He rose to a sitting position again, putting his weight on one straightened arm, and looked up at me. His answer made me shudder with a chill kind of horror. The insult had passed over him completely.

"But Mac," he said. "I wouldn't charge you anything this time. For old times past—please?"

I wanted to hit him, but shook my head again, not trusting myself to speak. And then I put one knee on the bed and bent over him. I put my two hands at the back of his head and lowered my face toward him.

So I stood for a long minute thinking of the crazy business life was, wondering about its twists and turns. I thought—oddly enough—of the baths of Caracalla in Rome. I remembered a line of poetry—Wilde's, perhaps—about his faun flashing out of the forest, and the poet not knowing which he should follow, shadow or song. I had a kind of world vision for an instant, seeing all of us fighting and loving and dying and starving and being happy and struggling—millions and millions of souls and bodies, white and yellow and brown and red and black, each engaged in its contest for something it did not want for long. I thought of religion and love and pain and death, and of myself and the uncounted numbers of other same-sex-loving insects with our tailored little egos seeking the feeble tickle that made us feel for a moment that we had found happiness. And suddenly I was aware, too, of the existence of a goal, when multiplied experience freed one from compulsion of any kind toward anyone or anything—the only real freedom worth aiming for, and the best reward.

His head turned uneasily between my hands and he murmured something I did not hear. The smell of his hot armpits was strong. It mixed with the sweetish scent of old powder, and faintly malodorous sheets that had been long slept on.

His arms reached around me but I drew away from them and kept my balance. Then, holding his head steadily between my hands, with my thumbs hooked into the porches of his ears, I leaned down and kissed him first on one cheek, and then the other.